M000222596

Murder in
Coweta County

Murder in Coweta County

by

Margaret Anne Barnes

PELICAN PUBLISHING COMPANY

Copyright © 1976
by Margaret Anne Barnes
All rights reserved

First published by Reader's Digest Press 1976
First Pocket Books edition 1977
First Pelican edition published 1983
First printing, January 1983
Second printing, March 1983

All rights reserved. Except for use in a review, the reproduction or utilization of this work in any form or by any electronic, mechanical, or other means, now known or hereafter invented, including xerography, photocopying, and recording, and in any information storage and retrieval system is forbidden without the written permission of the publisher.

Library of Congress Cataloging in Publication Data

Barnes, Margaret Anne
  Murder in Coweta County.

  I. Title.
P24.B258918Mu [PS3552.A683] 813'5'4 75-23340

Special acknowledgment is made to E. W. Thomasson, Editor of the Newnan *Times Herald*, for assistance with photographs.

Printed in the United States of America
by Rose Printing Company, Inc., Tallahassee, FL

Published by Pelican Publishing Company, Inc.
1101 Monroe Street, Gretna, Louisiana 70053

Consultant: Douglas M. Eason
Designed by Susan Schwalb

Contents

Author's Note

This is a true story, as it happened,
in Georgia, in 1948.

This book is dedicated
to the memory of
Sheriff Lamar Potts,
whose courage
made this story possible,
and
Bernice McCullar
for encouragement
to write it.

The Murder

Chapter One

Wilson Turner was doomed. Without benefit of trial, judge, or jury, he was going to die. Turner was certain of it. The only uncertainty was when.

That decision depended on John Wallace. Wallace wanted Turner dead, and in Meriwether County in 1948, John Wallace's word was law. If he decided a man needed killing, that was reason enough. Wilson Turner, his former tenant, had given him reason: He had stolen Wallace's cow.

In the Meriwether County jail that morning, Wilson Turner clutched the bars of his second-floor window. Desperate and hollow-eyed, he looked down for the hundredth time on the empty, unpaved street below.

Again there was no one . . . no help . . . nothing . . . only the soft April breeze stirring the leaves on the tree-lined street, the morning sun urging the flowers to respond to a warm Georgia spring.

Turner had been in jail since Sunday night. Neither his friends nor his family knew where he was. Tough, white-haired Sheriff Hardy Collier had denied him even a phone call to his young wife, Julia. Wallace would kill him and no one would ever know what had happened to him. There seemed no end to the nightmare.

It had begun in Carrollton on Sunday night when Chief of Police Threadgill arrested him for stealing one of John Wallace's registered Guernsey cows. By rights, Turner had convinced himself, the cow, or at least the money from selling her, was his. John Wallace owed him *something*. After Turner had worked for him for two and one-half years, Wallace had turned him out of his tenant house, taken his crops, and run him off his land.

Julia's uncle, Millard Rigsby, had warned Turner not to work for

Wallace. The first time he'd seen Wallace's farm, he'd gone there to help Millard haul some hogs to market. He had liked what he had seen . . . farming and cattle spread all over two thousand acres of pasture and pine.

"Man! I'd sure like working here," he'd exclaimed. "All that equipment! Hell! the barn's as big as the courthouse!"

"Forget it!" Millard had said. "John Wallace owns and runs Meriwether County like it was deeded to him."

"He sure seemed nice enough."

"He just *seems* thata way. Long as it suits him, you couldn't find no nicer man, but oh hell, look out if it don't suit him. He's one of them Stricklands . . . cross 'em and they'll kill you. And I mean to tell you, they kill you good."

"Yeah?"

"Yeah," Millard had replied, relishing the tales the county told about the Stricklands. "The worst of the bunch was old John Strickland. Some say he even wore his six-shooters in bed. The night he got killed by the revenooers he went down shootin' 'em both."

"Running liquor?"

"You know it! Used to be, they brought in sugar from New Orleans in carload lots, ran three shifts at the still around the clock, and shipped it out by rail."

"Aw, you gotta be kiddin'."

"Uh-uh! They shipped the liquor out in milk cans, put a false board siding on the rail car, and had the bill of lading marked 'lumber.' "

"Well, I'll be damned!"

"You will be, if you get mixed up with that outfit. Just stay the hell away from here."

But in John Wallace's place Turner had seen a chance to better himself. Growing up poor on a worn-out farm in Crawford County, he had watched his old man scratch a bare living from the soil. It was only when he entered the army that he learned what it was to have three whole meals a day and real sheets on the bed. He had promised himself he'd never go back to hand-to-mouth living, and when he got out he had taken a job at the cotton mill. But he found that all he had done was to trade the cotton field for the cotton mill. Living was just as poor in one as in the other. He had seen no way to get ahead until he chanced to haul Wallace's hogs with Millard that day.

Turner had gone back to the big farm in Meriwether County and asked Wallace for a job. He got it, and five months later, Wallace let him in on the liquor making. The arrangement worked fine until the

4

night Wallace learned that the Federal agents had discovered his still and were planning a raid. There were four hundred gallons of liquor ready to pull and twenty gallons ready to be run. Wallace went down to the swamp where his two Negro foremen, Albert Brooks and Robert Lee Gates, were working at the still with Turner. He told the three men to scratch the whole thing, that Sheriff Collier had said the Federal boys had the still spotted.

Turner was shocked. "You mean you're gonna give up the whole four hundred gallons of liquor!" He needed that money. He had a payment due on his new pickup truck. Both Julia and the baby had been sick, and Julia was pregnant again.

But Wallace was saying: "That's right. We're not taking any chances."

For a man who wasn't scared of Hell itself, Wallace was sure careful about the revenuers. From the beginning, he had told Turner that caution was absolutely necessary. He'd been caught twice and sent to the Federal penitentiary. He was out on a presidential pardon, but if he was caught again, they'd put him away for good.

"But we ain't gonna get caught," Wallace was fond of saying, "because ain't nobody gonna take enough chances to get caught."

"How about the twenty gallons that's ready?" Turner asked now.

"Leave it."

"The pickup is already set."

"Doesn't matter."

"Then how about givin' it to me?"

Wallace hooked his thumbs in his belt, reared his chest back. "You done got greedy, ain't you, boy? You done got a taste of money, and all you want is more."

"It ain't that, Mr. Wallace," Turner protested. "I just need the money . . . bad."

Albert and Robert Lee, seeing what looked like trouble coming, backed into the shadows. They had long ago learned not to have any part of white men's doings, particularly where Mr. Wallace was concerned. Once he'd made up his mind, he didn't want to hear no talk on the other side.

Turner was saying, "I just hate to see that liquor go to waste."

Wallace looked at him, a long, cold look. "Then run it, boy, it would likely do you good to get caught . . . learn you a lesson and teach you what caution means."

"I ain't gonna get caught."

He didn't get caught. He ran the liquor and got the money. But

5

when he showed it to Wallace and the two foremen, Wallace said, "All right, let's have that money."

Turner protested. "Mr. Wallace, you told me I could run the twenty gallons. You said. . . ."

"Pay up, boy."

Turner started to back off, returning the money to his pocket. But Wallace lunged for him, snatching him by the collar and holding him off the ground so that they were eyeball to eyeball. "You sonofabitch! Have you forgot who's boss here? Just 'cause you're white?" Turner could feel the heat and strength of Wallace's body, the burning anger in his eyes. "You ain't got no more rights than them niggers."

With one swift movement, Wallace threw Turner facedown in the soft, wet slime of the swamp. When he turned to get up, Wallace held his head down with his foot.

"You shoulda learned your lesson a long time ago. Tell him what that lesson is, boys." Wallace grinned, turning to Albert and Robert Lee.

"*Albert?*" Wallace said sharply.

"We gotta do what we're told," Albert recited.

"*Robert Lee?*"

"No matter what."

"You see, Turner, even these niggers are smarter than you. They done learnt their lesson, but I figure you ain't able to learn yours."

Wallace smashed one heavy shoe against Turner's head, then kicked him in the kidney with the other. "Now, get, goddammit, off my land before I decide to kill you instead."

Turner scrambled up out of the swamp slime and ran. He never looked back and he never stopped running until he reached his house. In panic, he got Julia and little John William into his truck and took off with them for Carrollton in the next county.

They moved in with Julia's Uncle Millard, but that wasn't satisfactory for long. Turner never felt right eating Millard's food and not putting any on the table himself, no matter what Millard said about not minding. Money was hard to come by, and it was impossible for Turner to get a job. Wallace had put the word out, and nobody dared hire him.

Growing up, desperation had been a way of life for Turner, but this was a new kind of despair. Now he had a wife, a baby, and another on the way, and no way to work to take care of them. At first, he tried sneaking a little liquor out of Wallace's still, so he would have something to sell, but after a few times somebody was there every night.

6

When Wallace ran him off, he had had to leave fifty acres of cotton and fifty acres of corn ready to be harvested, but there wasn't a way in God's world to get that now. Turner figured the only way he could get his money was to take a couple of Wallace's cows. Wallace had so many, he'd never miss them, and there was a ready market on cows. When he suggested to Millard that they go partners on the project, Millard refused.

"Wilson, why don't you quit while you're ahead?" Millard said. "You're lucky you didn't get shot over that twenty gallons of liquor. You start stealin' John Wallace's cows, and he'll kill you for sure."

"John Wallace won't even know who took 'em," Turner insisted. "I know just where them cows are at and just how to get 'em out of his pasture."

Millard shook his head. "Maybe you don't mind gettin' shot, but I sure as hell do. *You,* better'n anybody, ought to know what Wallace is like."

Turner knew what Wallace was like, all right. Once he got mad, he just couldn't seem to quit. One night at the barn, with all the work force assembled to watch, he had seen Wallace beat one of his Negro workers half to death for stealing a gallon of gasoline from the farm tank. Wallace had held a pistol in one hand and a bullwhip in the other, lashing the man with the whip time after time after time, ready with the pistol if he tried to run away.

"Why in the hell doesn't he go ahead and kill him?" Turner had asked the worker standing beside him. "The man's half dead already."

"Mr. Wallace don't want to *kill* him," the worker explained matter-of-factly, "he's too good a worker. Mr. Wallace just gonna whup him and teach him a lesson and let the rest learn theirs, lookin'."

It was different with the cows. "By rights," Turner told Millard Rigsby, "Wallace owes me those cows."

It took some talking, but he finally persuaded Millard. "I'll get Julia's brother, Tommy Windham, to come help," Turner said. "He can be lookout."

Their plan worked well. Millard had a hinged extension welded to the tailgate of his pickup truck, and they got two of Wallace's cows without even cutting the barbed-wire fence. Backing up to it, they let the extended tailgate down across the barbed wire, and ran cows up the improvised ramp.

When they had finished and all three of them, breathless, were back in the truck, Millard asked: "All right, Wilson, now you got 'em, what're you gonna do with 'em?"

"I thought I'd put one down in a pasture in Carrollton until I can sell her, and leave the other one over in Coweta County."

Millard smashed his fist down on the steering wheel. "I'll be goddamned if I'm gonna do that! Wilson, you're the dumbest bastard I ever seen! Do you know who's sheriff of Coweta County . . . *Lamar Potts!*"

"Now look, Millard, he ain't even gonna know. I got it all planned. I spotted a herd of Guernseys in Coweta where I can put that cow down and won't *nobody* know . . . not Lamar Potts . . . not nobody."

"Wilson, you ain't just dumb, you're stupid. Lamar Potts ain't no ordinary sheriff. There ain't nothin' that goes on in Coweta that he don't know. He's half bloodhound and half bulldog, and he ain't ever heard of the word *quit.* You get caught rustling cattle and you'll be in the *Federal* pen."

"There ain't no use in gettin' so riled up. . . ."

"Riled, hell!" Millard snapped. "If you're plannin' on takin' that cow to Coweta, you can start unloadin' now, 'cause she ain't goin' on *my* truck."

Millard obviously meant it. "All right," Turner said. "I'll take one cow to Carrollton and the other one down to my brother in Roberta."

"Where's that?"

"Crawford County."

"So what the hell we waitin' for?"

After leaving one cow in Roberta, they slipped the other into a herd of Guernseys on the outskirts of Carrollton. They figured the owner of the pasture wouldn't notice that an extra cow stood in his herd and that Wallace wouldn't realize his cows were missing until after they were sold.

They reckoned without Wallace's awareness. The very next morning he discovered his cows were gone. Immediately, he alerted every lawman in three counties . . . Lamar Potts in Coweta, Threadgill in Carrollton, Collier—and everybody else—in Meriwether. He even called in the Georgia Bureau of Investigation. He notified every livestock sales barn in Georgia, and when one of the cows was located in the Carrollton pasture on Wednesday, April 14, Wallace and Chief of Police Threadgill began a night watch, waiting for Turner to show up.

Aware of what Wallace was up to, Turner also watched the pasture. Every night when he saw Wallace go in, he went home. On Sunday, the eighteenth, Wallace failed to arrive at the usual time. When he still had not come at midnight, Turner and Millard Rigsby decided it was safe to take the cow out of the pasture.

While Millard waited in his pickup truck on a nearby dirt road, Turner led the cow out of the pasture. It was then that Chief of Police Threadgill caught him. Millard, waiting and waiting in the truck, didn't know what had happened.

John Wallace and his friend, Herring Sivell, arrived in town just as Threadgill and his men brought Turner in. At sight of Wallace, Turner broke and ran, but the police chased him down an alley, caught him and took him to jail.

For Turner, there must have been some small solace in being in the Carrollton jail. At least it wasn't Meriwether. Wallace couldn't very well kill him over here in Carrollton. Exhausted, he fell on the cell bunk. And he slept until a blazing circle of light on his face awakened him. Squinting against the glare, he could see only the outline of a man holding a flashlight. "Get up, Turner."

Turner recognized the voice . . . Sheriff Hardy Collier of Meriwether County.

"What for?"

"We're taking you to Meriwether County!"

"Why?"

"We got jurisdiction. That cow was stolen in Meriwether."

Suddenly, Wilson Turner was more afraid than he'd ever been in his life.

"I ain't goin'," he said.

"We got a warrant," Collier replied.

Turner turned to the jailer, who was standing in the doorway. "Don't let 'em take me. They'll kill me."

Sheriff Collier snapped the handcuffs on.

"Help!" Turner screamed. "Help! They're gonna kill me."

"Don't that make you sick?" Collier said to the jailer, "to see a man go hysterical like that?"

Turner screamed all the way out of the Carrollton jail and into Collier's patrol car, but there was no one to see him dragged out or to hear him scream except the prisoners in the jail cells, and they could only watch.

Behind the patrol car, John Wallace was waiting to drive Turner's pickup truck to the Meriwether County jail in Greenville. It was getting on toward daylight Monday morning when they arrived and locked Turner in a second-floor cell.

When the Negro trusty brought his breakfast, he jumped up from his bunk to receive the plate.

"Look, Bo, how 'bout doin' me a favor?"

The Negro trusty, small, black, and wrinkled, scowled. "My name ain't Bo. It's Jake. Jake Howard."

"Okay, Jake, how 'bout makin' a phone call for me?"

"Cain't do that."

"Look, man, I gotta get word to my wife. She don't know where I am. She's got one baby and another's on the way, and she ain't got no money for food."

"You ain't, neither."

"I can get her some if you'll just make a phone call for me."

"They won't let me use the phone."

"Then get me a pencil and paper and I'll write a note."

"I ain't got no pencil and no paper, and besides, I ain't gettin' Sheriff Collier and Mr. John Wallace riled up and killin' mad at me for the likes of you." Jake Howard stalked off down the corridor muttering: "Don't nobody mess with Mr. John Wallace's business, not nobody."

All day no one came, neither Sheriff Collier nor John Wallace. Restless, impatient, and agonized, Turner paced back and forth in his narrow cell. *There had to be a way to get word to somebody.*

Frantic at last, he stood on his cell bunk, clung to the bars of the high-ceilinged window, and yelled for help to the first, and only, passerby in the street below, an elderly woman with a shopping bag on her way to market. She stopped to listen, shading her eyes against the glare of the sun, and staring up at the window where Turner screamed and begged for help.

In the prison yard beside the jail, Mrs. Vivian Matthews, the assistant jailer, was hanging out her Monday wash. "Don't pay him no mind," Mrs. Matthews said to the elderly woman. "He's drunk."

The woman shook her head, continued on toward the market in town, and the street was deserted again. Except on Saturdays, when the country people came to town for supplies, very little traffic passed the jail, for it was located on a dirt road two blocks from Greenville, county seat of Meriwether County. Now that April had come, and farmers were busy plowing their fields, there was even less traffic than usual.

From his jail cell, Wilson Turner could hear the courthouse clock in the town striking the hours. Still he watched, waiting, hoping for some passerby who might bring him aid. None came. Only the elderly woman with the shopping bag, returning home. When Turner called to her this time, she did not even turn her head.

He sank down on his bunk, fished a red can of Prince Albert tobacco and a folder of papers from his pocket, and rolled himself a

10

cigarette. Searching for matches, he dug deep into the long pockets of his green army fatigue pants. He laid the wad of things beside him on the cell bunk: a crumpled rag that he had used to wipe the gasoline spills from his new pickup truck when he had it filled, a piece of dirty string, a rusty bolt, a penny matchbox with two matches left, and the stub of a pencil with a broken point.

A pencil! Now that's what his Ma would have called the Hand of God. It was barely an inch long and he had nothing to sharpen it with. His knife, wallet, and truck keys had been taken from him when he was arrested.

Taking the stub between his teeth, he gnawed the wood away from the lead until he had a point. It was stubby and uneven, but it would write. And he had the cigarette papers—more than enough for a note! He knew that Julia couldn't drive, and it was likely that Millard might also be in jail, so his best bet for getting help was Julia's brother James. Turner knew he could depend on James.

Removing the cigarette papers from the folder, he began to write: "James, I am asking you to go to Carrollton and go to Rigsby Bros. mule barn and ask for Frank Shack if he will take you to my house and James let Julia have 10 dollars if you will and when I get out I will pay you back and she are at your mama and will be more than glad to pay you for your trouble. James, she do not have any money and then she can the truck and get Tom to drive it to come here so I can get out. I am in jail, I hate to say. Always, Wilson Turner."

Looking back over what he had written, he added: "James, I left out part of it. If she is not at home, go to your mama and tell her and I will promise you that I will never bother you again in jail."

Satisfied, Wilson Turner put the folded note in his pocket and waited for the Negro trusty to come with his food.

"Evenin', Jake," he said pleasantly when the trusty arrived.

Jake was suspicious. "What's done come over you?"

"I found a pencil and some paper and wrote that note I was tellin' you about. Now, all that needs be is for you to pass it out for me."

"Not me," Jake replied, pushing the dinner plate through the door. "I done got to likin' livin' too much."

"Look, I'll give you some money."

"I ain't got noplace to spend money."

"Then I'll get you some liquor. I made it myself."

The trusty ignored Turner's outstretched hand holding the note through the bars. "Mr. Wallace got his reasons for keepin' you. I sho' ain't gonna give him no reason for killin' me."

He walked away, and Turner's last hope was gone. In the fading

11

light of the jail cell, he lay down on the dirty mattress and closed his eyes.

When the Negro trusty returned with his breakfast in the morning, Turner pushed it away. "I don't want food. I want help."

"There ain't no help here."

"Have you heard what they plan to do with me?"

"I ain't heard nothin', but you'll know when they do."

"Hell, it's Tuesday morning, and I been here since Sunday night. I want to know what's gonna happen."

"I don't know nuthin'. I just does what I'm told."

"Look, you gotta get word to my wife."

Jake Howard shook his head and turned away.

"You *got* to!" Turner yelled after him. "You *got* to! Nobody knows where I am." He clung to the bars of the cell door and sobbed.

Jake Howard didn't come back until just before noon. Then, with keys rattling, he walked down the corridor toward Turner's cell and unlocked the door.

"What're you doin'?" Turner asked. He was frightened.

"I'm turnin' you out."

"Why?"

" 'Cause Sheriff Collier said to, that's why."

Instantly, Turner was suspicious. "*Why* did Sheriff Collier say to turn me out?"

"He told Mrs. Matthews this mornin' that them cattle charges against you wuzn't enough to hold you and that she was to let you out right at twelve o'clock."

"Mrs. Matthews?"

"The assistant jailer. She's supposed to turn you out, but she's busy across the street helpin' a lady and she told me to do it."

"Why right at twelve o'clock?"

"How do I know why twelve o'clock? It's nearly 'bout twelve now, and I gotta go to town to meet the noon mail train."

"They let you do that?"

"Sho' they do."

"And you don't run away?"

Jake Howard's black face was set with resignation. "Where would I go that they wouldn't get me?"

Turner shrugged his shoulders.

"That's how I come to be a trusty," Jake explained. "Doin' what I'm told." He opened the cell door and stood beside it.

Wilson Turner hesitated. *Why* were they turning him loose? Were they waiting for him outside?

12

"You goin' or stayin'?" Jake asked. "If you take my advice, you better go while the goin's good. I done parked yore pickup truck outside in front of the jail. The key is in it."

Turner must have felt a stab of excited hope. If the truck was that close by, he could make a run for it. He followed Jake Howard through the corridor, down the stairs, and to the front door of the jail. Peering through the window, he saw no one, only his truck parked out front.

He walked out into the warm April sunshine. The street was empty. He looked around. No one was there. It was true. He was free. Really free.

Wilson Turner's hands began to tremble. He reached in his pocket for his tobacco can, hurriedly rolled a cigarette, and lit it with his last match. Tossing the empty matchbox away, he got in his pickup truck and switched on the ignition. The gas gauge was sitting on Empty, though he had filled the tank on Saturday night just before he was arrested.

He shrugged and grinned and started the engine. If all he lost out of this scrap was a tank of gas, he'd be damned lucky. He knew he could get gas at the Standard Oil station in the town, only two blocks away. For the first time in a long while, Wilson Turner felt aware of the warm sun on his back, the cool breeze on his cheek, the bright blue of the April sky . . . it was good to be alive.

As he reached the highway intersection, the Greenville courthouse clock struck the first stroke of twelve. He pulled up at the stop sign to turn left toward town. It was then that he saw John Wallace standing beside his car on the courthouse square, blocking his way toward home.

Turner knew then that it was a trap.

As he saw Wallace, Wallace saw him. In panic, Turner wheeled his truck around, toward Newnan and Coweta County.

Chapter Two

John Wallace had waited on the Greenville town square all morning. At the first stroke of noon by the courthouse clock, he and his friends were going to kill Wilson Turner. The plans were made, the signal set. Sheriff Collier had been told what to do.

No one in Meriwether County would question the killing, for as Millard Rigsby had told Turner, Wallace was one of the Strickland clan, a fierce tribe that had controlled the county for 150 years with fear, economic bondage, and an occasional dole.

Violence was a way of life for the Stricklands. Their deeds were legendary, and they had increased their fortunes through the manufacture of moonshine liquor. In the 1920s and 1930s, they had run the biggest illegal liquor operation in their part of the county, and at one time or another, most of them had spent time in the Federal penitentiary for conspiracy to violate the Internal Revenue laws.

John Wallace's uncle, John Strickland, had been the clan's most notorious leader. Colorful, clever, and ruthless, he costumed himself in balloon-sleeved white shirts, a black vest, and the pair of pearl-handled pistols that he never took off. No one dared cross him, and if they did, they didn't live to tell about it. Folks in Meriwether County remembered the day John Strickland shot his brother El to death in a duel over a mulatto woman in the front yard of the family home.

Later, when John Strickland himself was killed in the still yard by a Federal raiding officer named Hancock, the mantle of leadership passed to John Wallace. Although Wallace did not bear the family name, he had blood claims to the title from his mother, Miss Myrt Strickland. Years before, Miss Myrt had married a man named Wallace and lived with him in Alabama until he deserted her and

14

their two small children. She had then returned to her family home in Meriwether County, where she and her brothers undertook the education and training of her young son, whom she had named for her brother, John Strickland. John Wallace, now head of the clan, had learned his lessons well.

By rights, the leadership of the clan should have passed to Wallace's cousin, Tom Strickland. Tom, a tall, dark, sinister figure, had the necessary cruelty and lack of conscience to commit whatever deed was required to maintain family dominance, but his character was flawed by a tendency to break under pressure. Leadership required a cool detachment, an ability to function effectively under the most formidable circumstances. Tom Strickland didn't have it. John Wallace did.

In picking an heir apparent, the Stricklands put aside personal preferences and prejudices. Their key to survival was family solidarity. Whatever the crisis, they stood shoulder-to-shoulder, presenting an impregnable fortress to the world. To continue their rule of the county, the strongest clansman was selected, their sister's son, John Wallace.

John Wallace's reign was different from his uncle's. John Strickland's rule was based on absolute terror—even his friends were afraid of him. In an argument once, he had won his point by drawing his gun on a friend and warning: "Say just one more word, and I'll drag you down to my blacksmith shop and have my smitty beat your tongue just as thin as a dime."

Wallace had a different way of doing things. He tolerated nothing but blind obedience, but he coupled this with a spontaneous generosity so remarkable that his mother called him "Double John." "Because," Miss Myrt once explained, "he's the best boy and the worst boy I ever saw."

His paradoxical behavior caused confusion and division in the way people felt about him, but John Wallace courted this condition. He had long ago learned that people would forgive and overlook almost anything so long as a person was "nice." This meant courtesy in company, debts paid when due, and generous contributions to the church charities and to individuals in distress.

He was a master at presenting the unexpected gift and the dramatic dole . . . giving new pews to the church, replacing a widow's dead milk cow, rebuilding a farmer's burned-out barn. Whenever there was trouble, Wallace was always there, distributing whatever was needed from his great storehouse of possessions.

It unquestionably gave him pleasure, but more important, it gave

15

him power. The recipient accepting his generosity became beholden. He owed Wallace something. It might be years before Wallace called to reclaim the debt, but when he did, he wanted it paid in full—upon demand—in whatever coin he decided to collect.

To those who had never experienced his tyranny, his acts of generosity seemed like splendid, spontaneous charity. Others, who knew his cruelties, remembered the Sunday afternoon he drove to town and demanded of those idling on the courthouse square: "Where's the sheriff?"

When they said they didn't know, he told them: "Go find him and tell him to come out to my place right away. I had to kill a nigger a little while ago, and I want him to come down and take him away."

Nothing more was heard of this, no complaint, no charges, no investigation, nothing.

For the most part, however, when Meriwether people judged John Wallace, they balanced the atrocities they had heard about against the fine things they had seen happen with their own eyes, and decided that a man with such Christian virtues couldn't be *all* bad. And there were those who insisted that John Wallace was different from the rest of his clan. He didn't *look* like the Stricklands, he didn't *act* like the Stricklands, he wasn't even *named* Strickland.

In contrast to his dashing predecessor, John Wallace looked like an ordinary dirt farmer. He wore plain khaki work clothes and a broad-brimmed white hat to shade his sunburned face. What's more, he urged everyone to call him "John."

This was a liberty that most people did not care to take, considering who he was and what he was capable of doing. Out of deference to his request, most of them called him "Mr. John," which they considered a nice, safe balance between formality and familiarity.

Ordinary though he seemed, he was imposing. At fifty-two, he was a bear of a man . . . big, top-heavy, bullnecked, broad-shouldered . . . strong enough still to kill a man with his bare hands. His head was completely bald, his eyebrows and lashes so light he seemed to have none. His glacial blue eyes, hooded by folded lids, reflected no emotion, even when he was smiling.

Because he preferred a low profile, Wallace tried to be taken for "one of the boys," an image he developed by companionably talking cattle, crops, and corn to the men, and exhibiting courtly courtesy to the ladies. Predictably, their response was kind words in praise of his gentlemanly qualities.

16

Although the goodwill of the people was not necessary, Wallace found that it made his operation easier. Whenever there was any legal trouble, he had a drove of "upstanding citizens" whom he could call upon to testify on his behalf. It was like money in the bank, collecting interest while it lay idle, and a mighty reservoir if needed.

This currying of favor would have struck old John Strickland as an indignity beneath his stripe. In his day, Meriwether County had been as wild and wide open as the Old West. Domination required only daring and a fast gun. But no more. Times had changed since the twenties and thirties, and Meriwether with it. The men returning from World War II were not so easily swayed or intimidated, and law enforcement outside the county was getting tougher all the time. Control now required both cunning and cleverness, qualities with which John Wallace was heavily endowed.

Although the tactics had changed, the objectives of the Strickland family were the same as they had always been: continued control. From their half-moon corner of the county, which they openly and arrogantly called "the Kingdom," they ran their interlocking estates like feudal lords, dispensing favors and fear as they saw fit.

Compared to John Wallace and the Stricklands, the Ku Klux Klan was a Halloween charade. The Klan's target was subjugation of the Negroes and recalcitrant poor whites. John Wallace and the Stricklands subjugated everybody.

Even those who deplored the dark things that were happening, chose to leave a bad thing alone rather than start a sea of troubles. John Wallace was a powerful man. Left unprovoked, he was both generous and friendly; therefore nobody—absolutely nobody—interfered with John Wallace or his business, for there was no one to turn to for help. Meriwether County Sheriff Hardy Collier, without question or hesitation, did exactly what John Wallace told him to do.

On the morning of Tuesday, April 20, Sheriff Collier had received his instructions. At precisely the first stroke of noon by the Meriwether County courthouse clock, Sheriff Collier was to release Wilson Turner from jail. Turner's green-and-white pickup truck, impounded in the jail yard since his arrest, was to be drained of all but enough gasoline to get it started. Turner was to be told that he was being released for insufficient evidence, and that he could go home in the truck. At the highway intersection, Wallace and his friends would be waiting to chase him down and kill him. The story would be that Turner had broken jail and had been killed in an effort to capture him.

17

These arrangements, more elaborate than usual, were necessary because Turner was a white man and because too many people already knew about the trouble between him and Wallace.

Hiring Turner had been a mistake, and Wallace had done so against his better judgment. When Turner had come to him two and a half years ago, looking for a job, Wallace had at first refused. Workers were usually acquired under the peonage system. All his hired hands were Negroes, and Wallace told Turner he meant to keep it that way. Turner, assuming that Wallace took him for "poor white trash," took ninety dollars out of his pocket and fanned it out for Wallace to see.

"I got this much with me and thirty dollars more at home," he'd said, expecting the cash to prove him a man of worth.

Wallace refused again. Turner was not only white, he was a sickly-looking fellow weighing barely 125 pounds. He had the pinched, hungry look inbred in sharecroppers that no amount of plenty ever diminishes, and he didn't seem strong enough to do a day's work.

But when Turner told him that he had learned to be a top mechanic in the army and could keep anything running, Wallace hired him on a two-month trial basis. Good mechanics were hard to find.

Turner did his work fast and efficiently. Despite his frail appearance, he could do more in one hour than the others could do in eight. Wallace liked that. At the end of two months he decided to let Turner sharecrop, and gave him thirty acres of farmland—fifteen for cotton, fifteen for corn.

He waited longer to invite Turner to come along to the liquor still he was operating in the wooded swamp. Wallace chose with great care those who aided him there. Caution was the key in liquor making now. It was no longer possible to manufacture moonshine on the Stricklands' former scale. Wallace's operation was smaller, but more carefully managed. Whenever the Federal agents planned a raid, Sheriff Collier passed the information along to Wallace and all operations shut down no matter how much money or liquor was involved. Nothing was worth getting caught again.

Turner understood this and accepted the terms. For two years their arrangement worked well. Turner was a good liquor man. He had nerve and daring, he did what he was told, and he made enough money running liquor to buy himself a new pickup truck. That was all right because it gave him a means of making deliveries, but plenty was never enough for Turner. Wallace saw him getting fancy ideas about

18

bettering himself—buying store-bought clothes for his wife and kid, furniture for the house, and running to the doctor every time one of them got sick. As his expenses grew, he became reckless, willing to take greater and greater chances. Wallace was not.

When he had let Turner run those twenty gallons of liquor, Wallace had never expected him to succeed. He had been enraged by Turner's disobedience in refusing him the money, and after he had run the man off his land, he had had second thoughts. Just running Turner off could prove to be a fatal mistake. Turner knew too much. He might talk. He knew that he should have killed Turner while he had the opportunity.

Later, when Wallace learned that Turner was sneaking back to the still, stealing liquor to get some money to live on, he lay in wait for him, but was never able to catch him. It was at this time, wanting to get rid of Turner somehow, that he hit upon the masterful idea of calling in the Alcohol Tax Unit, reporting the still, and naming Turner as the culprit. That way, the Federal agents would be working *for* him.

The complaint was made through his Greenville attorney, Gus Huddleston. Federal Agent Earl Lucas was assigned to investigate the case. Wallace, playing the aggrieved innocent, explained to Lucas that his former tenant, Wilson Turner, was making liquor on his land. Although he had tried to stop Turner, he could not. He himself, Wallace pointed out, was under a presidential pardon and was afraid that Turner's activities might be mistaken as his own. He wanted Turner caught and arrested.

Unknown to Wallace, the still he reported had, for some time, been under surveillance by the Alcohol Tax Unit. Lucas, however, responded as requested and ran a stakeout at the still. Turner, hearing that a Federal officer had been called in, stayed away and no one was apprehended.

In the spring, when John Wallace discovered that two of his prize cows had been stolen from his pasture, his rage could not be contained. No man alive had ever stolen anything from Wallace and lived to tell about it. He was sure that Turner had stolen the cows, and Turner, he decided, would have to die.

Eighty-year-old Uncle Mozart Strickland, the clan's oldest male member, tried to dissuade Wallace from his far-reaching plan, but for Wallace, satisfaction could come only from killing Turner himself.

"I don't like it, John," Uncle Mozart warned. "Too many people know about the trouble between you and Turner."

Wallace shrugged indifferently. "Sharecropper tenants are a dime a dozen. Who the hell's gonna go looking if one turns up missing?"

Shortly after midnight on Sunday, April 18, soon after Chief of Police Threadgill had arrested Turner, Wallace arrived at the Carrollton jail to ask Threadgill's permission to transfer Turner to the Meriwether County jail on the pretext of venue, since the cow had been stolen in Meriwether County. Threadgill, unaware of Wallace's motives, agreed to this. His only stipulation was that Sheriff Collier bring a warrant when he came to make the transfer.

Wallace lost no time. By three o'clock in the morning, he and Sheriff Collier had returned to Carrollton to take Turner and his pickup truck back to Meriwether County. Threadgill was home in bed. Telephoning from the jail, Wallace told him that Collier had the warrant, and Threadgill released Turner to his custody.

Before dawn on Monday, Turner was locked up in the Meriwether County jail, to be held incommunicado until Tuesday, April 20. Wallace, meantime, completed his arrangements to kill him.

He had chosen with care the friends he needed to help him that Tuesday morning. All were beholden to him in one way or another. Herring Sivell, a fellow dairyman from the neighboring town of Chipley, had had his troubles some eight years before when he had killed a man named Pat Brooks in an argument over a poker game. Sivell had claimed Pat Brooks had given him provocation, but his act had been indefensible. He had left the poker game, returned with his gun, shot Brooks in the back and killed him. Wallace had applied enough political and financial pressure to have Sivell acquitted on the first-degree murder charges. Today, Sivell would drive one of the two cars needed to run Turner down. Wallace knew he could depend on Sivell. He had been crippled in a cattle accident but was tough and could get the job done.

Tom Strickland, Wallace's first cousin, was another choice. In the past, he had had his troubles, too. He and his wife had carried on a bitter controversy over a mulatto woman to whom Tom had taken a liking. When his wife was found dead in the bathhouse with five bullet holes in her abdomen, a coroner's inquest was called, and Tom, shaken, had turned to Wallace for help. The coroner's jury ruled the death a suicide.

Knowing his cousin's tendency to break under pressure, Wallace had assigned him to ride in the backup car, which was to be driven by Henry Mobley, a quiet, easygoing man who had once worked for Wallace and lived on Wallace's farm. Big, taciturn, and bald except for a cuff of hair that ran from ear to ear on the back of his head, Henry looked older than his thirty-six years. He had seen a lot of things that had happened down in the Kingdom, and Wallace knew

20

that he could depend on his remaining silent no matter what happened.

The only mistake in this morning's selection was Broughton Myhand, a budding young tough who ran a service station in nearby Chipley and did Wallace's mechanical work for him. Broughton was a boy by comparison with the others. Blinded by hero worship and eager to please, he had readily agreed to help with this morning's work. But when his wife, a forceful and formidable woman, had learned that the plan was to kill Turner, she had forbidden Broughton to go. More afraid of what his wife might do than what his friends might say, he had not shown up at the appointed hour.

This, Wallace decided when he heard the story, was just as well. Any man who would bend to a woman's will wasn't man enough to go along on the job this morning. Broughton would have to learn, if he had any hope of even hanging onto the edge of Wallace's inner-circle elite, that women were of use only in bed or in the kitchen. Once they were allowed to start talking, there was always trouble. With his own wife, Josephine, and his mistress, Young Missy, Wallace had no trouble. They never even made suggestions. They didn't dare.

John Wallace's arrival in Greenville that Tuesday morning was noted by idle storekeepers who had little to busy themselves with but looking out their shopwindows to see who was on the courthouse square, what they were doing, and why. Their interest was intensified when they saw that Wallace had been driven to Greenville by his friend Herring Sivell.

A short while later, the watching got more interesting when Tom Strickland arrived in Henry Mobley's car. After waiting for a while, Mobley walked into the Greenville Cafe. Strickland remained in the car, his long legs drawn up against the dashboard, his head resting against the seat, his black hair hanging in hanks, partially covering his sallow, unshaven face.

In the cafe, Henry Mobley ordered a Coca-Cola and spoke to the proprietress, Eula Baker, whom he had known since childhood.

"Watcha doin' in town on a Tuesday?" Mrs. Baker asked playfully.

Henry Mobley smiled. "Just messin' around."

Mrs. Baker intended to pursue her questioning, but a customer was standing at the cash register with a check to be paid. By the time she was finished, Mobley had left his half-finished Coke and returned to his car outside.

"Ain't that funny?" Mrs. Baker remarked to Willie Joe Copeland, the young Negro woman who helped in the cafe kitchen, "all four of them in town on a Tuesday?"

21

"Sho' seems funny," Willie Joe agreed.

When they later saw John Wallace go into the Production Credit Association, followed a short time later by Sivell, the spectators decided that Wallace and his friends had come to town on Tuesday about money. They saw Wallace come out on the square again, and as the morning wore on, they turned their attention to other things. It was nearly noon and time to go home for lunch.

Waiting on the courthouse square most of the morning had irritated John Wallace, who did not like waiting for anything, not even for the appropriate moment. His impatience, however, was in no way discernible to those who watched him. His ice-blue eyes reflected the unparalleled composure of one accustomed to having his own way. It had always been so, and John Wallace expected it to continue so forever.

Across the courthouse square he could see Sheriff Collier talking with Mrs. Stovall, the elderly, straitlaced editor who ran the *Meriwether Vindicator* for Judge Revel. Wallace was pleased. Collier had obviously completed the arrangements he had been told to make. Now he was establishing his alibi. He could not have found a more substantial witness to his being on the courthouse square at noon. Mrs. Stovall restricted her reporting to church news and civic activities and was forever trying to enlist someone in charity work.

Looking at his wristwatch and seeing that both hands were together at twelve o'clock, Wallace smiled. The hour had arrived. Shading his eyes against the noon sun's glare to look up at the courthouse clock, his eye caught sight of a pickup truck already at the intersection. It was Turner! Minutes before he should have been there.

The courthouse clock struck the first note of noon, rumbling its mighty sound across the quiet countryside. Wallace saw Turner swing his truck wildly away from town toward Newnan and Coweta County.

Sivell, cued to arrive back at the car just as the clock struck, was still on his way.

"Let's go!" Wallace shouted.

Sivell hobbled the last few steps, jumped behind the steering wheel, and headed after Turner. Mobley, seeing the sudden action, followed. The courthouse clock continued to strike the noon hour. The moment was marked.

On the narrow road, Sivell's strong, rough hands gripped the steering wheel as he swung his car around the curves.

"Get Turner before he gets to the Coweta line," Wallace barked. "That sheriff in Newnan is hell."

22

"Yeah, Lamar Potts." Sivell was concerned: "Folks in Coweta County brag like he was Wyatt Earp."

"Well, get the hell on down there and pull up alongside Turner. We'll edge him off the road."

But the narrow road wound around the red clay hills past freshly plowed cornfields and patches of woods in a tortuous route. Despite Sivell's skill, the grades of the curves allowed no real speed. Turner, with the advantage of a moment's lead, stayed ahead just enough so that his truck came in sight only as it disappeared around the next curve.

"You keep this up, Herring, and you'll let him get away. Coweta's only seventeen miles, and we musta come ten already." Wallace's hand closed on the sawed-off shotgun that lay beside him on the seat, loaded and ready to use the moment they captured Turner.

"You said Collier had drained his gas tank."

Wallace scowled angrily. "I *told* Collier to drain his gas tank. I also told him to turn Turner out of jail at exactly the first stroke of twelve. Damn if I know what happened."

Ahead, on a downhill grade, the road straightened out for a quarter of a mile. Sivell, anxious now and determined, stomped down on the accelerator so that the car leaped forward, closing the distance between him and Turner's truck. Turner, driving faster, rounded the next turn with the truck's tires squealing as they gripped the inside curve. The State Highway Department was repairing one lane of the road and he had barely missed their blockade.

Sivell grinned. "If he keeps this up, you won't have to kill him. He'll kill himself."

"I wouldn't like that," Wallace said, taking Sivell's .44 pearl-handled pistol from the glove compartment. "This is somethin' personal. I want to do it myself."

Leaning out of the car window, he took aim and began firing at Turner's truck, trying to hit the tires. Turner, now riding the middle of the road, began swinging wildly from left to right to dodge the bullets. Wallace fired again and again, but the truck raced on.

"John, what the hell's the matter with you?"

Wallace sank back on the seat to change the gun clip and wiped his wet eyes. "Damn wind is whipping in my face so bad, it's making my eyes water and I can't get aim."

"You better hurry. The county line is just ahead."

"You just keep Turner in sight. I'll get him," Wallace said.

As Turner rounded the curve ahead, there was again a shrieking of brakes and a squealing of tires. Sivell hit his brakes, too, and pulled over just as an oncoming Purina Feed truck plunged over the hill and toward him. Turner, run off the road, pulled back an instant before Sivell reached him, and they raced across the Coweta County line with Turner only ten feet ahead.

"That sonofabitch," Wallace said, hanging out the window with the pistol ready to fire.

"Hold off shooting, John," Sivell warned. "We've crossed the county line. We'll catch him."

But before Sivell could overtake him, Turner swung his truck off the road to a tourist camp on the right. The sign said: SUNSET TOURIST CAMP, RESTAURANT AND CABINS, STEVE SMITH, PROPRIETOR. The restaurant was an old, oblong building with a roof overhang above the gas pumps. Small, white-frame cabins clustered in a grove of pine trees behind the restaurant, and noonday diners had parked their cars in the gravel drive out front.

Turner swung past the parked cars, sprang from his truck, and ran screaming toward the restaurant door. "Help! Help! Somebody get some help. They're gonna kill me!"

Sivell, almost bumper to bumper with the truck, pulled in after it and screeched to a stop beside the white picket fence that divided the tourist camp property from the house next door. A startled old man, leaning on his walking cane, stood still in his garden behind the picket fence. He saw Wallace snatch his sawed-off shotgun from the car seat and take aim at Turner scrambling for the door.

A shrill shriek pierced the air. A woman's voice from across the road screamed: "Don't kill him!"

Reflex made Wallace look back. Flinging up his hand, he motioned to the woman to hush. In that moment, Turner reached the restaurant door, clawing at the screen to get it open.

Sivell, his pearl-handled pistol in his hand, ran from his car, caught Turner, grabbed him by his trouser belt, and began beating him with the gun. Though half Sivell's size, Turner fought like a trapped animal, kicking, flailing, screaming.

Hurrying to help Sivell, Wallace grabbed Turner by one arm. Sivell took the other. Together they dragged him toward the car.

Inside the restaurant, the diners, hearing Turner's cries, had crowded to the door. Proprietor Steve Smith, tall, tough, with the build of a bouncer, pushed past them and walked outside. "What the hell's goin' on here?" he demanded.

Wallace shot him an irritated glance. "We're officers," he said. "This man's an escaped prisoner. Dangerous. Wanted for murder."

24

Steve Smith looked at the two big, burly men dressed in khaki work clothes beating a small, frail man. Wiping his hands on his long white apron, Smith said: "Why don't you handcuff him, then?"

"Don't let them kill me," Turner cried.

Wallace jerked him to the car, but Turner, writhing and twisting, dug his heels in the dirt. Beating and prodding him with their guns, Wallace and Sivell tried to force him through the car door they had left open in their rush to catch him. Frantically, Turner grabbed hold of the door frame with his hands, one foot braced against the car, the other on the ground, using his body as leverage. Despite their pelting blows, they could not force him in.

Wallace, red-faced, sweating, and enraged, took his sawed-off shotgun in both hands, swinging it overhead as though it were an ax. With his full force, he brought the barrel down against Turner's head. So powerful was the blow that when the barrel struck the back of Turner's head, the gun went off, the explosion shattering the air.

Turner collapsed, falling forward onto the rear floor of the car, his feet hanging limply out the door, his screams silenced. Sivell grabbed Turner's heels, stuffed them inside, and ran around to the driver's seat. Wallace climbed into the back seat over Turner's lifeless body. His anger unappeased, he continued the pummeling as Sivell spun the car around in the gravel drive and sped back toward Meriwether County.

Standing in a little group outside the Sunset Tourist Camp restaurant, the eight eyewitnesses watched wordlessly as the green Ford disappeared.

"What're you gonna do, Steve?" one of them asked at last.

Steve Smith wiped his big hands on his apron. "I'm gonna call Sheriff Potts."

The Sheriff

Chapter Three

Lamar Potts had been sheriff of Coweta County for twelve years. At forty-seven, he was lean, muscular, and agile as a college athlete. A man of few words, he kept his own counsel, viewing the world steadily from beneath the brim of his hat, which he always wore pulled down to his brow. He was considered a man of conscience and integrity, trusted by the citizens and respected by the criminals. His intent was to keep the peace and enforce the law. To this end, he devoted all his energies and eighteen hours a day.

As a result, Coweta County enjoyed the lowest crime rate in the state of Georgia, something due in large measure to the sheriff's success in anticipating problems. To accomplish this, he made it his business to know everyone and everything that was going on everywhere in the county.

Assisted in this effort by his only deputy, his brother J.H., he constantly rode the back roads of the county, stopping to talk with whomever he saw, listening to what was said, and observing any changes that had taken place. If there was so much as a fresh footprint in the county, Lamar Potts knew about it.

Although this situation benefited the people, it was the despair of the criminal, petty crook, and moonshiner. All but the most foolhardy had moved their operation to more accommodating locations outside Coweta County.

Those in the criminal community agreed, however, that if they *did* get caught, it was better to be arrested by Sheriff Potts than by anyone else. He took care of his prisoners, would see to it that a man had a fair trial, and would help him get started again once he had served his time. Most important of all, he steadfastly held to the principle that every human being—white or black, rich or poor—was entitled to full

29

justice under the law, and that neither money, power, nor influence should dilute that right.

Beyond law enforcement, the sheriff's special concern was the welfare of his people. In time of trouble, need, or stress, their first reaction was to "call the sheriff." His response was always the same: total commitment to solving the problem. Because of this, a rare relationship developed between the citizens and their sheriff. Knowing that their confidence was safe with him, they did not hesitate to call him or to disclose any information that might be useful in keeping the peace.

When the telephone rang in Newnan during the noon hour on Tuesday, April 20, Sheriff Potts was standing on the courthouse steps talking with the old men who spent their time on the courthouse square. They were a tattered, threadbare group who had outlived their usefulness and now sought daytime shelter in the courthouse, warming themselves at the flow of life that had passed them by. Despite some objections from the town's Beautification Committee, Sheriff Potts allowed them to stay. For this they were grateful, and whenever the opportunity arose, they clustered around to talk to him.

When the phone rang again, Sheriff Potts walked inside and answered: "Sheriff's office."

"Lamar? This is Steve Smith down at Sunset Tourist Camp."

"Yeah, Steve, what you got?"

"I think we just seen a killin'."

"Where?"

"Right here in front of my place at Sunset."

"Do you know who it was?"

"No, not for sure, but they headed back toward Meriwether County."

"Anyone else see this?"

"Yeah, eight of us."

"Have them stay there. I'll be right out."

Sheriff Potts looked at his watch. It was twelve thirty-five. J.H. had not yet returned from a trip to the Crime Lab in Atlanta. He'd leave him a note. Picking up the phone, he called Sergeant Otwell at State Patrol Headquarters, told him there'd been trouble down near the county line, that he might need him.

Otwell, a vigorous man in his thirties, was a good officer. Enthusiastic, thorough, and dependable, he assisted the sheriff's office when additional help was needed. "Yes, sir, Sheriff," he answered now. "I'm on my way."

He was just rounding the corner in his gray State Patrol car as

30

Sheriff Potts walked down the courthouse steps. Nodding to him, Potts got into his own car. "Let's go," he said.

At the Sunset Tourist Camp, they found Steve Smith and the others standing beside a green-and-white pickup truck parked outside the restaurant. A thin, middle-aged woman darted from the group toward the sheriff's car. It was Merle Hannah, bursting to tell what she had seen.

"Sheriff, I saw it all," she said breathlessly. "I was standing over yonder across the road. . . ."

"Slow down, Merle," Sheriff Potts said quietly, taking her by the elbow and guiding her back to the others. "You're going to get yourself all out of breath talking so fast."

"Sheriff, he killed that man . . . I know he did . . . I saw him do it."

"Merle!" Steve Smith said sharply. "Will you wait a damn minute and let's get the facts straight!" Merle Hannah was his cousin, and when he spoke, she stopped immediately.

"Are these the witnesses, Steve?" Sheriff Potts asked, indicating the five men and two women clustered around him.

"Yes, sir. Geneva Yaeger"—he nodded toward the waitress standing beside him—"and I were serving these four customers when it happened. Merle was across the street, and Mr. Wilson, here, was standing in his garden behind the picket fence, right where they pulled in. Mr. Wilson lives next door. He saw it all."

Sheriff Potts looked at the old, old man with the drawn yellow skin and sunken eyes, leaning on his cane for support. The violence of what he had seen had left him frightened and faint and unable to talk.

Resting a gentle hand on the ancient arm, Sheriff Potts told him: "There's nothing to worry about. It's over now." Turning to Otwell, "Take Mr. Wilson back to his house and see that he's comfortable. We can take his testimony later."

The old man's clouded gray eyes misted and his chin trembled an acknowledgment as Otwell took his arm and led him to his house.

"Now, Steve," Sheriff Potts said, "tell me what happened."

He was told in detail to the point where the two men from the green Ford sedan had started beating the little fellow from the truck with guns. Then the sheriff interrupted.

"What kind of guns?"

"One man had a sawed-off shotgun, the other had a pearl-handled pistol."

"Did you recognize either one of them?"

"Not to know them. The one with the sawed-off shotgun was big

31

and bald-headed. The other one had a reddish crew cut. They said they were officers. Both were wearing khaki clothes like prison guards, but I couldn't figure out why they were beatin' on him so bad. In fact, I asked them why in the hell they didn't just handcuff that fellow."

"What did they say?"

"They said he was an escaped prisoner . . . wanted for murder."

"Did you know the man they caught?"

"No, but he put up one helluva fight for a little fellow." Steve went on with his account, telling what had happened at the door to the car, how the big bald-headed one had got mad, raised his shotgun with both hands, like an ax, and cracked the little fellow across the back of the head so hard that the gun went off.

"Did he hit him with the barrel of the gun?"

"Just as hard as he could. Then that fellow fell forward into the car and never made another sound. I'm sure he was dead. They quick stuffed his feet in the car and took off."

Sheriff Potts nodded, reflecting on what he had been told. "Steve, on the phone you said that they left going toward Meriwether County."

"That's right. They hightailed it outa here so fast, it's a wonder to me that the tires didn't come offa that car."

"Were you able to get the license number?"

"Only part of it." Steve Smith took an order pad from his apron pocket and handed it to Sheriff Potts. "I got only the last three numbers. The others were covered over by a homemade trailer hitch."

Merle Hannah had fidgeted impatiently while Steve Smith reported. Aware that her imposed silence was becoming unendurable, Sheriff Potts turned to her and said: "Now, Merle, what is it you want to say?"

"Well, it's like I told you, Sheriff. I was across the road and I saw the big bald-headed man take aim at that little fellow while he was running. I yelled, 'Don't kill him!' That's when the man with the gun turned around and motioned me to be quiet."

"Ain't that just like Merle?" Steve Smith interrupted. "She can't keep her mouth shut even in the middle of a killin'."

Merle scowled at him and continued: "By this time, the other man, the one that was driving, had got out with his pistol and they all ended up scrambling at the screen door. The rest is just like Steve said."

"Did you know any of them, Merle?"

"No. The little fellow they caught was a scrawny thing . . . couldn't have weighed more'n a hundred twenty-five pounds . . . black hair and peaked-looking."

"How about the other two?"

"Seems like I've seen that bald-headed fellow somewhere before. Somehow the livestock auction comes to mind."

Steve Smith was reaching in his pocket. "Here's the keys to the truck," he said. "When they were going through all that scuffling, that fellow musta dropped them. We found them over there near the cafe door."

Sheriff Potts reached in and turned on the ignition. The gas gauge was empty. "They chased that fellow as far as he could go," he told Otwell. "The gas tank is bone dry. Go over the truck good, and see what you can come up with. I'm going inside to call Sheriff Collier in Meriwether County."

Steve Smith started back toward the cafe. "I'll show you where the phone is."

Sheriff Collier himself answered the call to the Meriwether County Courthouse.

"Sheriff Collier? Lamar Potts here. Have you had anything on a prison break down there in Meriwether County?"

"Prison break?" Collier repeated the words as though they did not make sense.

Sheriff Potts's tone was slow and deliberate. "Have you had anyone escape?"

"No, indeed. What've you got?"

"Witnesses at Sunset Tourist Camp, just over the Coweta County line, saw two men who claimed to be prison guards run a fellow down and haul him off toward Meriwether County."

"I have no knowledge of such a thing."

Collier's formal and restrained reply had the ring of deceit.

"How about a black-haired fellow weighing a hundred twenty-five pounds, driving a green-and-white pickup truck? Do you know anything about him?"

Collier's reply was prompt. "No, sir, I can't help you a bit."

"If you get anything on this, would you let me know?"

"I'll be glad to."

Steve Smith had busied himself near the phone so that he could overhear the conversation. "What did he say, Sheriff?"

"Says he knows nothing about it."

"What do you think?"

Sheriff Potts's eyes lingered on Steve Smith's face for a moment. "I think Sheriff Collier is lying."

Outside, Sergeant Otwell had completed his search of the pickup truck. "Did you find anything, Otwell?" Sheriff Potts asked.

"Not much. Just this from under the seat." Otwell handed him a pink matchbook lettered in gold, advertising the Crepe Myrtle Motel in Carrollton, Georgia.

Sheriff Potts studied the book of matches for a moment, then slipped it in his pocket. "Anything else?"

"The truck's license plate frame says LaGrange Motor Company."

"There's a possibility. Get me the motor number, and I'll call right now to check the registration."

Since the truck was a new model, the salesman in LaGrange was able to quickly locate the information. "That truck is registered in the name of Wilson Turner, who gave his address as Meriwether County with a post office box in Greenville," he reported. "Will that help you, Sheriff?"

"Just what I needed. Thank you very much."

Otwell was standing beside the telephone. "Whose truck is it?" he asked.

"It belongs to Wilson Turner, a tenant on John Wallace's place in Meriwether County."

Otwell's eyes widened. "Do you think *John Wallace* was the one who ran Turner down?"

"He fits the witnesses' description."

"What're you gonna do?"

"Start checking. I want you to cruise down through Meriwether County. Pick up any information you can find and meet be back at the courthouse in Newnan."

Driving back to Newnan, Sheriff Potts began fitting the fragments together . . . Wallace . . . Turner . . . Sheriff Collier's strange reluctance to talk. A lot of things went on in Meriwether County, *but a public killing with an alibi by the sheriff?*

Sheriff Potts already knew there was trouble between Wallace and Turner. Earl Lucas, the Federal agent assigned to Wallace's territory, had told him that Wallace had reported Turner for making liquor on his land. Added to this was the report of cattle theft in Meriwether County that Sheriff Potts had received a week ago on Monday, April 12. The complainant: *John Wallace.*

The afternoon sun was blazing against his office window when Sheriff Potts got back to the courthouse. J.H. was waiting for him.

Four years younger and forty pounds heavier than his brother, J.H. had a middle-age paunch that hung over his belt. Unlike Lamar, he never wore a tie. His open-neck white shirt, though freshly starched, seemed rumpled even at the beginning of the day. His hat, worn on the back of his head, was floppy and shapeless as a sunbonnet.

34

"I got your note," J.H. said, pushing himself out of the brown swivel chair with some difficulty. "What's up at Sunset?"

"Looks like a killing." Sheriff Potts filled him in on the details. "I want you to call the Bureau of Motor Vehicles in Atlanta and get them to trace this license tag," he added. "Steve Smith was only able to get the last three numbers."

"Anything else?"

"Not yet."

Taking out the pink matchbook that Otwell had found in Turner's truck, Sheriff Potts ran his thumb across the gold letters: *Crepe Myrtle Motel, Carrollton, Georgia.* Jim Hillin, agent for the Georgia Bureau of Investigation, had Carrollton in his territory. Sheriff Potts picked up the phone: "Operator, get me GBI headquarters in Carrollton."

"I'd like you to check with Chief of Police Threadgill," Sheriff Potts told Hillin after briefing him on the background. "He doesn't miss much. If Turner's been in Carrollton, he'll know about it."

"I'll see what I can do for you, Sheriff," Jim Hillin said.

"Good. I'll appreciate that."

As Sheriff Potts put the receiver down, J.H. walked back in the office, fanning himself with his hat. "You got anything else?"

"No. But I'm going to get in touch with Earl Lucas now to find out what's happening with the liquor traffic in Meriwether County."

When Sheriff Potts had Lucas on the phone, he asked: "What's the latest on the John Wallace case in Meriwether?"

"We still have his place under surveillance."

"What about his tenant, Wilson Turner?"

"Wallace wants us to catch him."

"For running liquor?"

"That's what he says," Lucas replied, "but I'm 'most sure it's just to get Turner out of the way. Wallace told me if we did *not* get Turner, he was going to kill him."

"I think he already has."

"When?"

"This afternoon."

"What are you going to do about it?"

"Go after him."

"He'll be hell to catch."

"I know."

"Let me know if you need any help."

"I will."

The courthouse clock was striking five when Otwell arrived back in Newnan from his trip into Meriwether County.

"Any luck?" Sheriff Potts asked.

"Not much. I stopped and talked to a gang of road workers from the State Highway Department. They're repairing the highway between Greenville and the Coweta County line."

"Yeah?"

"One of the workers, Leon Flournoy, told me that they had seen *two* cars chasing a pickup truck toward Sunset at a little after twelve o'clock."

"What do you mean *two* cars? According to the witnesses at Sunset there was only one . . . a green Ford."

"The highway workers saw two . . . a green Ford *and* a black Ford. Only the green Ford returned, *and*," Otwell added, "the driver was alone."

"Could they give you a description of him?"

"Yes, it matches the one who drove the green Ford to Sunset . . . middle-aged . . . sandy-haired crew cut . . . khaki clothes."

"What time did they see that car return?"

"About forty minutes from the time they saw them all racing toward the Coweta County line."

Sheriff Potts leaned back in his brown swivel chair. Propping one foot on the bottom drawer of his kneehole desk, he cupped his chin in his hand and considered this latest information. The time factor did not fit. Forty minutes was too long to pass the point of road construction, abduct Turner at Sunset, and return. Something had happened in between . . . but what? Wallace had obviously transferred Turner to a second car that the witnesses at Sunset hadn't seen . . . but why? To avoid being seen by the highway workers again?

Otwell leaned forward in his chair, studying Sheriff Potts's face. "What do you think, Sheriff?"

"I think Wallace switched Turner from the green Ford to the black Ford and took him back to Greenville down one of those little backcountry roads to avoid the main highway."

J.H., leaning against the door frame, asked: "What now, Lamar?"

"Collect all the facts, then have Collier bring in Wallace and the man who helped him."

J.H. swept his hat off and ran his handkerchief over the top of his head. "I hope to Christ you get enough indisputable evidence so that Wallace can't weasel out of this one. He's the kind who could turn it around and get you for false arrest."

"Not likely," Sheriff Potts said. "I'll wait to hear from Jim Hillin in Carrollton and from Motor Vehicles in Atlanta. By then, we'll have enough evidence to go on."

36

Outside, the town was quiet. The old men who spent their time on the courthouse steps were returning home for the day. Shopkeepers on the square were winding up their street awnings. Otwell stood up. "If there's nothing more I can do, I'll check back in at Patrol Headquarters."

"That's all for now, Otwell. Much obliged."

When he had gone, Sheriff Potts reached in his shirt pocket and pulled out the small spiral notebook he used for daily reminders. There were two entries for today: *Britches for Berryman Brown—Noise in Miss Agnes's barn.*

He had noticed Berryman walking to school that morning, straggling behind the others, his shoulders drooping, his britches so small he walked stiff-legged. Poor and proud, Berryman never complained, but the too-tight britches were an obvious indignity that made him ashamed and self-conscious: Something could be done about that.

"J.H., there's not much more we can do here but wait for those phone calls. Could I get you to do an errand for me before the stores close?"

"Sure. What do you need?"

"Berryman Brown needs a new pair of pants. I'd like you to buy them for me and take them out to his mother."

"Right in the middle of all this . . ."

"What happened today has nothing to do with Berryman. His morale is low, and his britches are too tight. I want something done about it."

J.H. sighed. "Okay, Lamar, what size?"

Sheriff Potts took some money out of his billfold. "Better get him a size fourteen. He's a big boy for twelve."

The courthouse was dark except for the light in the sheriff's office when J.H. returned. "Did you hear anything, Lamar?" he asked.

"Jim Hillin called from Carrollton."

"What did he find out?"

"More than I expected. Remember that cattle-theft notice we got last week from Meriwether County on two registered Guernsey cows?"

"Sure. They belonged to John Wallace, didn't they?"

"Right. Hillin says that Threadgill found one of them in a Carrollton pasture last Wednesday. Wallace requested a stakeout until whoever stole the cow tried to remove it. On Sunday night Threadgill caught Turner trying to move the cow, arrested him, and took him back to the Carrollton jail. Wallace showed up just as they were bringing Turner in. He wanted Sheriff Collier to transfer Turner to the Meriwether County jail. Threadgill agreed if Collier came with a warrant."

"Did Collier come get Turner?" J.H. asked.

"About three A.M. he and Wallace took Turner and his pickup truck back to Meriwether County. That was the last that Threadgill heard of Turner until this afternoon."

"What happened then?"

"Wallace and Collier drove over to Carrollton and told Threadgill that they had released Turner because they didn't have enough evidence to prosecute."

"Hell!" J.H. exclaimed, snatching off his hat and smashing it against his knee. "Collier told you on the phone that he knew nothing about a green-and-white pickup truck or a man fitting Turner's description!"

Sheriff Potts nodded.

"Why?"

"I expect he's involved."

"Damn that kind of business," J.H. snorted, smacking his hat back on his head. "Are you going to swear out a warrant now?"

"Not until I've heard from Motor Vehicles. I want to know who was driving that car for Wallace."

"Do you think we'll hear today?"

"We can wait awhile longer. Meantime, I've got one more errand."

"What's that?"

"I promised Miss Agnes I'd come down tonight and check out those noises she's been hearing in her barn."

J.H. drew his mouth into an exasperated line. "You just don't ever quit, do you?"

Sheriff Potts stood up. "Well, checking her barn won't take long. You stay here by the phone, and I'll be back in a little bit."

Miss Agnes's barn was an ancient structure that now served no useful purpose, but because of its sentimental value, she could not bring herself to have it torn down. A quick check with the flashlight spotted the trouble. The upstairs loft door was ajar and banging against the side of the barn.

When Sheriff Potts reported this to Miss Agnes, she reached out and touched his arm with a frail, wrinkled hand. "What a relief! I haven't been able to sleep for worrying about who might be at the barn. Thank you, Lamar."

"No need to worry anymore, Miss Agnes."

When he got back to the courthouse, J.H. told him there had been no word on the registration. Sheriff Potts looked at his watch. "We may as well call it a day."

"Suits me," J.H. said.

At ten-thirty the next morning, the Bureau of Motor Vehicles called with the owner identification.

"Whose car is it?" J.H. asked.

"It belongs to Herring Sivell."

"Hey! Isn't that Wallace's friend . . . the one who was indicted for murder over in Troup County several years ago?"

Sheriff Potts nodded. "I had a fairly good idea that it was Sivell who was helping Wallace after I heard the witnesses' description of him yesterday. I just had to be sure."

"What next?"

"We've got enough evidence to have Collier bring them in."

"When?"

"Now."

Sheriff Potts picked up the phone. "Operator, get me Sheriff Collier in Meriwether County."

Chapter Four

When the telephone rang in the Meriwether County jail, Mrs. Vivian Matthews was leaning against the kitchen sink, peeling potatoes for the prisoners' noon meal. Although she had been assistant jailer for the past fourteen years, her duties were more domestic than official.

Officially, Mrs. Matthews was supposed to lock up and release the prisoners and enter this in the jail's log. Sheriff Collier had never been too particular about keeping the records, so Mrs. Matthews got around to that whenever she could . . . after she finished the cooking and cleaning, or if she chanced to remember while dusting the sheriff's ground-floor office.

What Sheriff Collier *was* particular about was having his meals well prepared and on time. Since the death of his wife, he had lived upstairs in the quarters over the jail, and Mrs. Matthews, who lived downstairs with her family, kept house for him.

The phone rang again. Mrs. Matthews, a buxom woman in her midthirties, pushed aside a strand of carelessly pinned-back red hair and savagely slashed at the potato she was peeling. She had no intention of stopping what she was doing to cross the hall and answer the phone when Sheriff Collier and John Wallace were sitting there beside it. All morning long they had been there, just talking.

Ever since Sheriff Collier had brought that Turner fellow over from the Carrollton jail, things had been in a turmoil. Sometime way before daylight Monday morning Mrs. Matthews had heard the cars drive up, but having no clock, she hadn't known what time it was. Besides, the baby had cried most of the night and she had sunk back into an exhausted sleep.

Before seven o'clock that same morning, the telephone was ringing. *Mrs. Turner wanted to speak to her husband!* Sheriff Collier had left

40

word that he couldn't receive any calls, and Mrs. Matthews told her so, but she just wouldn't listen. She kept calling and calling, thinking that begging was going to change Mrs. Matthews's mind. *Well!* She finally learned that when Mrs. Matthews said something, she meant it. Julia Turner never got to talk to her husband, but Mrs. Matthews never caught up with her Monday chores, either.

Tuesday was even worse. Mrs. Matthews had promised to do an upholstery job for Mrs. Jarrell across the street, but Sheriff Collier wanted her to stop whatever she was doing at noontime and let Turner out of jail. "Right at the first stroke of twelve by the courthouse clock," he told her, and then he took off for town.

As it got toward twelve o'clock, Mrs. Matthews, busy with the upholstery job, called Jake Howard, the Negro trusty at the jail, and told *him* to let Turner out. Jake had to meet the noon mail train in town . . . as he always did . . . so he let Turner out just a little before twelve . . . just a little.

That's when the trouble began. In all the fourteen years Mrs. Matthews had been working at the jail, she had never seen Sheriff Collier so mad. What she couldn't figure out was why. *What difference could a few minutes make one way or another?* It certainly couldn't be important enough to have a fit like the sheriff had had this morning. Why, having heart trouble like he did, he was liable to have a stroke.

Now when the phone in the office rang for the third time, Sheriff Collier called from across the hall: "Vivian, come answer this phone."

Mrs. Matthews threw down the potato and paring knife, wiped her hands on her apron, and walked over to the sheriff's office with quick, angry steps.

John Wallace, sitting across the desk from the sheriff, followed her with his eyes, and Mrs. Matthews found that her anger had suddenly melted into self-consciousness. With those pale eyes, there was no way of knowing what Wallace was thinking, and Mrs. Matthews suddenly felt uneasy.

The phone rang again. She picked it up. "Sheriff's office . . . yes, Sheriff Potts?"

She looked at Sheriff Collier. He glanced at John Wallace, then shook his head.

"Sheriff Collier is not in the office right now," Mrs. Matthews said. "Yes, I'll have him call you in Newnan just as soon as he comes in."

When she had hung up, Sheriff Collier waved his hand in dismissal and started talking to Wallace again.

Mrs. Matthews was furious. Calling her away from her work to answer the telephone when they were only talking and she had

41

important work to do. As she turned on her heel to go, she found Wallace's eyes still fastened on her and her uneasiness edged toward fear.

John Wallace kept his eyes on Vivian Matthews until she had scurried across the hall and was back in the kitchen. "If it was up to me," he said, leaning forward and propping his massive arms on the sheriff's desk, "I'd get rid of that goddamn woman."

Hardy Collier, a small man in his midsixties, shrunk further into the large swivel chair behind the desk. The pain in his chest was like a knife being turned, and the more they talked about what happened yesterday, the worse the pain got.

"Now, John," he said, tugging at the collar of his white shirt and slightly loosening his black bow tie, "there ain't no use in killin' Vivian."

"That's not exactly what I had in mind," Wallace said. "I meant I'd fire her."

A frown creased Hardy Collier's red face. "Vivian didn't *intend* to cause trouble."

"It doesn't make a good goddamn what she *intended* to do. The fact is that she didn't do what she was told."

"I'm afraid that's my fault," Collier apologized. "I didn't let on how important it was to let Turner out at exactly noon. I thought it was better that she didn't know."

A tidal wave of anger rose in Wallace's face. "And then that Negro trusty didn't do what *he* was told!"

Hardy Collier grieved at his failure. He had been Wallace's good and devoted friend for years. Any request Wallace had ever made, he'd seen to it that it was done immediately and without hesitation . . . no matter what. Somehow, yesterday, everything went wrong.

"Well, he didn't know, either. He had to meet the noon mail train."

Wallace sprang from his chair, smashing his hard, wide fist down on the desk between them.

"What kind of goddamn place are you running here, Collier, when the hired help decides when and what they will do? I gave you some simple instructions. You didn't do a goddamn thing right but establish your own alibi."

The anger in his eyes cut like a laser beam. Collier twisted miserably in his chair. "John, I'm sorry. It was just a mix-up."

"I can't afford mix-ups like that. Now I got Lamar Potts breathing down my neck, and I don't like it . . . not worth a damn."

Collier waved his hand, brushing aside this absurdity. "Lamar

42

Potts don't know nothing. He's just nosing around. Hell, John, we ain't never had no trouble. *Nobody* meddles with the folks in Meriwether."

"Can't count on that. Potts won't let this thing rest. You remember that nigger that shot his wife and chopped off her legs? That nigger went clear to Kansas . . . hid out on a farm in the middle of nowhere. Potts never let up. He tracked him down, found him, and brought him back for trial."

"So damn what?" Collier scoffed. "That wasn't nothing but a nigger."

"How about that old man they found dead when his house burned down? The coroner ruled it accidental death, but Potts wasn't satisfied. He kept on searching till he found the bullet that killed the old man, proved the fire was deliberately set, and caught the killers as they were boarding a bus for Atlanta."

"Niggers. All of 'em were niggers."

"Nigger or not, it don't matter to Potts. He'd go after *anybody* that starts messin' around in Coweta County."

Sheriff Collier sighed. The pain in his chest just wouldn't let up and neither would Wallace. And this was ridiculous, talking about niggers.

"Now look, John, be reasonable," he said. "*No sheriff* in his right mind would think of hauling a man of your prominence into court . . . especially for some no-good nothing like Turner. Hell, nobody's even gonna miss him, much less go lookin' for him. Just ignore the whole thing. Just wait till it dies down."

"Not a chance. I want you to get on that phone and find out what Potts knows."

"Now?"

"Right now."

"John, I don't see a bit of use in. . . ." Wallace's look stopped him in midsentence. Collier reached for the phone. "Get me Sheriff Potts in Coweta County."

Wallace walked into the hall, picked up the telephone extension, and listened.

"Sheriff Potts, this is Hardy Collier in Meriwether County. Mrs. Matthews said you had called."

"Right," Sheriff Potts replied in that soft, even drawl, so calm it was always hard to tell how close he was to what he was after. "It's about that noon abduction yesterday at Sunset Tourist Camp."

"I see," Collier said cautiously. "What can I do for you?"

"Bring John Wallace in. I want to talk to him."

"*John Wallace!* Why, man, you're way off. He wasn't at Sunset yesterday at noon because he was sitting right here having dinner with me."

"Couldn't have been," Sheriff Potts said evenly.

"Right here at my own dinner table, I can vouch for that."

"I don't want you to vouch for him. I want you to bring him in."

"Now see here, Potts, John Wallace is a big man down here. You don't just go hauling him in like you would anybody else."

"I have substantial evidence that both he and his friend, Herring Sivell, were involved in that Turner killing. I want to talk to both of them. Now, either you bring them in or I'll come down there and get them."

"I can't do that."

The silence on the other end of the line was ominous. Hardy Collier hurried to explain: "Wallace has gone out of town . . . on business."

"Then you'd better find him . . . fast."

"I'll see what I can do." Collier agreed reluctantly.

"I'll be waiting," Sheriff Potts said.

Collier hung up the phone and closed his eyes. The pain in his chest seemed to worsen with the situation. He was feeling in his pocket for his heart pills, when Wallace reentered the room.

"*Well!*" Wallace's tone was an accusation. "You sure as hell had that figured out all ass-backward. I told you, Potts wasn't gonna let it rest." He smashed his fist into the palm of his hand. "I ain't never failed to figure a man yet . . . and Potts is one of those relentless kind."

"John, he won't try to bring his law enforcement to Meriwether County. *Nobody* meddles with the folks in Meriwether. Any law officer looking for information wouldn't be able to find out the time of day, let alone incriminating evidence. Potts can't prove a thing."

Wallace glowered at the sheriff. "I'm not taking any more chances. I'm gonna see Gus Huddleston."

"What you gonna tell him?"

"As little as possible." Wallace picked up his hat. "I'll be back. You wait here."

Gus Huddleston, a Greenville lawyer who had done Wallace's legal work for years, had his office on the courthouse square, only two blocks away. When Wallace returned from seeing him, Collier, overcome with anxiety, sprang from his chair. "What did Gus say?"

Wallace's face had a stiff, set-in-cement look. "Says it's serious. Says I should have you arrest me on suspicion."

"What!" Collier cried. *"Me* arrest *you!* What kind of damn-fool advice is that?"

"So if Potts does pursue this, Meriwether County will have jurisdiction."

"Gus is crazy as hell. Nobody's gonna charge you. What the hell have they got to go on? Somebody saw Turner get snatched at Sunset yesterday, but that don't mean nothing. Like I said, I'd ignore the whole thing."

Wallace shook his head. "Not with Potts."

"All right," Collier sighed. "What do you want me to do? Arrest you?"

Wallace's eyes were almost smiling. "Not yet. I got a better idea."

Collier looked up quickly. "What have you got in mind?"

"To be tried for murder in this state, corpus delicti has to be established, right?"

"Right."

"To establish corpus delicti, you gotta find a body, right?"

A grin of admiration and relief washed the anguish from Collier's red face. "By God, John, I knew you'd think of something. What do you want me to do?"

"Stall Lamar Potts," Wallace said. "I'll make damn sure he doesn't find the body."

Since late morning, John Wallace had searched the woods and wild undergrowth on his 2,000-acre farm for the abandoned well where just yesterday he had dumped Turner's body. Despite his efforts, he could find no trace of it. It was as though the earth had covered it over to torment him.

Deeply superstitious, Wallace always resorted to premonition and animal instinct to guide him through any misfortune, relying upon signs and omens to warn him of danger. So far, nothing had appeared to help him, and he attributed this circumstance to an inexplicable caprice of Fate. Try as he might, he could not make the earth yield its secret. *Was there no way to rid himself finally and forever of this troublesome tenant?*

He had begun by trying to retrace the path that he and Tom Strickland had taken yesterday through the green jungle of swamp, trees, and undergrowth to the well where he had thrown Turner's body. Abandoned wells pockmarked the old plantation, and at the time, he had made no effort to remember the location of this one, thinking that here, at last, was the end of Turner. But now, only a day later, he was back trying to find where he had been only yesterday. For hours, he had gone around in circles, searching, looking, probing.

He knew the well was located on land no longer under cultivation. Like the others, it had once served a tenant house, but years ago the constant cotton crops had stripped the surrounding fields of fertility. The tenant had moved, the deserted house had collapsed and disappeared, the swamp and the woods had reclaimed the land. Only the well remained. Somewhere in this green profusion, Wilson Turner lay at the bottom of that abandoned well, but where was it? *Where?*

Scratched by briars and the dense brush, angry and uncertain, Wallace came at last on a small branch of White Sulphur Creek, cutting its way through the woods. Here he removed his hat and sat down on the mossy green bank to smoke a cigarette. Soothed by the unexpected coolness, he leaned back against a tree and tried to decide on a course of action. Before him, the white vapor rose from the stream like the boiling brew of a witch's caldron. Was it an omen? A warning? What did it mean? Why had he chanced upon this particular spot?

He closed his eyes and tried to remember yesterday. *Exactly* what had happened after they left Sunset? Memory came in snatches of sensation . . . the concern when Sivell's car had a flat tire . . . the rush to transfer Turner into the other car with Henry Mobley and Tom Strickland . . . the indecision as they drove down back roads searching for an isolated spot . . . the weight of Turner's body when he hoisted him over his shoulder and walked through the woods . . . the sticky feel of blood as Turner's head bounced against his back . . . the relief as he unburdened himself of the dead body and threw Turner headfirst into the well . . . the final fit of anger when he dropped the enormous boulder in on top of him. Wallace could remember all these things, but the well, he could neither remember nor find.

It seemed incredible. Laying aside instinct and premonition for the moment, Wallace reasoned that if he couldn't find the well on his own property, then Lamar Potts wouldn't be able to find it, either. Why, then, look further?

He took one last drag on his cigarette and flipped it into the stream. Perhaps Collier was right after all. Maybe it was best just to forget the whole thing until it died down. The swamp was virtually impenetrable, its secrets hidden forever.

He watched the cigarette float smoothly downstream through the rising mist on the creek. It was almost out of sight when it ran against a rock jutting out from the water. Its passage blocked, the cigarette rolled against the rock until it disintegrated and sank out of sight. Wallace stared horrified at the spot where his cigarette had disappeared. In the dark, remote woods this, too, seemed an omen.

Picking up his hat, he hurried back to his car. He had to know whether or not Turner's body would be found. Only one person could give him the answer to that: Mayhayley Lancaster, an ancient, self-styled mystic who lived in a handhewn cabin built in 1830, in a wilderness area of Heard County, thirty miles away. She had one artificial eye and was said to be a witch—for she cast spells, conjured up visions, and was inexplicably successful in predicting the future and finding lost or stolen objects. For years she had served the countryside as seer and spellcaster.

Wallace himself had been at Miss Mayhayley's backwoods cabin only the week before to ask her help in locating his stolen cows. After he had crossed her palm with the required dollar and a dime, she had told him that Wilson Turner had stolen his cows, that one would be found, and that Turner would be caught. It had happened exactly as she had said it would.

As he drove into her yard, Miss Mayhayley's pack of dogs bounded off the porch and over the forty bales of cotton strewn like shipwreck remnants around the grassless yard. Years before, she had taken the cotton in payment for timber she had sold off her land. The bales had remained where they were thrown, providing bedding for her dogs and pecking places for the flock of chickens that wandered in and out of her open cabin door.

Wallace blew his horn and Miss Mayhayley came out on the lean-to porch, shading her eyes with her hand. She wore, as always, her dead brother's World War I army cap, an ankle-length wool skirt, and turn-of-the-century high-button shoes.

"Who's there?" she called.

"John Wallace. Call off your dogs."

Miss Mayhayley attempted a feeble whistle. "Come here, you critters." The dogs, wagging their tails, turned back toward the house, and Wallace followed her through the door.

Miss Sally, Mayhayley's seventy-year-old spinster sister, was standing by the wood-burning stove, stirring up a pan of corn bread for supper while the flock of chickens clucked and pecked at the cornmeal droppings around her feet. When Wallace entered, she looked around, smiled shyly, and turned back to her work.

Miss Mayhayley sat down in her cane-bottom chair in front of the fireplace, picked up a blackened iron poker, and stirred the fire in the grate. Wallace watched her without a word. Mayhayley did not like to have her thoughts interrupted when she was concentrating. Any violation of this unspoken rule could bring down her scathing wrath. When she indicated a chair, Wallace sat down beside her.

Without looking up, Miss Mayhayley said: "You killed him anyway, didn't you?"

"Who, Miss Mayhayley?"

Mayhayley turned her head and fixed him with her one good eye. "Turner."

"Who told you that?"

"The fire."

"What else does the fire tell you?"

"That you've lost the body and can't find it."

Wallace remained motionless, his face expressionless, determined not to let her know the impact of her words. Her tone had been accusing, but he could not be certain if she had spoken in anger or disgust.

"Where *is* the body, Miss Mayhayley?" he asked cautiously.

"I warned you, John Wallace! I warn you again! *Danger! Death! Destruction!*" Using the poker, Mayhayley punctuated each of the three prophetic words with a black soot mark on the hearth. "The three Fates surround you!"

Angry to hear her say what he already feared, Wallace blurted out: "Don't give me that hocus-pocus. All I want is the body. *Where is it?*"

Mayhayley squinted her eyes to angry slits, and Wallace regretted his impatience. Mayhayley deferred to no man. Independent, outspoken, acid, she was capable of bringing down Black Fate to block a man's path. He respected her power. Apology was difficult but he forced the unaccustomed words. "Forgive me. It's just that I'm in a hurry."

Mayhayley's anger swarmed around him. "Hurry will do you no good, John Wallace. The hands of the Fates have joined. This evil deed will see the light."

"Not if I can find the body."

Mayhayley shook her head. " 'Twill do no good."

He insisted. "Where is the body, Miss Mayhayley?"

"Deep in a well. Deep in the woods. The well is lost, but not for good."

Wallace tried to control himself. *"I know that. How can I find it?"*

"Alone, you can't. You must have help. Soon others will be looking."

"Will *they* find the body?"

Mayhayley stirred the fire and concentrated on the flames. Wallace leaned forward. "The truth, Miss Mayhayley, the truth!"

Mayhayley spat in the fire, then turned her head to listen to the crack and sizzle as the spittle hit the flame. Rocking slightly back and forth, she began to chant: "Run, run, the trouble's begun. They'll get you, too, before it's all done."

Wallace gripped the seat of his chair with both hands. "*Will* they find the body?"

Mayhayley only repeated her hypnotic chant: "Run, run, the trouble's begun, they'll get you, too, before it's all done."

He would have liked to grab the old witch and shake an answer from her toothless mouth, and she, still taunting him with the singsong rhyme, staring with that dark and terrible look, knew he didn't dare.

"Goddammit," he exploded, "can't you give a straight answer to anything? I want to know *who* will find the body."

Mayhayley's eyes were hard. "A man who is brave, a man who is true, a man who is just as determined as you!"

Potts. She was talking about Potts.

"Damned if he will!" Wallace upset his chair as he got up to go.

"Damned if he won't!" Mayhayley predicted.

"I'll get Turner's body back if I have to tear up hell and half of Georgia."

Mayhayley's thin lips stretched into a leer. "Try as you may, try as you might, the evil deed will see the light."

Wallace would listen to no more. He stormed out of the house, scattering dogs and chickens from his path. Getting in his car, he raced back toward Meriwether County.

There was still time. Potts wasn't even looking yet. Besides, Collier was going to stall him.

Chapter Five

In Coweta County, Sheriff Potts had spent Wednesday in the courthouse, taking care of routine business and waiting for Sheriff Collier to call. By afternoon, his cigarette pack was empty, his ashtray was full, and his patience was gone.

Collier was obviously not going to cooperate, figuring perhaps that if he did nothing, nothing would be done. *Collier should have known better than that.*

A sheriff had jurisdiction anywhere in the state. Customarily, with a suspect from another county, that county's sheriff was contacted and requested to bring the suspect in. Collier had been afforded that courtesy this morning.

As the courthouse clock struck three, Sheriff Potts opened a drawer of his desk and took out his .38 revolver. The time for waiting had passed.

"I'm going after Wallace myself," he told J.H.

J.H. watched him snap his gun into his holster. The occasions on which his brother wore his gun were so rare that J.H. could remember them all.

"Want me to go with you?" J.H. asked.

"No, I'll take Otwell. You stay here by the phone in case Collier calls."

"And if he does?"

"Tell him I'm on my way down."

An hour later, Sheriff Potts and Sergeant Otwell arrived in Meriwether County. On the surface, Greenville seemed no different from any of the hundreds of little rural towns that dotted the South. Its hallmark as a county seat was the courthouse, an antebellum brick

50

structure, mortared with pride and passion, that rose in white-columned splendor above the surrounding wooded countryside.

Beneath its Southern slumber lay violence and injustice of the cruelest kind. There were those who were above the law, those who were beyond the law, and those who were at the mercy of the law. Wilson Turner was one of these last. The people of Meriwether County preferred to dwell on the happier times when Franklin Roosevelt occupied the Little White House in Warm Springs, nine miles south of Greenville. When the presidential motorcade came down the Federal Highway from Atlanta, they lined the streets and cheered. Roosevelt's warm response delighted them and they claimed him as their own.

Judge Revel, county politician and owner of the *Meriwether Vindicator*, had known Franklin Roosevelt well. When he had first come to Warm Springs for polio treatments, it was Judge Revel, a self-appointed host, who had welcomed him to the town. And the judge always claimed that it was he who had first suggested that FDR run for President. No one in Greenville disputed the claim because it gave the town a distinction they liked to think was so.

For the people in Meriwether County, these were cherished memories. These were the things they were willing to talk about. What they would not talk about were the hard realities and the dark deeds done in the name of the law. The Meriwether County jail housed those who did.

Anything could be made a valid charge. The casually kept records ensured that no one quite knew where a prisoner was, when he had been arrested, or if he had been released. If any discrepancy arose, there was a blind justice of the peace who could be counted on to correct the record by signing whatever affidavit was put before him.

The architecture of the Meriwether County jail was as unusual as the conduct of its business. Built of brick on a scrap of lawn behind a wrought-iron fence, it resembled a child's building-block castle with rectangles, turrets, and towers. Sheriff Potts parked on the gravel beside the jail. Walking with Otwell up the steps, he knocked on the screen door.

Inside a baby cried, and Mrs. Matthews, pinning her dress over her chest, came to the door, her face drawn with fatigue. "Yes?" Her voice was sharp and irritable.

"I'm Sheriff Potts. This is Sergeant Otwell, State Patrol. I'd like to see Sheriff Collier."

"He's not here."

51

"Can you tell me where I can find him?"

"No."

"When do you expect him back?"

"I don't know," Mrs. Matthews said crossly.

Sheriff Potts kept his voice even and courteous. "Mrs. Matthews, aren't you the assistant jailer?"

"Yes," Mrs. Matthews's tone was suddenly defensive. "But Sheriff Collier never says where he's going or when he'll be back."

"When did you see him last?"

"This morning. He left after he talked with you, and I haven't seen him since."

Sheriff Potts looked at Otwell and back at Mrs. Matthews. "When Sheriff Collier comes back," he said, "tell him I'm looking for him."

Her eyes quickened with apprehension. "Yes, sir, I will." She hung on the screen door, watching until they drove away.

"No help there," Otwell said, shaking his head. "What now?"

"We'll take a look around town."

Two blocks away, Sheriff Potts parked his car on the Greenville town square. The streets were quiet as Sunday afternoon. "Maybe we can find out something in that café across the street," he said.

A plump woman, past middle age, wearing a ruffled white apron and steel-rimmed glasses, was standing behind the café's long counter. A small sign pasted on the front of the cash register said: MRS. EULA BAKER, PROPRIETOR.

Without speaking, the woman poured the coffee they asked for. The cups rattled as she set them down and coffee sloshed over on the counter.

"Sorry," she said shortly, taking a rag from beneath the counter and wiping up the spill. Sheriff Potts noticed that her hand trembled.

"Are you Mrs. Baker?" he asked.

Her eyes behind the glasses darkened with anxiety. "Yes, I'm Mrs. Baker."

"We're looking for Sheriff Collier, Mrs. Baker. Have you seen him?"

"Not today."

"How about the deputies? Have you seen any of them?"

Mrs. Baker shook her head. She was holding onto the edge of the counter.

"No one?"

"Only Cecil Perkerson," she admitted hesitantly.

"Where can I find him?"

"He was on the courthouse square a little while ago."

Sheriff Potts paid for the coffee and got up. "Thank you, Mrs. Baker."

"For what?" she asked nervously. "I didn't tell you nothing."

"No, you didn't."

As they started for the door, Mrs. Baker said, "Don't tell Cecil I said where he was." Her voice quavered. "He won't like that."

"Don't worry, Mrs. Baker, he won't even know we talked."

When they were outside, Otwell asked: "What's with this Cecil Perkerson fellow? That woman seemed tore all to pieces just talking about him."

Sheriff Potts squinted against the blazing sunlight. "Cecil is part of the setup down here. He's Herring Sivell's brother-in-law. . . . Like Wallace and Sivell he runs a dairy, makes moonshine liquor, and for a while was one of Collier's regular deputies. Now he's an acting deputy—he only goes after those he's interested in."

"Hell's fire!" Otwell exclaimed. "That's like a license to hunt."

"Damn right. The biggest game of all."

They walked around the square and on the opposite side found Cecil Perkerson on the courthouse steps, leaning against a tall, white column, a toothpick clamped between his teeth. When he saw Sheriff Potts and Otwell approaching, he grinned.

"Hello, Cecil," Sheriff Potts said.

"Howdy, Sheriff," Cecil drawled deliberately. "What brings you to this neck of the woods?"

"I'm looking for a Meriwether deputy."

"You just found one," Cecil said, shifting the toothpick to the side of his mouth. "What can I do for you?"

"I want to find John Wallace."

"What for?"

"I want to talk to him."

Cecil moved forward. "What about?"

"That killing at Sunset yesterday."

Cecil shifted his toothpick again, leaned back against the court-house column, his eyes full of challenge. "You know somethin', Sheriff, you ain't got a hope in hell of gettin' *anybody* in Meriwether County to help you find John Wallace. He's a powerful man in these parts, and he don't like *nobody* messin' in *his* business."

"When he crossed that county line into Coweta yesterday, he made it *my* business," Sheriff Potts shot back.

Cecil pursed his lips, wrinkled his brow, and shook his head disapprovingly. "I tell you what, Sheriff, I sure as hell ain't gonna go lookin' for him, and if you know what's good for you, you won't, neither."

"Is that a warning, Cecil?" Sheriff Potts kept his voice calm and even.

Cecil Perkerson shrugged his shoulders. "Just friendly advice."

"Then I reckon you'd better save it for your friends."

Sheriff Potts turned and walked down the steps to his car. Around the square, faces that had been pressed to shopwindows faded back into the shadows. With Otwell beside him, he headed his car in the direction of Warm Springs and Wallace's farm.

"Old Cecil is a pretty tough char-ac-ter," Otwell said, lighting a cigar and watching the gray smoke swirl into rings.

Sheriff Potts smiled. "Cecil likes to think so, but without Wallace to back him up, he's not worth a damn."

Five miles out of Greenville, he turned down a rutted dirt road that cut through red clay hills grown thick with Georgia pine.

"Is this where Wallace lives?" Otwell asked.

"Somewhere down here."

Up ahead, an old Negro in worn, frayed overalls walked up the road, his gnarled hands clutching a burlap bag slung across his shoulder. His back bent under his burden. Sheriff Potts pulled up beside him. "Can you tell me where Mr. John Wallace lives?"

The Negro looked at Otwell's State Patrol uniform. He did not reply, but took one hand off the burlap bag and pointed down the road where the turn forked left.

"Thank you." Sheriff Potts drove on.

"He ain't saying nothing, either," Otwell observed.

"None of them will. They're scared to."

"Do you think you can find Wallace's house?"

Sheriff Potts nodded. "It sits right beside a forty-acre lake."

"A forty-acre lake!" Otwell exclaimed. "Maybe he dumped Wilson Turner in there."

"Not likely. Wallace is too smart for something so obvious as that."

The road wound now through lush green meadows. Behind barbed-wire fences, herds of Guernsey cows grazed, raising their heads, blinking their eyes, as the sheriff's car drove by. Off to the right, the lake, cut out of the woodland, glittered in the fading afternoon sunlight. On a hill beside it was a modest white-frame house, nestled in a grove of pecan trees.

"Wallace lives *here?*"

Sheriff Potts nodded.

"I thought his house would be a good deal grander than *this*."

"Used to be. The big house burned some years ago," Sheriff Potts explained. "Wallace never bothered to rebuild it."

"Wonder why?"

"Wallace is interested only in power, not in its trappings. The only car he owns is a 'Twenty-nine A model. That's why they drove Sivell's car yesterday. He couldn't have caught an ox cart in his."

Otwell looked around the quiet, well-kept yard, a rose garden in the front and flower beds edging all sides of the house. "Don't look like anybody's here."

"Let's see." Sheriff Potts got out and went to the door.

His knock was answered by a big Negro woman with a wide, pleasant face. Wiping her hands on her white cook's apron, she opened the door. "Yassuh?"

"I'm looking for Mr. Wallace," Sheriff Potts said. "Is he at home?"

"Nawsuh, he ain't."

"Do you know where I can find him?"

Her eyes went past him and rested on Otwell's uniform. "Nawsuh, I don't."

"Is Mrs. Wallace home?"

The cook took up the end of her apron and began to wring it in her hands. "Nawsuh, Miss Josephine went to visit her sister."

"When was the last time you saw Mr. Wallace?"

"I ain't seed Mr. Wallace since yestiddy . . . yestiddy mawnin'."

"Not since yesterday . . . Tuesday morning?" Sheriff Potts was puzzled and frowned over the answer.

The question seemed an accusation to the frightened cook.

"Nawsuh, not since yestiddy. I ain't seen him, and fo' God, I don't know where he is."

"That's all right," Sheriff Potts reassured her.

She released her pent-up breath. "Who must I tell him come?"

"Sheriff Potts, Coweta County."

When they returned to the courthouse in Newnan, J.H. was still waiting beside the phone.

"Heard anything from Sheriff Collier?" Sheriff Potts asked.

"Not a word."

Sheriff Potts considered this for a moment, cupping his chin in his hand, rubbing his bottom lip with his thumb. Collier was a fool to think hiding out would solve his problem. "J.H., get me a justice of the peace."

Otwell and J.H. exchanged glances. The waiting was over, the search was about to begin.

"Which one?"

"Doesn't matter. Mr. Carswell or Mr. Brown, either one will do."

A short while later, Mr. Brown waddled in, wearing his official expression, shuffling the papers he carried. "You want a warrant sworn out, Lamar?"

Sheriff Potts pulled up a chair for him to sit down. "That's right."

"Who for?"

"John Wallace and Herring Sivell."

Mr. Brown's beetle brows tilted up like a tent, his small mouth pursed in a little round *o*. "Lamar, are you *sure* you want to do this?"

Sheriff Potts nodded.

"What's the charge?"

"Kidnapping and murder."

The Body

Chapter Six

The setting sun was touching the treetops, ready to slide out of sight, when John Wallace reached home Wednesday afternoon. As he walked into the house, he heard the cook padding toward him.

"Mr. Wallace? Is dat you, Mr. Wallace?"

"It's me, Florine."

Florine's eyes were worried. "The sheriff's been here lookin' fo' you, suh. Dat one from Coweta County . . . Sheriff Potts."

Wallace's fury rose. *What the hell had happened to Collier this time? He was supposed to stall Potts.*

"All right, Florine, go on back to cooking," Wallace said, "I'll see about it."

But Mayhayley's words returned to haunt him . . . *Run, run, the trouble's begun. . . .* He knew he could not wait until morning. He would have to start searching for Turner's body tonight.

Down at the dairy barn, the milking would have been done and the Negro field hands would be putting away the tools for the night, waiting for someone to call quitting time. Wallace walked out of the house toward the barn, rolling down his sleeves.

"You may as well go home, boys," he said. "Albert, you and Robert Lee wait."

As the others left, Albert Brooks climbed down off the tractor and walked over to Robert Lee. "Looks like we's in fer it tonight."

Robert Lee Gates shook his head and wiped the sweat from his thin black face on his sleeve.

"Oh, Lawd!" he moaned under his breath, "what you reckon he wants wid us tonight?"

Albert, big and yellow-skinned, in contrast, chewed off the end of

59

the cigar stump he held between his teeth and spat it on the ground. "Ain't nooo tellin'."

"I sho' hopes we ain't diggin' no still tonight," Robert Lee clasped his back with both hands. "I'se wore out from plantin' cotton all day."

Albert and Robert Lee were Wallace's two liquor foremen, expert at digging the pits where barrels of mash brewed, tending the fires, and running off the liquor in gallon jugs when the time was right. Loyal and trustworthy, they could be depended upon to do anything. Time had proved that. Even when the Federal agents caught them, they never talked. Tried and convicted, they served their time in the penitentiary and returned to work. For this, Wallace rewarded them with a special status that set them apart from the other field hands.

From their liquor-making experiences together, an informal camaraderie had emerged, which the two Negroes treasured and Wallace enjoyed. When his mood was light, he indulged Robert Lee's comic complaints, and then Robert Lee, tall, thin, and black as freshly poured tar, "played the fool" with joy and gestures that made Wallace laugh, and Albert join in. Sensitive as a weathervane to Wallace's mercurial moods, Robert Lee knew when to start and when to stop his foolishness. There was joking and fun only when Wallace allowed it.

This time, when Wallace said to him and Albert, "Well, boys, we got a little job to do tonight," Robert Lee asked: "Ain't we gonna eat supper?" And then squirmed under Wallace's stony stare.

"I'se hawngry, Mr. Wallace," he whined, "so hawngry my stomach thinks my throat's cut."

"Keep that up and I'll cut it for you."

Albert laughed and Robert Lee grinned broadly, his white-toothed smile dividing his face almost in half. The game had begun and they enjoyed their joke before business began. After that, they resumed their roles of the haves and the have-to-dos.

Wallace smiled companionably at his own joke. "All right, Robert Lee, go on home and eat your supper. We'll pick you up later."

"Thankee, Mr. Wallace," Robert Lee grinned again.

"Get out of here," Wallace said in mock gruffness, waving him away.

He turned to Albert. "Albert, go get two five-gallon milk cans. Fill them with gasoline and set them in my car. I've got to get some things from the toolshed and I'll meet you there."

Albert was his favorite and as much a man as Wallace himself. Because of this they had a special regard for each other that lifted their relationship out of the Negro–White Man ratio, but even at that, Albert knew his "place," never crossing the invisible line, never

60

equating himself with Wallace or asserting his own opinions. He listened to what Wallace said, did what he was told, and when Wallace asked, told him what he thought. When Wallace chose, he used Albert as a confidant, knowing full well that anything he said would never be disclosed to anyone.

Over the years they had been through a lot together . . . making liquor, time in prison, even getting married. Wallace and Josephine had been married on a New Year's Eve; Albert and Lola Mae on that New Year's Day. Although he and Josephine had no children, Wallace took a custodial interest in Albert's eight offspring, seeing to it that they had clothes to wear, plenty to eat, and an occasional nickel to spend at the country store.

Albert already had the milk cans in the ancient 1929 A-Model when Wallace came up with his toolbox, a bucket, ropes, and a burlap sheet made from feed bags sewn together. He put these in the back of his car and drove down the road toward his Uncle Mozart Strickland's house.

"We got some work to do for Mr. Mozart?" Albert asked cautiously.

"No, we're gonna borrow his pickup truck."

Albert said no more, sensing something strange in Wallace's attitude, something he didn't understand, but something he knew it was best not to ask about. Years of working for Wallace had taught him not to cross him. Wallace had a quick temper and a fast gun, and Albert had seen them both in action.

People said John Wallace was nothing like his uncle John Strickland, but Albert knew better. He had worked for both of them. Mr. John Strickland liked to talk big and flash his pair of pistols around and use 'em every chance he got. Mr. Wallace wasn't that way. He talked quiet and polite to people and carried his gun in his pocket so nobody noticed, but Albert *knew* John Wallace would kill you just as quick as John Strickland would . . . you just didn't realize it.

Over the years there had been trouble between Wallace and Albert only once, and that was over a Negro girl that Albert was going with at the time. One day when the girl's daddy had sent her to Wallace's barn with a mule, Wallace caught her in the stall. Hearing her scream, Albert ran to the barn and lunged for Wallace, but Wallace warded off Albert's big fists.

"Look out, now, boy," Wallace said, "I was just funnin' with her."

"That's *my* girl, Mr. Wallace, and I don't want nobody funnin' wid her."

61

Wallace and Albert stood facing each other. Albert, much the same size and weight as Wallace, thought then he might kill him and he was ready to fight, but Wallace's look held him where he stood.

"Ain't no harm done," Wallace said, and waited until Albert turned away.

The incident was never mentioned again, but whenever Wallace referred to Albert as a "tough nigger," Albert took it as a compliment, not an offense.

This evening he remained silent until they got to Mr. Mozart's house and Wallace went inside. Ted Turner, Mozart's Negro field hand, husband of Mozart's cook, Mary, was squatted on his haunches, his back against a tree in the yard.

"You waitin' for Mary?" Albert asked, getting out to talk to him.

"Just waitin'," Ted Turner said. "Mr. Mozart said Mr. Wallace might want me for some work."

"Wonder whut?"

"Don't you know?"

Albert shook his head. "I thought maybe we wuz gonna put down another likker still."

Wallace came out on the porch. "Albert, take Mr. Mozart's truck, go down to his woodpile, and get me two cords of pine wood. Ted, you go with him to help."

When the two Negroes returned with the wood, Wallace said: "You can go now, Ted. Albert, put those two cans of gasoline and the other things in my car on that truck and we'll get Robert Lee."

At Robert Lee's house, Wallace honked the horn. Still eating a piece of corn bread, Robert Lee hurried out, grinning, and got in the truck. Sensing Wallace's changed mood, Robert Lee was aware that the earlier attitude of joking was gone. Things had got serious again. In silence they rode down to the swamp on an old log mill road. At the edge of the woods, Wallace directed them to unload the tools, the burlap sheet and the ropes, the cans of gasoline, and the two cords of pine wood.

Getting back in the truck, he drove to Albert's house. "Albert," he said, "go get those well drags I let you have and meet us down at the pasture gap. Wait for us there."

The strange activity had begun to worry both Albert and Robert Lee. They exchanged anxious glances, and as Albert got out of the truck, Robert Lee started to follow him.

"You come along with me in the truck, Robert Lee," Wallace said.

He drove back to his barn and parked the truck. "Now, Robert

Lee," he said, "you go down to the paddock and catch my saddle horse and Old Nell."

"Hawses?" Robert Lee asked. "What's us gone do wid hawses?"

"Just go get the goddamn horses."

"Whut must I do wid 'em?"

"Saddle them, you idiot."

Robert Lee looked dumbfounded. He could understand neither Wallace's sudden, sharp tone nor his strange requests.

"Now!" Wallace snapped.

A few minutes later, Albert saw them riding toward him, and opened the gap, a passage through the fence where the barbed wire could be hooked back onto the post. When they had gone through, he closed it and followed them on foot through the pasture into the woods.

Daylight was gone now and the woods were dark. Leading the way on his saddle horse, Wallace pushed through dense growth until the horses could go no farther.

Here, Wallace asked, "How far would you say we've come?"

Robert Lee scratched his head.

"I reckon 'bout three-quarters of a mile," Albert answered.

"That sounds about right." Wallace dismounted and took his flashlight out of his saddlebag. "We'll tie the horses up here on this high place, and leave the well drags," he said.

Robert Lee slid off Old Nell and whispered to Albert: "Whut you reckon he aims to do?"

"I dunno."

"Whut us gonna do?" Robert Lee asked, his voice high with tension.

"We're gonna look for a package."

"A package!" Robert Lee and Albert exclaimed together.

"Yeah, a package."

"Whut kinda package?" Robert Lee insisted.

"Just a package," Wallace replied. "It's down here somewhere in some plum trees and briars, and I got to find it."

It was his way never to tell them in advance what his plans were, waiting until the last moment to say what it was he wanted done. This avoided any reluctance or passive resistance, and gave Robert Lee, who was easily frightened and childlike in his hysteria, no time for anticipation.

"What size package?" Albert asked.

"Just a good-sized package."

"How's us gonna find sumpthin' when us don't know whut us is lookin' fer?" Robert Lee complained.

"You'll know it when you find it," Wallace assured them. *"Now get to looking."*

The main thing was to keep moving and not get Mr. Wallace mad. Albert and Robert Lee got busy looking—for what, they didn't know. The three of them fanned out and section by section searched through the trees, under the bushes, and in the briar patches. At midnight, the package still had not been found.

Robert Lee edged over to Albert's section and whispered: "Albert, whut you reckon he's lookin' fer?"

"I dunno," Albert replied, "but he sho' aims to find it."

Hearing their voices in the night's stillness, Wallace called out: "Hey, boys, have you found the package?"

"Nawsuh," Albert called back. "We ain't found nuthin' noplace."

"Well, we got to find it if it takes all night."

"Mr. Wallace, I'se tired," Robert Lee complained.

Wallace held his watch under the flashlight. It was past twelve o'clock. "All right, we'll stop to rest for a while. But we *have* to keep looking. We've *got* to find that package."

Sitting down on a fallen log, Wallace took out his cigarettes and handed one to Robert Lee and one to Albert. Lighting up, they stretched out and smoked in silence. Finally, Albert asked: "Mr. Wallace, do you know for sho' that package is down here in dese woods?"

"It's for sure down here," Wallace said. "I just can't find it. It's in a thick place down in a well."

"Down in a well? You ain't never said it was down in a well!"

"That's where it is. Down in a well in a bunch of plum trees and briars."

"If *that's* whut you's lookin' fer," Albert said, "I can go show you a well right now."

"Let's go," Wallace said, getting up.

They followed Albert through the woods to a thicket of plum trees and briars. "Here's the well right here."

Wallace came forward with his flashlight, holding the beam down in the well. "This looks like the right place, but there's nothing in it. Maybe it's done caved in."

"Nawsuh, this well ain't caved."

"Are there any more wells?"

"Yassuh, there's annuder one over that hill yonder."

"Let's take a look."

64

When they came to the second well, Wallace shook his head. "Not this one. It's too small. We'll have to keep looking."

The moon had risen and filtered like silver filigree through the trees as it traced its path across the sky toward morning. Still they found nothing. Robert Lee, having neither Albert's stamina nor Wallace's interest, grew more weary with each passing hour. Finally, he sank down on the ground beside a tree, his voice edging toward hysteria. "Mr. Wallace, I'se purely broke down."

"What in the hell is the matter with you?" Wallace demanded.

"I ain't able to go no mo'," Robert Lee wailed. "I'se plowed all day and looked all night." His voice broke in a sob. "We ain't never gonna find no more wells 'cause there ain't none."

Robert Lee's despairing words unleashed the frustrated anger Wallace had tried all night to control. Driven on by desperation, gnawed by Mayhayley's prediction and Potts's persistence, he had channeled his suppressed rage at Turner, hidden someplace beneath the ground, defying him even in death. Wallace wanted to shake the earth, tear down the trees, and so thoroughly destroy Turner that no trace of him would ever be left to bedevil his soul and reduce him to such absurdities as searching the swamp in the middle of the night with two frightened Negroes and a flashlight. *How could he . . . John Wallace . . . have come to this?*

Robert Lee, realizing that he had triggered Wallace's wrath, crouched on the ground and quivered, waiting for the blow to fall.

"Get up from there, you black bastard, and keep looking."

"I ain't able," Robert Lee cried, scrambling on his hands and knees to get out of Wallace's way.

Wallace drew back his hand.

"Don't kill me, Mr. Wallace, don't kill me!"

The screamed words sobered him. Striking Robert Lee would do no good. Besides, he needed him. There was no one, other than Robert Lee and Albert, whom he could trust to do the job that had to be done.

"Shut that nigger mouth of yours," he said. He snatched Robert Lee off the ground and stood him up. "You know goddamn well I'm not gonna kill you . . . you ain't worth killin'."

"Yassuh," Robert Lee agreed meekly.

Wallace had reduced him to docility; there was no need to force him further. It was time to quit. In the morning they could begin again. Shining the flashlight on his watch, Wallace saw that it was now past three o'clock.

"Go find Albert," he said, releasing his hold. "We'll go home and rest for a while and come back at first light when we can see what we're doing."

"Praise Gawd!" Robert Lee said, rolling his eyes toward heaven. He ran through the woods calling to Albert: "Praise Gawd, we'se goin' home at last!"

Bone-weary, Albert had reached a state of resignation—he no longer cared why they were there or what they had to do. He just wanted to get it over and done with. When he heard they were going home, he didn't even ask Robert Lee why. He just followed him back to where Wallace waited.

When the three of them had worked their way back to the height where the horses were tied up, Albert started to gather the well drags they had left there. "Leave them," Wallace said, "we'll need those things in the morning."

He mounted his saddle horse and Robert Lee climbed up on Old Nell. "Want to ride wid me, Albert?" he asked.

"Not me," Albert answered. Dragged long ago by a runaway mule, Albert had vowed never to ride again. Tired as he was, he followed the horses home on foot.

At sunup Thursday morning, Wallace drove Albert and Robert Lee in Mozart Strickland's truck toward the woods they had searched the night before.

"Albert, you and Robert Lee get out and go wait for me on that hill where we left the well drags. I'm going to go by Wilson Wood's house. He may know of another well."

Wilson Wood, an ancient Negro who had spent his life on the family plantation, lived in a tenant house close by. Albert and Robert Lee got out of the truck and climbed the hill as they were told.

Sitting down to wait, Albert pulled up a long blade of grass and chewed on it, saying nothing. Robert Lee worried over the silence for a while and when it began to oppress him he asked: "Albert, what you studyin' over?"

"I feel trouble comin'. Sumpthin's up. I ain't never seed Mr. Wallace like this befo'."

"Me neither," said Robert Lee.

Just then, they heard Wallace coming through the woods. And he was whistling.

"Uh-oh. He done found what he's after."

Robert Lee trembled. "Albert, I'se scart."

Albert pushed himself to his feet. "Who ain't?"

Wallace's face glowed with achievement. Last night's anger and

66

aggravation gone, he was again good-humored and gay, ready to trade teasing words with Robert Lee. But Robert Lee, unwilling to risk Wallace's wrath again, did not join in.

"Well, boys," he said, clapping his hands together, "get the well drags and let's go. Wilson Wood told me right where to look."

"How far?" Albert asked.

"Not far. Almost where we were at last night."

"How'd he know?" Robert Lee asked.

"He's hunted these woods for years . . . knows every fox, possum, and bird . . . but he says he don't hunt this area anymore."

"Why not?" Robert Lee wanted to know.

"Says it's too dangerous by himself . . . afraid he might fall in a well and wouldn't nobody know."

For the first time, things began to make sense to Albert. Maybe the danger was why Mr. Wallace wanted him and Robert Lee with him to help look.

Relief had brought a peaceful look to Robert Lee's black face. "Now you know where it's at, I reckon you don't need us no mo'," he said, ready to return to his day's work in the field.

"You boys gotta help me get it out."

"Get whut outa where?"

"The package out of the well," Wallace said. "Get your tools and come along." Pushing aside the saplings, he began making his way through the woods.

Obediently, Albert and Robert Lee followed him. Their relief had lasted for only a moment. Whatever it was, it wasn't over yet.

Finally, Wallace stopped in a clearing. "Here it is!" he said triumphantly. "Right here!"

Robert Lee rushed forward and looked into the well. What he saw transformed his eagerness into horror. His eyes protruded, his mouth twisted open and his shriek tore through the woods. Hearing it, Albert felt terror strike to his marrow.

"God and Jesus!" Robert Lee shrieked again, starting to run away.

"Hold it!" Wallace commanded, dropping his hand to the pocket where he kept his gun.

Years of obedience and fear stopped Robert Lee's flight.

"Ain't nothing in *there* gonna hurt you," Wallace said. "Now come on back." His tone was one of enticement to lure a wayward dog.

Robert Lee cringed and whimpered.

"Robert Lee . . ."

Robert Lee dragged himself back. He struggled to do what he was told, but the act was an agony.

"Albert . . ." Wallace's voice commanded.

Albert felt his feet move forward against his will. Every instinct urged him to run the other way. He edged up to the well and looked down. A pair of thin, white legs were propped upside down against the wall of the well, the britches fallen to the knees. The feet, clad in bloody brogans, were twisted in death's unnatural repose.

Even though the darkness at the bottom of the well concealed the remainder of the body, Albert knew who it was . . . it was Wilson Turner . . . he recognized his feet . . . the smallest man-foot Albert had ever seen. Oh, he knew this would happen. The night Turner took the money for the twenty gallons of liquor, Mr. Wallace was fightin' mad. When Turner stole the cows, Mr. Wallace was killin' mad. He had said he was gonna get Turner, and Albert knew he would . . . but not *this* way. A warm pool of sickness collected in Albert's mouth, ran down his throat, and spread across his stomach. He had seen dead men before, but never one like this.

"Let's get moving," Wallace said, the crack of the whip in his voice. "We gotta get this 'package' out of here."

Throughout the search, and even now, "package" was the term Wallace persisted in using to designate the dead body. By definition alone, he expected to depersonalize it into a "thing," denying its humanity and thereby removing the stigma of desecration. Despite his attempts to force this concept on the two Negroes, they could not adopt his callous denial of what had once been a man. To Wallace, this was of little consequence. Unemotionally and efficiently, he continued the task he had set out to do.

"Albert, go back to the old mill road and get the ropes and the burlap sheet. Robert Lee, see if you can hook the package with those well drags."

Robert Lee rolled his thick, black lips inside his mouth and bit down as he picked up the long hemp rope and dangled the drag into the dark hole. Fishing it up and down, he finally snagged one of the prongs into the sole of Turner's shoe. But when Albert returned with the ropes and the sheet, Robert Lee still had not managed to lasso the legs.

"Give it to me." Wallace took the rope. Expertly, he looped it several times around the legs until they were securely tied. Then, turning his back to the well, he drew the rope over his shoulder. "Grab ahold, boys. Let's pull this package out."

Albert and Robert Lee fell into line behind him, hanging onto the rope and driving their legs into the ground . . . pulling, tugging, straining with all their might, inching the body out.

68

"Heave!" Wallace said, and with that last hard effort, Albert felt the body slide over the top of the well and onto the ground.

Slowly, Albert looked back and there was Wilson Turner stretched out before him. His face, pale yellow and smudged with dirt, bore no marks of violence, but something terrible was wrong with his head. It lay at a strange, low angle like it was resting in a hole. Bending down for a closer look, Albert saw that the back of Turner's head was gone, that blood and brains had poured down his shoulders and neck.

A dead man was no novelty to Albert. He had seen them after they had been shot, knifed, drowned, and hanged, but he'd never seen a man killed this way before. Lying there like that, the rope still tying his feet, Turner no longer even looked like a man. He looked like an animal that had fallen prey to a trap in the woods . . . mutilated, dead, and still.

A cold sweat began to run down Albert's face and armpits. He had never, in all their years together, been afraid of Mr. Wallace before . . . not until now.

"Hurry up!" Wallace snapped, as though delay would allow them time for recognition. "Wrap the package up."

Albert and Robert Lee dropped the sheet Albert had brought over the body and rolled it over and over until they had a long, lumpy bundle lying on the ground.

"Now! Tie it up with the ropes."

Lifting the legs, wrapping the ropes around, feeling the dead weight of the body, Robert Lee was seized with so violent a tremor that his shaking hands could no longer knot the rope.

"Robert Lee, let Albert finish it," Wallace said impatiently. "You go cut a pole . . . a long one."

"A pole?" Robert Lee's face wore a senseless look. "What kinda pole?"

Wallace reddened with exasperation. "You dumb black bastard, get the ax and go over there and cut down that pine sapling."

Robert Lee, moving mechanically, cut the sapling, stripped the limbs, and brought it back to Wallace.

"Give me a hand, Albert," Wallace said. He ran the pole through the ropes so that the bundle was skewered like a pig on a barbecue spit.

"Now," he told the two Negroes, "pick it up, and let's get out of here."

Robert Lee took the front end of the pole, Albert the rear. Together they lifted their burden and laid the ends of the pole on their shoulders. With Turner's trussed body swinging between them, they followed Wallace through the woods. By the time they reached the clearing on the hill, from which they had set out that morning, the sun was climbing toward noon.

"Lay the package over there in that ditch," Wallace said, "and cut some brush to cover it in case somebody happens by."

Sweating, and still out of breath from the trek, Albert cut the brush with his knife while Robert Lee laid it over the body.

When he was satisfied that the camouflage was complete, Wallace told Robert Lee: "The truck is parked down by Wilson Wood's house. Get it and go back to the barn. Catch my saddle horse and Old Nell and bring them back here. Me and Albert will wait for you."

Watching Robert Lee trudge down the bank and onto the road, Albert felt a sinking sensation. In all their years together, through all the things they had done, Albert had never felt uncomfortable with Wallace. Now he did. The silence between them was like a person sitting there. Sensing this, Wallace said: "Sit down, Albert, and have a cigarette."

Albert refused the offered pack. "Nawsuh, I just as soon have a puff off my cigar." He felt in his pocket and took out the stump he saved for special occasions, lighting it carefully so as not to waste any of the precious tobacco leaves. That done, he sank down on a fallen log beside Wallace. They smoked in silence, each occupied with his own thoughts. After a while, Wallace turned toward him.

"Albert, I got to get rid of that package." His voice was low and confidential, as though he didn't even want the trees to hear what he was saying. "I got to get rid of it so good, won't nobody ever know what happened to it or where it's at. Understand?"

Albert nodded.

"Now . . . if you had such a problem with a package, what would you do with it?"

Albert studied the look in Wallace's eyes, trying to figure if he really wanted to know or if this was some sort of loyalty test.

"Well, I tell you the truff, Mr. Wallace," he said, "if it wuz me, I'd go right over there to that pe-can orchard and dig me a hole just as deep as I could go. Then I'd bury it."

Wallace started to shake his head, but Albert continued: "Then I'd kivver it up good and commence ta plowin' and harrowin' over it. Then I'd plant me a corn crop so's nobody could tell."

Wallace seemed to consider the suggestion for a moment, then shook his head. "Uh-uh. You got the wrong idea."

"How come you say dat?"

"Somebody would find it."

"Wouldn't nobody know."

Wallace smiled, his face full of cunning. "Mayhayley would, and just sure'n hell, somebody would go and ask her and she'd tell 'em it was buried in the pecan orchard."

"Whut you gonna do wit it, den?"

"Burn it," Wallace replied.

The horror of the suggestion tore down layers of restraint that Albert had built up over the years to protect himself. "Oh, Mr. Wallace," he protested, "I wouldn't do *nuthin' like that* if I wuz you."

Wallace's eyes were adamant, his face hard and cold. "That's what I'm gonna do . . . burn it!"

Chapter Seven

In Coweta County, a stillness had settled over the courthouse. It hung in the dark-green leaves of the magnolia trees that shaded the four corners of the square. It softened to whispers the voices of the curious who clustered on the low brick wall that guarded the apron of grass surrounding the courthouse. It silenced the footsteps inside the cool corridors.

All Thursday morning, everyone's attention had been riveted on the sheriff's office. They knew that a warrant had been sworn for the arrest of John Wallace and his friend Herring Sivell, and they knew that Sheriff Potts had been unable to locate them. They waited now to see what the sheriff would do about it.

The old men who spent their days on the courthouse square, crowded beneath his open window, straining to hear what was going on inside. If anything chanced to happen, they would be the first to know.

Sheriff Potts, bending over his desk, was telling the long-distance operator: "I don't care how many times Mrs. Matthews says Sheriff Collier is not home, keep calling until you get him." Before the warrant could be served, John Wallace had to be found, and Sheriff Potts had made up his mind to force Sheriff Collier to do the finding.

For J.H., sitting in the chair across from his brother, the waiting had become an endurance test. "Do you think Collier knows that you have a warrant out for Wallace and Sivell?"

"Not yet."

"He doesn't seem to be in any hurry to find him."

"Collier damn well better get himself in a hurry, or I'll get a warrant for him, too."

"Do you think he's *that* involved?"

"Hell, yes. He made himself an accessory after the fact when he swore that Wallace was eating dinner with him at the time of the killing on Tuesday. We *know* that was a lie. I'm beginning to believe he was also an accessory *before* the fact, but I can't prove that yet."

J.H. frowned. "That's going out on one helluva limb to help a friend."

"He's doing much more than helping a friend. He's obstructing justice, and by God, that won't do." Sheriff Potts looked reflectively out the open window. After a while, he folded his hands and said: "A sheriff should serve without fear or favor. Collier is both awed by and indebted to Wallace, and he's using his office to shield Wallace and do his bidding. Wallace issues the orders and Collier carries them out. That's breaking the law in the worst kind of way. That sort of business discredits every law officer everywhere."

"Do you think you'll be able to get enough evidence on Collier for a warrant?"

"I don't know, but if I do, I'll haul him into court so fast. . . ." The telephone rang and Sheriff Potts reached for it.

"Sheriff Potts?" Collier's voice was light and pleasant. "Mrs. Matthews tells me you've been trying to get in touch with me."

"Ever since yesterday," Sheriff Potts replied.

"What can I do for you?"

"I have a warrant for the arrest of John Wallace and Herring Sivell."

Sheriff Potts could hear a quick intake of breath. Then Collier said: "I told you yesterday that Wallace was out of town."

"You haven't been able to find him?"

"Not yet."

"Neither have I. I was down there yesterday."

"I guess we'll just have to wait," Collier said, the smile in his voice coming over the phone.

"Well," Sheriff Potts began in his soft drawl, "I wouldn't want to do anything like that. I'll just have to put out an All-Points-Pickup on him."

"A general alarm on John Wallace?" Sheriff Collier's voice was shocked.

"On John Wallace."

"Man, have you any idea who . . ."

"Save it, Collier. I've heard it all before. If you can't find Wallace, I can. I'll call the All-Points in right now."

Collier hesitated. "I need a little more time."

"How much?"

"A couple of days."

"I'll give you one hour," Sheriff Potts said, looking at his watch. "That will be twelve o'clock noon."

The courthouse clock was striking noon when the phone rang again, but it was not Sheriff Collier.

"Sheriff Potts?" The voice was professional and pleasant. "This is Gus Huddleston in Greenville. I'm attorney for John Wallace. I understand that you have warrants for him and Herring Sivell."

"That's right."

"We have managed to locate John, and Sivell, too."

"Good."

"If you can hold off till morning, I'll bring them to your office in my custody."

"Nine o'clock," Sheriff Potts said.

"Nine o'clock we will be there."

"I'll be expecting them."

In Meriwether County, time was running out and John Wallace's job was only half done. Waiting with Albert on the hilltop overlooking the road, he paced impatiently.

The surrounding land, owned by him and his kinsmen, was divided in half by a red clay road that curved in a scarlet scar across the green fields and woods on either side. Spotted along the roadway were the family residences, and scattered in between were the tumbledown tenant houses with fields of cotton and corn under cultivation.

The success of Wallace's plan depended upon taking Turner's body across this road at the right time . . . during the noon hour when all the field hands would be home having dinner. It was now half-past twelve and Robert Lee still had not returned with the horses.

"That's the slowest goddamn nigger God ever gave life to," Wallace said.

Albert rocked his head up and down, but said nothing. He had spent his time looking at the ant holes in the ground, at the wood moss, the fallen pine needles . . . anything but the mound in the ditch where Turner's mutilated body lay under a cover of cut green foliage.

When Robert Lee, riding Old Nell and leading Wallace's horse, rounded the curve, the noonday sun glazed glints of gold on his black face. With each clop of the horses' hooves, little red puffs of dust rose from the clay road, the sound echoing across the quiet fields. Reaching the steep embankment, Robert Lee kicked Old Nell in the sides, urging her up to the hilltop.

74

"It's about damn time," Wallace snapped. "Did anybody see you coming down the road?"

"Nawsuh, most everybody is home eatin' dinner."

"We have to work fast," Wallace said, throwing off the brush that covered Turner's body. "We got to load this package up on Old Nell and get across the road before afternoon plowing starts." He motioned to Robert Lee. "Bring Old Nell over here. Albert, get the ropes. We got to tie this package on good."

Albert and Robert Lee struggled to follow Wallace's instructions, but the body, frozen in death's last pose, was stiff and hard to manage when they tried to balance it across Old Nell's saddle.

"We'll just have to tie the package down as best we can," Wallace said, "and you boys will have to walk alongside to make sure it doesn't slide off."

"Where's us gonna go wid it?" Robert Lee wanted to know.

"Across the road and down to the swamp on the other side."

Puzzled by Wallace's reply, Robert Lee looked to Albert for an answer, but Albert turned away from his inquiring look. It was better for Robert Lee not to know what was about to happen. Mr. Wallace was going to make them do it anyway, and if Robert Lee knew, he was liable to go all to pieces.

When the body was at last lashed down, Wallace mounted his horse and led the way over the wooded embankment paralleling the road, looking for a safe place to cross to the other side. Albert and Robert Lee struggled to keep up, pushing aside the saplings, working their way through the hanging vines and close-set trees. The body, bundled in burlap, snagged on the branches, twisted, tottered, and turned on its precarious perch.

Wallace looked back at the two Negroes. "We're not moving fast enough."

"It's the trees, Mr. Wallace," Albert said. "They's most too close to get through."

Wallace looked around for easier passage. "We'll go down in the creek," he said, "and follow the creek bed for a while. That's wide enough to get through."

Albert and Robert Lee, holding onto the body, led Old Nell down into the water, then let her pick her way through the slime-slick rocks, slipping, sliding, trying to maintain her balance with the unsteady package lashed to her back.

As they labored along, the water steadily became deeper . . . ankle-deep, knee-deep, hip-deep . . . ending finally in a deep pool surrounded by dense woods. Unable to go farther, Wallace rode his horse to the top of the bank to take a look at the road below.

Coming back, he said: "We can't cross here. Someone's already plowing in that field. We'll have to backtrack until we find a better place."

Turning the horses, they started back. Wallace again rode to the hilltop to check the road. "Bring Old Nell on up," he told Albert and Robert Lee. "We can cross here."

Albert threw the reins on the horse's neck, giving her her head. Holding onto Turner's body, he and Robert Lee ran alongside as she scrambled up the bank.

"Remember," Wallace told them when they reached the top, "it's important that we don't draw notice. I'll ride on across and wait for you at the edge of the woods on the other side. You boys go slow and easy . . . understand?"

They nodded, and Wallace cantered down the hill, across the road, and into the woods. From there, he watched Albert and Robert Lee progress slowly across the same path.

"Good work, boys, " he said, when they reached him, "now follow me."

For nearly two miles they continued their tortured trek through the woods, until the forest growth made passage impossible. "We'll have to go on foot now," Wallace said, getting down off his horse. "Robert Lee, go cut me another pole."

"Like befo'?"

Wallace nodded, and with no further questions, they repeated the process they had gone through at the well: laying the body on the ground, taking the pole and working it through the ropes.

"Now, Albert," Wallace said, putting him in charge, "you and Robert Lee take the package, just like you did before, and go down through the woods here for about half a mile till you come to that old liquor still pit by the branch. I'll take the horses, circle back through the field, and meet you there."

"Whut must us do if you ain't there when us get there?" Robert Lee asked anxiously.

"Lay it up on the side of the hill by the pit and cover it over with brush, like this morning."

As they walked along with Turner's body swinging from the pole that rested on their shoulders, Robert Lee said: "When I thinks about whut us is doin', I gets the spooky creeps."

"Shut yo' mouth," Albert said irritably, "else you'll give them creeps to me, too."

76

The pit was deep in the woods where the trees of a virgin forest grew to a height of sixty feet. Their dense foliage so shaded out the sunlight that it looked like dark in the middle of the day. A mist hovered over the dark water in the branch nearby, and an owl, mistaking the hour, hooted high in a tree.

Albert and Robert Lee hurriedly laid the body on the hillside above the pit, and cut brush to cover it.

"Come on, Albert," Robert Lee said when they had finished. "Let's get outa here."

"Make tracks, man," Albert replied.

Then together they started to run, dashing through the woods toward the daylight. Almost at the edge of the field they met Wallace coming toward them with the horses.

"Did you get the package to the pit?"

Breathless, Robert Lee nodded.

"Covered it over so no one can see?"

Robert Lee nodded again, gulping for air.

"All right, boys, you can go on back and start to planting cotton." Wallace handed Old Nell's reins to Robert Lee. To Albert he said: "Be ready tonight an hour before sundown. I'll meet you at Robert Lee's house."

They watched him gallop away on his horse, a flash of chestnut and four white feet flying across the soft green of the sunlit field.

"You know sumpthin', Robert Lee? Wouldn't nobody know from lookin' that he'd been up to nuthin' more'n ridin' his hoss out in the field." Albert's green eyes hardened as he watched Wallace disappear. "And he ain't finished yet."

"Whut you mean . . . ain't finished yet?"

"We gotta come back an hour fo' sundown."

"Whut fo'?"

"To finish up wid dat package."

Robert Lee's black face began to knot again with fear. "What's he gonna do wid it?"

"Burn it."

"Ahhhhhhhhhhhhh . . ." Robert Lee shrieked and began running again from the dark of the woods toward the sunlight.

Albert ran after him, tackled him out in the open field and pinned him to the ground. "Listen to me, nigger," he said. "You get aholt 'a yoreself. If Mr. Wallace wuz to hear you squallin' like that and see you so tore to pieces, he'd come back and kill the both of us."

Robert Lee tried to get up. Then gave way to the force of Albert's big, coarse hands on his shoulders.

"You better not say nuthin' 'bout this," Albert warned, "not to nobody no time."

Robert Lee lay limp and frightened, his eyes fixed on Albert's face.

"Just one word," Albert said, getting up, "and I'll string yore guts out like a clothesline."

Tears ran down Robert Lee's ravaged black cheeks. He rolled over and hid his face in the soft green grass. He was now afraid of everything . . . Turner's dead body, Mr. Wallace, and Albert, too.

Old Nell had bolted and run, and Albert stalked off to find her. Angry as he was, he felt halfway ashamed of jumping on Robert Lee like that. He didn't feel no better about what they had done than Robert Lee did, but carrying on like that wasn't going to help a thing. When it came to getting nerved up, Robert Lee wasn't no better than a woman.

Old Nell was standing by the pasture fence, nibbling tender green leaves from the trees. "Come on, ol' gurl," Albert said, easing up and picking up the reins. "We gotta go home for dinner."

Albert's wife, Lola Mae, was standing on the porch waiting for him when he got home. Her dark purple lips were puffed out in a pout, her round face set, her eyes flashing fire.

"Where in the name of de Lawd is you been, Albert?" she demanded. "It's way past dinnertime."

"Me and Robert Lee been helpin' Mr. Wallace fix up an old barn," Albert lied.

"Come on so's I can feed you."

Albert followed her into the kitchen, took a pint bottle of moonshine liquor off the shelf, and had slugged down half of it before she saw what he was doing.

"Albert! Whut's done got into you, drinkin' like that in the middle of the day?"

"My stomach's uneasy."

Lola Mae propped her hands on her hips, her eyes full of accusation. "You ain't looked right to me since yestiddy. Whut you been up to?"

"I ain't been up to nuthin'."

"Sayin' and doin' is two diffunt things," Lola Mae said skeptically. She sloshed beans and corn bread on his plate and sat down to watch him eat.

Trying hard to look unworried and innocent under her relentless glare, Albert choked down his dinner. But he knew there was no

78

fooling Lola Mae. She knew trouble like it was her blood brother. She could sense it coming.

That afternoon, while he planted cotton in the field, Albert's worries ballooned. There was what he had done and what he had yet to do, Lola Mae's suspicions, and worse yet, there was Mable, Robert Lee's wife. If Mable plowed into Robert Lee like Lola Mae had done him, Robert Lee was liable to let the whole thing out, and they'd really be in for it. Mable was the kind that couldn't stand nuthin' on her mind. She had to pass it on to somebody else.

Long before sunset, Albert was hankering for another swig of moonshine, but put it off until just before time to meet Wallace. While Lola Mae was out minding the children, he slipped inside and finished the bottle, then walked down the road to Robert Lee's house.

Like all the other tenants, Robert Lee lived in a one-room weathered-gray frame house with a kitchen attached to the back and a porch across the front. Built on brick pilings, with space underneath for chickens and dogs, it stood off the road in a field of corn.

Robert Lee was sitting in a depressed heap on the edge of the porch, his arms propped behind him, his chin on his chest, his feet dangling over the side. When Albert walked up, he did not even look up.

"I didn't mean to get rough wid ya today," Albert said apologetically, sitting down beside him.

Robert Lee swung his feet back and forth and did not answer, his lips pushed out in a pout.

"We gotta be careful," Albert cautioned, "else us'll both get kilt."

Robert Lee raised hurt eyes to look at him.

"Things done got dane-jus," Albert insisted.

Robert Lee's chin trembled and he opened his mouth to speak, but Mr. Wallace, in Mr. Mozart's truck, was blowing the horn out front. Wallace said nothing when they got in, nor did he speak as he drove down the old log mill road where they had thrown off the two cords of pine wood and left the gasoline the day before. Here, he stopped the truck and leaned forward on the steering wheel so that he could look directly at both Albert and Robert Lee seated beside him.

"Boys, we got a job to do." His tone told them there would be no resistance. "I want you to take the gasoline and cordwood we brought down here yesterday and bring it to the pit where you left the package this morning. When you get it there, I'll rack the wood up myself. Any questions?"

Robert Lee, looking straight ahead, shook his head. He had come through anxiety, fear, and hysteria to docile submission.

"Albert?"

"Nawsuh, I ain't got no questions." Albert had reached resignation. He tried not to think about what Wallace was going to make them do. He was into it now, with no way out. The only thing to do was to get the job done before he was caught doing it.

They carried the cordwood through the woods to the liquor-still pit, a rectangular excavation twelve feet long, six feet wide, and two feet deep, dug from a hillside that sloped down to the nearby stream. Here, at an earlier time, the barrels of mash, nestled against the bank in a bed of sawdust and sand, had brewed to maturity. Now, Wallace laid the six-foot lengths of pine side by side, filling the bottom of the pit, crossing the second layer, and crisscrossing the next until the piled wood reached a height of three feet.

Wiping the sweat from his face, Wallace asked: "How much more wood is there?"

" 'Bout three or four more turns," Albert answered.

"All right, you and Robert Lee go up on the bank and bring the package down. Lay it straight up and down this pile of wood."

Wordlessly, they obeyed.

"Now," Wallace said, "take off his shoes."

Stunned, Albert and Robert Lee looked at each other and back at Wallace.

"Go on!" he commanded. "Take off his shoes and lay them right there beside him."

It was the first time since the search had begun that Wallace had referred to Turner's body as anything but a "package." Hearing him personalize it brought the realization back . . . what they were about to do was burn a human body. Removing the brogans that they had always seen Turner wear when he worked for Wallace, touching his cold, white feet was almost more than Albert and Robert Lee could force themselves to do.

"Get on with it!" Wallace snapped. "We'll be here all night just getting his shoes off."

Albert couldn't figure why the shoes should be removed and didn't dare ask, for the tension of the task was beginning to show on Wallace. The veins in his thick, sunburned neck stood out like well ropes, and his chin, drawn tensely back, disappeared into the layers of flesh around his throat. Albert's own nerves had begun to unravel. He had done lots of things in his lifetime, but he had never before violated the dead, and he began to have the awful feeling that the Lord was looking.

After they had managed to get Turner's brogans off and had set them beside him, Wallace told them to get the rest of the cordwood and the two five-gallon cans of gasoline. When they had done so, he piled the remaining wood carefully, sandwiching the body in between the layers. Taking the cans one at a time, he poured the gasoline over the body and across the stack of wood. When he finished, sweat was pouring over his eyes, down his neck, and into his shirt collar. Taking off his hat, he wiped his wet face on his shirtsleeve, then took a penny box of matches from his pocket.

"Albert, you and Robert Lee get back in the woods out of the way."

The two Negroes ran for a ditch and dived into the dirt. Lying flat on their faces, they covered their heads with their arms and waited. Albert heard Wallace strike the match. Opening one eye, he watched Wallace toss the lighted match on the pyre he had built and step back behind a tree.

The forest exploded. The blast shook the ground and trembled the trees. A column of bright orange flames ran to the tops of the sixty-foot trees, consuming bark and branches with a deafening crackle and a fearful roar.

Deer, rabbits, and squirrels rushed from their hiding places to escape incineration. Coveys of birds flew skyward. The furnace-like heat became so intense that Albert and Robert Lee were forced to edge out of the ditch and move farther back into the woods.

From where he lay on the ground, Albert could see Wallace standing beside the tree. Throughout the holocaust, he had remained where he was, the red glow of the flames licking his face, his eyes fixed and intent on the burning body, his teeth gritted together in a strange, grim, satisfied smile.

From overhead, they heard the roar of a plane. Wallace jerked his head toward them. "Don't look up!"

Albert and Robert Lee buried their faces in the ground where they lay. "Albert," Robert Lee whispered, "why you reckon he said dat?"

"Ain't no tellin'. Maybe he thinks somebody up there's gonna see whut us is doin'."

"From way up there?"

Albert raised up and gave Robert Lee a dark look. "If you can figger somethin' better, you figger, but when I figger, don't worry me wid trifles."

"Ain't no use to get so nerved up."

"Who's nerved up?" Albert asked crossly.

When the fire had burned down to a steady glow, Wallace called them back. They rose and walked toward him reluctantly, trying not to look at the fire that had burned away the burlap cover, leaving the dim outline of the man lying there in the flames. The fire had drawn up the arms and legs into a grotesque agony, and Turner's head, in black silhouette, was outlined against the orange flames.

Sickened by what he saw, Albert turned away. Beside him, Robert Lee began to cry, silent tears running down his cheeks.

"We can go home now," Wallace was saying. "The fire will finish this up tonight. In the morning I want you boys to come back with some feed sacks and a shovel. I want all the ashes cleaned out of the pit and dumped in that stream over yonder. Make it look like the pit's been scraped out to make liquor. That way, nobody will get suspicious."

"What about the boom it made and that big blaze?" Albert asked. "Folks for miles round are bound to've noticed that."

"They'll just think it was the revenooers blowing up another still," Wallace replied confidently. "Forget it."

"We got a lot of forgettin' to do," Albert said sorrowfully.

"Now, Albert," Wallace said, giving him a friendly slap on the back, "you oughtn't to feel that way. My ma always told me: 'Do what you gotta do, and don't let your conscience get in your way.' "

"That's Miss Myrt's sayin'?"

Wallace nodded. "She brought me up on that saying, and it never once guided me wrong."

Albert looked down at the ground and didn't reply. Robert Lee looked down at the ground, too.

"Don't worry, boys," Wallace brushed aside their concern with a return to joviality. "By morning the job will be over and done with."

Albert could not accept his lighthearted disregard of what had happened. There was a heaviness in his chest, and his shoulders felt bent down with the heaviest burden he had ever known. There was no way to lighten the load, for this was a burden on his soul.

Even after he had left the pit and gone home, Albert still felt a deep, brooding sadness. It was like going to a funeral where they buried your ma, your wife, your kids, and everything that had ever meant something to you. He had been forced to take part in something evil, something that had scarred his soul and left him with no promise of heaven and no hope in hell.

When Friday morning came, Albert and Robert Lee returned to the pit with the feed sacks and shovel to carry out Wallace's orders.

"You know sumpthin'?" Robert Lee said as they trudged along side by side. "Mr. Wallace ain't never said a word about that

82

likker-still pit, but I knowed the minute I seen it yestiddy that it was the same pit what Mr. Turner dug for him when they wuz makin' likker together."

"I knowed it, too, soon as I seen it."

Robert Lee's black face reflected the irony. "That's whut you call diggin' yore own grave, sho' nuff."

"Sho' is."

The smell of burned leaves and smoke hung thick in the woods around them. The blackened bark of charred trees bore grim witness to what had been done there the night before. The pit lay before them, silent and still.

"Come on, Robert Lee. Let's get it over wid."

"I'se scart."

"Whut of? Ain't nuthin' left."

Robert Lee's eyes widened with a fear he could not name. "Whut about the heart? I heered tell ain't no way to buhn up de heart."

"See fo' yoreself. Ain't nuthin' but ashes."

In the pit a pile of gray-white ashes lay undisturbed, like those in a hearth after a winter night's fire. Albert took the shovel and laid it on top of the ashes. The pile collapsed in a cloud of gray dust.

"See there, Robert Lee. Ain't nuthin' left. Now let's get to work. I'll shovel and you hold the bag."

They had filled two bags and part of the third when the hot ashes near the bottom of the pit began to crackle and pop with shooting sparks.

"Watch out wid it." Robert Lee slapped out a spark that was burning the fuzzy fiber of the burlap. "You'll set this here bag afire."

"Ain't no likelihood of dat," Albert said. "We'ze already down to the dirt, and that's goin' in wid it, too."

When they had completely cleaned the pit, scraped it, and filled up the third bag with the debris, Albert and Robert Lee took all the bags down to the stream and dumped the contents. Some of the blackened ash floated on top of the water for a while. Standing on the bank with the empty feed sacks, they watched it move downstream.

"Ain't that somethin'," Albert said. "That there's the last of Mr. Turner."

Robert Lee shook his head. "No it ain't."

"What you mean 'ain't'?"

"Mr. Turner ain't nearly 'bout gonna rest easy, gettin' put away like that. I always heered tell that the ghost'll come back and spook a man to death."

As Albert nodded a grim acknowledgment, they heard the crackle of footsteps coming through the woods. Gripped with fear, Robert Lee whirled around: "Whut's dat?"

"Hey, boys," Wallace's voice called, "you still down here?"

"Yassuh, Mr. Wallace," Albert answered. "We'ze here."

"Lawd have mercy God," Robert Lee exclaimed, holding his hand to his heart. "I thought Jedgment was comin'."

Together they walked back to the still pit where Wallace was inspecting their work. "Looks like you did a good job," he said, running his hand over the smooth dirt. "I can't find a trace of anything." He looked up and smiled. "Not a trace."

Albert picked up the shovel they had used, and Robert Lee took the empty feed bags. "Whut must us do now?" Albert asked.

"Get rid of those things," Wallace told them, "and go back to planting cotton. I got to go to Newnan this morning. Mr. Huddleston and I got some business to tend to."

The Search

Chapter Eight

Gus Huddleston, attorney for John Wallace, was a successful country lawyer. He used his talents, recognized his limitations, and never tried to go beyond what he knew he could do.

He was good at drawing wills, making transfer deeds, and presiding over the settlement of an estate. When the heirs squabbled, Gus Huddleston would cross his long legs, hook his thumbs in his vest pockets, and peer over the top of his steel-rimmed glasses in an attitude of fixed concentration. After the storm had subsided, he would rise from his chair. Six feet three inches tall, he knew the psychological advantage of height, and therefore delivered an opinion standing up. As he towered above his listeners, his brief and ordinary words seemed profound.

Although this technique had settled many a dispute in Greenville, Gus Huddleston had little hope of its helping him this morning when he took Wallace and Sivell in custody to the sheriff of Coweta County. Potts was tough and smart, strong on law and order, and could see through duplicity like an X-ray machine. Despite this, Wallace expected Gus to make short work of the sheriff.

"Fix it up, Gus," Wallace said. "That's what you're paid for."

There wasn't any "fixing it up." Wallace had his way in Meriwether County because of power and prestige. That didn't count for anything with Lamar Potts, which was a fact that Wallace wouldn't accept. Wallace expected a simple denial in a face-to-face confrontation to resolve the whole thing.

Gus had been uncertain about what course to take. He had suggested to Wallace that they call in a Newnan lawyer to help with the case. If charges were pressed in Coweta County, it would be a distinct advantage to have a local attorney. Besides, it would be far less abrasive to phone Sheriff Potts from a lawyer's office than for Wallace to traipse into the courthouse like a fugitive.

Wallace had agreed to the suggestion. Fortunately, he had had earlier dealings with Walt Sanders, one of Newnan's most successful criminal lawyers. Comfortably established and in his midforties, Walter Sanders was popular with the people in his area. Having him as counsel for John Wallace would be a decided asset.

Wallace had met Walt Sanders years before when a Coweta County widow had had her license to ship milk revoked after a state inspection had revealed too high a bacterial count in her product. The widow, anxious not to lose her milk allotment, had heard of a dairyman named John Wallace in Meriwether County who might be willing to ship her milk until she was able to meet the state requirements. She had asked Walt Sanders, whom she had known for years, to go with her to Meriwether County to talk to Wallace. When the situation was explained, Wallace had agreed to help.

Favorably impressed at the time, Walt Sanders remembered the incident when Gus Huddleston asked him to help represent Wallace in the Turner case. His current work load, Sanders explained, was too heavy for him to take on another case at this time, but he agreed to let Huddleston bring Wallace and Sivell to his office in Newnan on Friday morning.

Wallace, driving his ancient A-Model, was the first to arrive at Gus Huddleston's office that morning. Radiating confidence, his eyes sparkling with satisfaction, Wallace slapped Huddleston on the back. "Don't look so glum, Gus. Things aren't all that bad."

"When did they change?" Gus asked, remembering Wallace's earlier anxiety.

Wallace grinned. "Things have a way of changing, Gus. What's bad today is not so bad tomorrow."

Gus was peering at him over the top of his glasses when Herring Sivell walked in. Sivell, obviously angry and resentful, did not seem to share Wallace's optimism. He nodded curtly and waited silently.

Gathering up the last of his papers and putting them in his briefcase, Gus Huddleston was ready to leave when Wallace held out a hand to stop him. "Wait awhile," Wallace said, "Collier wants to go, too."

To confront the Coweta County sheriff with Wallace's arrogant self-confidence, Sivell's sullen anger, and Hardy Collier's banty-cock attitude was clearly more than Gus Huddleston was prepared to cope with. "I don't think Collier's presence will help a bit," he said.

"Collier feels like it will strengthen the case to say I was having dinner with him."

Exasperation overcame Huddleston's controlled patience. "John, please let me handle the legal affairs. After all . . ."

"Hell, it won't hurt nothing. Besides, here he is now."

Before Huddleston could protest further, Wallace, Sivell, and Collier were deciding whose car they should go in. Wallace's A-Model was too small, and Collier didn't want to use the sheriff's car because it would look as though Wallace were being "brought in."

"We can use mine," Sivell said.

"What about the blood?" Wallace asked.

"I took it to the service station this morning and had it cleaned out."

Gus Huddleston was profoundly shocked. "You took that car to a *public* service station to have it cleaned?"

Sivell's words were saturated with insolence. "Why not?"

"Because," Gus Huddleston said, deploring their utter contempt for the law and what it could do, "it's dangerous to be so damned arrogant."

Arriving in Newnan before nine o'clock, they climbed the stairs to Walt Sanders's second-floor office on the courthouse square. After a round of introductions, Sanders called the sheriff's office.

"Lamar, this is Walt. Gus Huddleston has John Wallace and Herring Sivell in my office."

Lamar Potts and Walt Sanders had been good friends and bird-hunting buddies for years. This morning, their conversation was unusually formal and restrained. This morning, the call was official.

Walt Sanders hung up and said, "He's on his way over to get you." At that, Wallace suddenly decided to go to the sheriff's office unescorted. Before Huddleston could stop him, he was halfway down the stairs. At the foot he met Sheriff Potts.

"Mr. Wallace . . ."

"Sheriff Potts . . ."

"Come with me."

Wallace followed Sheriff Potts across the street to his office in the courthouse. Huddleston, Sivell, and Sheriff Collier had no choice but to straggle along.

"John Wallace," Sheriff Potts said, "I'm arresting you for the kidnapping and murder of one Wilson Turner."

"Murder!" Wallace shouted. His hooded eyes bulged and the small veins beneath the skin of his fleshy face turned purple. "What d'ya mean, *murder*?"

Gus Huddleston stepped forward to intervene before things got out of hand. "Sheriff Potts, I understood the charge was for kidnapping."

"I don't know who you understood that from, Mr. Huddleston. The warrant is for kidnapping and murder."

Herring Sivell, silent until now, limped forward, his face hostile. "I ain't had nothing to do with no kidnapping and murder," he barked.

Sheriff Potts looked at Sivell as though he were adding a column of figures. "You're Herring Sivell?"

Sivell gave an affirmative snap of his head.

"I have a warrant for your arrest for the kidnapping and murder of Wilson Turner."

Sivell opened his mouth to protest, but Wallace rode across his words. "How in the hell can there be murder?" Wallace demanded. "Where's the body?"

Sheriff Potts leveled a look at him. "That's what I want you to tell me."

"This is ridiculous!" Sheriff Collier's agitated face was flushed with rage, his arms were rigid at his sides, his thumbs clasped inside his fists. "I told you before, Potts, that John Wallace was sitting at my table having dinner with me when this thing happened at Sunset."

Wallace shouldered Sheriff Collier aside. "I don't know a damn thing about any kidnapping and murder."

"Not me neither," Sivell snarled.

Sheriff Potts looked at his brother, who was standing in the doorway. "J.H., bring in Steve Smith."

Big and broad-shouldered, Steve Smith made the room seem smaller when he walked in.

"Gentlemen," Sheriff Potts said, "Steve Smith is the proprietor of Sunset Tourist Camp. He is one of eight witnesses who saw what happened to Wilson Turner on Tuesday." To Steve Smith he said: "Can you identify any of these men?"

"Yes, sir," Steve Smith replied, indicating Wallace and Sivell. "They're the ones that done it. I seen 'em do it."

Sheriff Potts nodded a dismissal. Turning to his brother, he said, "All right, J.H., let's lock 'em up."

Gus Huddleston, who had been relying on his usual method of listening and then making a pronouncement, never got a chance. The whole thing seemed to go to hell in a hurry. Sheriff Potts was snapping handcuffs on John Wallace; J.H. was snapping them on Herring Sivell.

"Just a minute, Sheriff," Gus Huddleston said, trying to assert himself. "I had expected to arrange some sort of bail."

"They're being held without bond."

"Now, Sheriff," Huddleston said, attempting a confidential tone, "I don't think you realize the situation. John Wallace is a man of position and prestige. He can't be put in jail like an ordinary criminal. He's got too much money."

Sheriff Potts stopped what he was doing to look at Huddleston. "Then I'll put Wallace in jail and his money too. J.H., did you check out the numbers on that license plate?"

"They checked out," J.H. replied.

"Mr. Sivell, is that your 1947 Ford parked outside?"

Sivell's gray-green eyes, never able to fix on any one thing, shifted like the carriage of a typewriter. "That's my car. Why?"

"I am impounding it as material evidence."

Bristling with hostility, Collier jutted out his chin. "Now see here, Potts!"

Sheriff Potts looked down at him. "I'll see to it that you have transportation back to Meriwether County."

"You'll see to no such thing," Collier snapped. "I'll have my own deputy bring a car. Where's the phone?"

Sheriff Potts pointed toward his desk. "Help yourself." Taking Wallace by the arm, he said: "All right, let's go."

At the Coweta County jail, a block down from the courthouse, Wallace and Sivell were put in separate cells on the same floor. As Sheriff Potts turned the key in the lock, Wallace warned him from the other side of the bars: "You're making a grave mistake, Sheriff."

"Not likely."

"What plans have you got for proving your allegations?"

"I have a warrant to search your house and premises."

Wallace smiled. "My wife will be there. She'll be glad to show you around the place. Look all you want. You won't find a thing."

Sheriff Potts dropped the key in his pocket. "We'll see."

Sheriff Potts had never met Wallace's wife. His arrival at her house with a search warrant was sure to be an inconvenience and an intrusion, and he cautioned his deputies to use the utmost consideration in their search. He expected her to be resentful or hostile. He was entirely unprepared for what he found.

Josephine Leath Wallace was a beautiful woman with a slender hold on reality. When Wallace brought her from Florida to Meriwether County to be his bride, she was a glowing nineteen-year-old beauty full of enthusiasms and girlish expectations.

At their wedding reception, given on New Year's Eve night at the resort hotel in White Sulphur Springs, Josephine had, at Wallace's insistence, danced into the night, winning the heart of every man there. Wallace himself did not dance. He contented himself with watching the others admire his latest possession.

Josephine had not been married long when she learned that she shared her husband with another woman, a woman who had been, and who remained his good friend. Wallace even brought this woman to their house, and Josephine, gentle and well-bred, endured the indignity with quiet restraint.

Unhappy in her marriage, she attempted to interest herself in other things, but all her efforts failed. She liked to ride, but Miss Myrt, Wallace's mother, objected. Like her brothers, Miss Myrt always carried a gun, and rumor had it that she would beat a Negro half to death with a stick of stovewood for not dusting the furniture right. This notwithstanding, she fancied herself an authority on propriety.

"How can you ride horses and call yourself a lady?" Miss Myrt demanded of Josephine. "Only men ride horses."

Later, Josephine wanted to open a dress shop, but Wallace refused to finance the venture. When she sought capital elsewhere, the little building she planned to use for her shop mysteriously burned down.

In despair, Josephine surrendered to her circumstances. She was restricted to the confines of her childless home, limited in her pursuits, and the years gradually eroded her enthusiasms and ended her expectations. Overwhelmed by the harsh way of life inside "the Kingdom," she retreated into a world of her own creation, an imaginative world inhabited by little animals and happy children, about whom she wrote in songs and stories under the pen name "Worldye." No one objected to this harmless pursuit, nor did they understand the need for it.

As time passed, Josephine withdrew farther into her dream world. Floating aimlessly about the house, composing at the piano or writing at her desk, she grew both more beautiful and more oblivious of what happened around her.

When Sheriff Potts arrived at John Wallace's modest frame house, Josephine herself answered the door.

"Mrs. Wallace?"

She smiled an uncertain acknowledgment, and he noted that her doelike eyes were vague.

"I'm Sheriff Potts of Coweta County." He indicated the others: "My deputy, J. H. Potts, Sergeant Otwell of the Georgia State Patrol, and Jim Hillin, from the Georgia Bureau of Investigation."

Josephine nodded to the introductions and waited expectantly.

"I'm sorry to inconvenience you," he said, "but I have a warrant to search your house and premises."

"Search the house?" The request seemed beyond her understanding.

"Yes, ma'am."

Suddenly, Josephine smiled, as though the confusion had cleared away. "Go right ahead," she said. "Help yourself." Without another word, she walked out to the garden and began picking flowers.

Puzzled by her strange reaction, the other officers looked at the sheriff questioningly. But he shook his head, refusing a reply.

"Otwell, you and Hillin go down to the barn. J.H. and I will search here."

The house was shining clean and orderly, ruffled curtains at the windows and freshly baked tea cakes on the kitchen table. Systematically, Sheriff Potts and J.H searched each room, closet, and cupboard. On the back porch, near a washtub and scrub board, J.H. found a basket of soiled clothes . . . dirty towels, sheets, dresses, and men's work clothes. At the bottom of the basket lay a pair of khaki pants and a khaki shirt, both heavily stained with blood.

"Hey, Lamar," he called, "come take a look at this."

Taking up the clothes, the sheriff examined them. The shirt, splattered with dried blotches of blood in the front, had a large black stain running down the back of the right shoulder to the waistline, which had been creased by a tightened belt. The back of the pants were bloodstained from the waistband to the right hip, with splatters down the trouser leg. He was studying the pattern of the bloodstains when Otwell came back from the barn. "Nothing out there," he said. Then: "What's that you've got?"

"Looks like the clothes Wallace wore the day he ran Turner down. J.H. found them at the bottom of the laundry basket."

Otwell frowned. "Why would Wallace leave them there? Seems to me like he would have gotten rid of them."

"He never expected to have anybody come looking." Sheriff Potts fitted the back of the trousers to the waist of the shirt so that the black blood became one long, continuous line from shoulder to hip. "The bloodstains indicate that he carried Turner across his right shoulder, possibly for some distance."

"Why do you say that?" J.H. asked.

"Bloodstains are on the *inside* of the trouser legs," the sheriff explained. "Carrying a bleeding man slung across the back, the drops of blood would splatter the legs, particularly the inside left if the body is being carried on the right."

"Damn if you ain't right!" Otwell agreed. "You can just about tell from those splotches how Wallace was walking."

Sheriff Potts nodded. "J.H., go find Hillin and see if he has turned up anything. I want to go talk to Mrs. Wallace."

Josephine was still in the garden gathering late spring flowers. Standing on the hillside in the sunshine, the breeze blowing the honey-blond hair that fell to her shoulders, her face had a childlike quality.

"Mrs. Wallace . . ." Sheriff Potts called from the porch.

Josephine looked up, smiling.

"I'd like to ask you some questions, if you don't mind."

"Certainly, I'll be right there."

On her way from the garden, Josephine took the bouquet of flowers she had gathered and left them on the dashboard of the sheriff's car.

"I thought the other officers might like to have some flowers," she explained. "I brought a special one for you." She handed him a bright red geranium. "I think geraniums look so brave." She paused a moment and her eyes searched his face. "You look like you're brave, too, Mr. Potts. Are you?"

She asked the question with a child's directness. Sheriff Potts took the flower she offered him. "Thank you, Mrs. Wallace, you're very kind."

Josephine smiled, pleased that her offering had been accepted.

"Mrs. Wallace, could you tell me if these clothes belong to your husband?"

Recognition lit her face. "Why yes, those are John's clothes. He left them in the laundry hamper two or three days ago."

"Can you remember which day?"

Josephine struggled to recollect. "Tuesday or Wednesday, I can't be sure."

"Why haven't they been laundered?"

Josephine's face clouded, then grew serious. "Why, *Monday* is washday," she explained, as though pointing out the obvious, "and today's only Friday."

"Of course," Sheriff Potts replied. "Monday is washday." Realizing the futility of burdening her with further questions, he moved toward the door to call out the others.

"You're lucky, though," Josephine said, her smile breaking through again. "Friday is baking day and I have some freshly baked tea cakes. I'll make a pot of coffee and you can all have some refreshments."

"That's very hospitable of you, Mrs. Wallace, but we have some business back in Newnan."

94

"Can't it wait?" Josephine asked—with a child's disappointment at the failure of a party to materialize.

"I'm afraid not, but we're much obliged for the offer."

"Maybe next time?"

"Maybe next time," Sheriff Potts replied.

On the way back to Newnan, Otwell sat in front beside Sheriff Potts, holding the bouquet of flowers that Josephine had left on the dashboard. "Don't that beat all you ever saw?" he asked, turning toward J.H. and Jim Hillin in the back seat. "That lady's just like a little girl that ain't ever grown up . . . talking about tea cakes and flowers and her husband in jail for murder."

Hillin shook his head. "Doesn't make sense."

Sheriff Potts, with his eyes on the road ahead, only half heard the conversation. His mind was on Wallace. Wallace was the one who didn't make sense. Why did he leave the bloody clothes in the laundry hamper? Why didn't he burn them, or throw them away, or at least leave instructions to have them washed immediately? Was he really so confident he wouldn't be caught that this damaging evidence was of no consequence? What *possible* explanation could Wallace give?

"J.H., when we get back," Sheriff Potts said, "I want you to go over Herring Sivell's car. If Wallace is *this* careless about the clothes he wore, likely, Sivell has been careless, too."

The red-brick rectangle that was the Coweta County jail had absorbed the heat of the late-afternoon sun when Sheriff Potts arrived. Inside, hot, dusty shafts of sunlight cut across the corridors. Wallace, with his hands on the bars, was looking out the cell window and did not hear him approach.

"Mr. Wallace . . ."

"Ah, Sheriff . . ." Wallace turned around, poised and collected beside his bunk. "Did you find anything?"

"These." Sheriff Potts opened the cell door and handed Wallace the bloody shirt and pants. "Are they yours?"

Wallace took the clothes and turned them over in his thick, coarse hands. He seemed neither flustered nor afraid, nor even mildly disturbed.

"They're mine," he said, handing them back, his manner as casual as though he had been shown a lost glove.

"Can you explain all these bloodstains?"

Wallace chuckled. "Of course. I was riding my horse in the pasture and cut my hand on some briars." Three thin scratches, barely big enough to scab over, ran across the back of Wallace's right hand. He held it up for Potts to see.

Annoyed with Wallace's flippancy, Sheriff Potts fixed him with a look. "Can't you think of a better excuse than that?"

Wallace neither flinched nor changed expression. "Why should I?" His voice was edged with arrogance. "That's exactly what happened."

"Are you prepared to tell that to a jury?"

A smile curled the corner of Wallace's mouth. "If it comes to that."

"Hey, Otwell," Sheriff Potts called up the stairs to Sergeant Otwell, who was waiting there.

"Yes, sir, Sheriff."

"Get me an official photographer. I want a good photo taken of Mr. Wallace exhibiting the scratches on his right hand. We'll enter it as material evidence."

There was a flare to Wallace's nostrils, and the curl on his lips had turned into a snarl. "Very interesting, Sheriff, but what's that going to prove?"

"It will establish for the court that the insignificant size of the scratches you have shown me could in no way have produced the amount of blood found on the back of this shirt and this pair of pants."

A flicker of amusement glinted in Wallace's cold eyes. "For all you know, Sheriff, that might be hog's blood."

"We'll just see about that," Sheriff Potts said. He rolled the clothes into a tight bundle and put them under his arm. "I'm sending these things to the Crime Lab in Atlanta for analysis. Dr. Jones is well equipped to determine the difference between hog blood and human blood."

Chapter Nine

Wallace's bloody clothes were not the only carelessly concealed evidence. In the glove compartment of Herring Sivell's car, J.H. found the pearl-handled pistol that had been used in Turner's abduction.

"Can you beat that, Lamar!" J.H. held out the pistol wrapped in a handkerchief. "It's still got bloodstains on it. They drove the getaway car right into Coweta County with a bloodstained pistol in the glove compartment!"

Sheriff Potts took the gun and turned it over in his hand. "I'll be damned! Either they're the biggest fools I ever saw or they think we are. Did you find anything else?"

"Looks like there might have been bloodstains on the door panel and in the back seat. The car's been washed out, so it's hard to tell."

"We'll have Dr. Jones find that out, too."

Dr. Herman Jones, head of the Fulton County Crime Lab in Atlanta, was an expert analyst of material related to criminal cases . . . guns, bullets, burglary tools, and blood. He serviced all state law enforcement agencies and over the years had worked often with Sheriff Potts. This morning, when the sheriff called to request tests for human blood on the collected evidence, Jones told him to send everything up to the lab by deputy.

"You want me to take the car up there, Lamar?" J.H. asked.

"No. We're taking a posse into Meriwether County tomorrow to look for Turner. I'll need you to round up the men for it. Call Pete Bedenbaugh and ask if he can take those things to Dr. Jones."

Since all law enforcement agencies were undermanned, there was an exchange of officers among them. Sheriff Potts sometimes assisted the state agents in raiding liquor stills. In return, Pete Bedenbaugh, a state revenue agent for the Alcohol Tax Unit, helped him if he needed an additional deputy.

When J.H. had reported that Pete could deliver the car the next morning, the sheriff gave his brother further instructions: "Take Sivell's car down to the County Farm," he said, referring to the high-security county prison. "Ask them to lock up the car for safekeeping tonight and arrange for us to use the bloodhounds tomorrow." The sheriff got up to leave, too. "I'm going over to Carroll County and try to locate Mrs. Turner."

"Wilson Turner's wife?"

"Yeah. I've heard she and Turner were living over there with relatives. I expect Chief Threadgill will know where to find her."

In Carrollton, twenty-two miles away, Chief Threadgill direced Sheriff Potts to a back-road tenant shack near the village of Bowdon in Carroll County. The last scarlet light of day was silhouetting the tumbledown, one-room house against the sky as he turned into the rutted clay drive. Rusted tin tubs, broken toys, and worn-out tools littered the yard. No one answered his knock on the weathered door. Smoke came from the chimney and there was a smell of food cooking, but the house had fallen silent.

Sheriff Potts knocked again. When there still was no answer, he called out: "This is Sheriff Potts. Coweta County. I'm looking for Mrs. Turner."

A ragged curtain at the window was pulled aside and someone peered out.

"Mrs. Turner?" Sheriff Potts said.

The door opened a crack and a voice from inside said: "Did you say *Coweta* County?"

"Yes. Sheriff Potts, Coweta County."

The door opened. An emaciated young woman in her early twenties stood there. Her dark-brown eyes were crossed and her hair had been twisted into short, fuzzy curls by a cheap permanent wave. "I'm Mrs. Turner," she said nervously. "Come in."

Removing his hat, Sheriff Potts went inside. A number of children and several adults, all motionless and frightened, sat around the room on beds and chairs. A little boy of two sat in the middle of the splintered floor, chewing up bits of paper that he had torn from a seed catalog. Mrs. Turner picked him up and placed him on her hip.

"This is my son," she said, "John William."

Sheriff Potts gave the boy's grubby fist a friendly shake and was rewarded with a wet smile. "He's a fine boy, Mrs. Turner."

"Looks like his daddy," she said, turning toward the cheaply framed picture of a dark-haired young man that stood on the mantelpiece.

"That's what I'm here for, Mrs. Turner," Sheriff Potts began. "I'm looking for your husband."

Anguish crossed her thin, sallow face. "I ain't seen Wilson since Sunday, Sheriff, when they arrested him in Carrollton. I knowed they took him to the Meriwether County jail, but when I went over there, they wouldn't let me see him."

"Who wouldn't let you see him?"

"That lady jailer at the Meriwether County jail . . . Mrs. Matthews. She wouldn't let me see him and she wouldn't let me talk to him . . . not even on the phone."

Mrs. Turner's disclosure reinforced Sheriff Potts's growing belief that Sheriff Collier had aided Wallace in the killing of Wilson Turner.

"What day was this, Mrs. Turner?"

"Monday, when he was in jail. We were gonna go back Tuesday, but before we got there, we wuz told that he'd been turned out. We ain't seen him yet." She tightened her grip on John William. "I'm afraid something's done happened to Wilson."

"We'll do all we can to find out," the sheriff said reassuringly. "To begin with, I'll need a piece of Wilson's clothing."

She caught her breath and searched his face. "You gonna look for him with the bloodhounds?"

He nodded.

Two tears rolled down her thin cheeks. His reply had confirmed her fears. They wouldn't be looking for Wilson, they'd be looking for his body. She put John William on the floor, gave his head a gentle pat, and brought out a pair of her husband's worn overalls to show the sheriff. "It's all I got left."

"These will be fine," he said. He took them and moved toward the door. "I'll keep you informed, Mrs. Turner."

On Saturday morning, the courthouse square in Newnan was so filled with the posse's cars that a city policeman had been summoned to direct traffic around them.

"Looks like you did a good job rounding up a posse," Sheriff Potts said to J.H.

Glad of the recognition, J.H. grinned. "Looks like about seventy-five men—I got some of the County Farm boys. The dogs are outside in the truck, barking like hell."

Sheriff Potts fitted his .38 pistol into his holster and walked out of the courthouse. When they saw him, the men in the posse who had been waiting outside moved forward, the confidence they felt in their sheriff reflected in their faces. With J.H. beside him, he spoke to them from the top of the courthouse steps.

"Men, you all know what we're after," he said. "A man, we believe, has been murdered, his body concealed. We're going into Meriwether County this morning to look for it."

Seeing his listeners edge closer, he raised his voice so that everyone could hear. "When we get there," he instructed them, "we'll divide up into groups. An officer . . . State Patrol, GBI, or State Revenue . . . will be in charge of each group with a search area assigned. That way, we won't waste time with random looking." He paused a moment. "Any questions?"

When no one replied, Sheriff Potts said: "Let's go."

In the surge toward the waiting automobiles he took Otwell aside. "I want you to follow me until we get to Greenville," he said. "Then I want you to lead the posse on down to Wallace's farm and get started. I'm going by to see Sheriff Collier."

Otwell grinned. "You gonna have him join the search?"

"Hell, yes. It's *his* county and *his* duty."

Sheriff Potts, with J.H. beside him, drove to the Meriwether County jail according to plan. But he failed to see Sheriff Collier.

"He's in bed, sick," Mrs. Matthews explained at the door. "His heart trouble's been acting up bad on him for the past few days."

"I'm sorry to hear that. Are there any deputies around?"

"Not here. Cecil Perkerson might be on the square."

Sheriff Potts found Cecil Perkerson standing in his accustomed place on the courthouse steps. He walked down to the car as the sheriff pulled to the curb.

"What are you boys up to this morning?" Cecil asked. "I just seen a whole passel of cars full of strangers pass by."

"We've brought a posse to search for Wilson Turner's body."

"You're wasting your time." Cecil's voice was arrogant.

"A man has been murdered," Sheriff Potts said seriously. "Wallace is in jail."

Cecil Perkerson leaned back, sliding his hands into his back pockets. "I'll tell you the same thing anybody down here will tell you . . . if John Wallace kills a man, he's got *good* reason."

"Not in my county," Sheriff Potts replied firmly, pulling away from the curb. Cecil Perkerson stood looking after him.

At Wallace's two-thousand-acre farm, the posse searched buildings, fields, swamps, and woods. Through the day and into the night, the bloodhounds barked and bounded over the countryside, but no trace of Turner was found.

When dark had fallen and the white mists shrouded the swamps, Sheriff Potts thanked the posse and released it. "Those of you who can," he added, "meet at the courthouse in the morning. We'll try again."

When Sheriff Potts and his deputies gathered in his office in Newnan, Otwell remarked: "I ain't never seen such an awful place in my life. Swamp and muck and mud and woods so thick a man can't hardly get through. Hell, we could look from now till Christmas and never find Turner."

Sheriff Potts took his lower lip between his thumb and forefinger. "We got to have more help," he agreed thoughtfully.

"How we gonna get more help?" J.H. asked. "We already got everybody that's not nailed down to the floor."

"I'm going to call the governor," the sheriff said. "I'm going to tell him what's happening and I'm going to ask for state help." He lifted the phone. "Operator, I want to speak to Governor Thompson at the State House in Atlanta."

When the governor had come on the line and had heard Sheriff Potts out, he was quick to respond. Already familiar with the case, he said: "You can have all the state help you need, as many men as you want. Request them by name, if you like."

On Sunday morning, before the church bells began to chime, units from the Georgia State Patrol, Georgia Bureau of Investigation, and the State Alcohol Tax Unit from all over the state converged on the courthouse square in Newnan to join the posse. When the long cavalcade reached Greenville, the people there lined the streets to watch it drive past the Meriwether County courthouse toward John Wallace's farm.

The search for Wilson Turner's body began again. This time, the area was enlarged, the effort intensified. From the people in Meriwether County, the officers could learn nothing. Those who were Wallace's friends were hostile; these who were not were afraid. Either they refused to talk or they claimed they had seen nothing, heard nothing, and knew nothing. When Sunday's search ended, no trace of Turner had been found.

On the way back to Newnan, Sheriff Potts, J.H., Jim Hillin, and Otwell stopped at a roadside café for coffee. As they sat around the table, J.H. asked: "What are you gonna do tomorrow, Lamar? Keep looking?"

"We got to until somebody talks."

Otwell shook his head. "Those people in Meriwether are clammed up so tight they won't even tell you what county they're in. They're scared to death of John Wallace."

"That's right," Hillin said, "they know you got him in jail, but they're not a bit sure you're gonna keep him there, and nobody's gonna take a chance on talking."

The mathematical odds against finding Turner in so large a search area were enormous. With no cooperation from Meriwether County, the job was doubly difficult.

"Well," Sheriff Potts said slowly, "we're just gonna even up the odds by offering a reward. Five hundred dollars . . . out of my own pocket . . . for information leading to the discovery of Wilson Turner's body."

Otwell whistled. "You damn sure want to find him, don't you?"

"Bad," the sheriff answered. "The preliminary hearing has been set for Tuesday morning. That's only two days away."

"How're you gonna get the word out about the reward?" J.H. asked. "You know damn well they won't let you post it in Meriwether County."

"I'm going to call it in to the Atlanta papers tonight. Meanwhile, we've got to keep on talking to people. Ask them questions. Try to get them to help. There isn't any way in the world to keep a killing like this a secret. Somebody is bound to know something."

"Where do we start?"

"When we leave here," Sheriff Potts said, "you and I, J.H., will go south to the Harris City area. Otwell, you and Hillin head west toward LaGrange. See what you can find out, and meet us back in my office at midnight."

At midnight, Sheriff Potts and J.H., their own efforts having produced nothing, were waiting in the courthouse for Otwell and Hillin to return. But Otwell telephoned instead:

"Say, Sheriff, I got one piece of information, only I don't think it amounts to much. A fellow down here in LaGrange told us that John Wallace has been going to that fortune-teller over in Heard County."

"Mayhayley Lancaster?"

"Yeah, that's her."

"That might be a good lead. You and Hillin go over there and see what you can find out."

"Hell, Sheriff, I heard she was a witch."

Sheriff Potts laughed. "She might look like one, but you'd be surprised at the number of people . . . well-known, educated people

102

. . . who take stock in what Miss Mayhayley says. I want you to check it out."

"*Now?*"

"Now, Otwell, now. We've only got two more days. If we don't come up with some solid evidence at the hearing, we could lose the whole thing."

When Otwell left the phone, he went out to the car where Hillin was waiting. "You ain't gonna believe this, Hillin, but the sheriff wants us to go see that fortune-teller."

"*Now?*"

"He said, right now."

The night was black. A pale, white moon, high above in the midnight sky, shed no light on the earth below. Only the twin beams from Sergeant Otwell's patrol car pierced the blackness of the deserted dirt road that led to Mayhayley's cabin in the woods.

Even though Otwell could not see Hillin sitting beside him, it was reassuring to know he was there. Hillin was not only tall, he was big . . . 250 pounds of tough muscle and bone ready to do any job that came his way. Mayhayley, Otwell had been told, was unpredictable. Sometimes she would cooperate, sometimes she would not, and sometimes, when riled, she would cast a spell that was said to last for seven years. Otwell didn't believe this, of course, but it gave him no comfort to think about it.

Following the directions he had been given in LaGrange, Otwell found Mayhayley's log cabin in its grove of pine trees, a glimmer of firelight flickering in its window. As the patrol car stopped, Mayhayley's pack of dogs bounded toward it, barking, holding it at bay.

"Hand me that billy stick in the back seat," Otwell said. "If one of them comes close, I'll hit him so hard he'll be in hell for breakfast."

Both men eased out of the car, Otwell swinging the stick in a hard half-circle, Hillin swinging his gun by the barrel. Together, as the dogs backed away, they walked up onto the porch of Mayhayley's cabin, the board floor groaning under their weight. Otwell knocked on the door, heard the soft swish of footsteps, then a croaking voice.

"Who comes to my door at this hour?"

"The law," Otwell answered.

"What law? God's law?"

"The state law."

"What business have you here with me? The hour is late. The cock has not yet crew."

"Sounds like some sort of damn spook," Hillin whispered.

"Shhhh," Otwell cautioned. Addressing himself to the closed door again, he said: "I'm sorry about the hour, Miss Mayhayley, but I can't wait. I got to ask you some questions."

"About what?"

"Murder."

"Aiiiiiiiii!" The sound was like a stab in the dark. The dogs began howling and baying again in chorus.

"Miss Mayhayley," Otwell insisted, "you've got to let us come in."

There was a silence on the other side of the door, a padding of feet, and then: "Show yourself at the window, so I can know you are who you say you are."

"Come on," Otwell caught Hillin's sleeve and walked with him to the paned window at the far end of the porch. A grotesque figure was silhouetted there by the firelight, but they could not see the face that peered out at them until a lighted lantern was lifted shoulder-high.

Mayhayley stood framed in the window before them. Her artificial eye glowed orange in the lantern light, the other was lost in a shadow. Heavy gold earrings pulled holes in her earlobes. Her nose seemed a thin, crooked fish hook, her toothless mouth, a dark, open hole.

"Holy Christ!" Hillin breathed. "I believe she *is* a witch!"

Mayhayley disappeared from the window, then they heard the turning of a rusted lock. The door creaked open and firelight fell on the porch outside.

The voice said: "Enter."

They moved through the open door. Mayhayley stood in the middle of the one-room cabin, her dead brother's army cap shadowing her face, her shoulders bowed under layers of fringed gypsy shawls. She held out a shriveled, yellow hand.

"I have seen your uniform," she said to Otwell, "show me your badge."

Otwell held it up for Mayhayley to see. "J. C. Otwell, Georgia State Patrol."

Mayhayley turned toward Hillin. "Who," she asked, "is he?"

Hillin stepped forward with his badge. "Jim Hillin, Georgia Bureau of Investigation."

Mayhayley nodded her head. "Can't be too careful these days . . . so much badness abroad. I got thirty-three dogs and been robbed twenty-two times."

Walking to the fireplace, she sat down in a cane-bottomed chair by the hearth, indicating two other chairs to Otwell and Hillin.

"What," she asked, "do you want of me?"

"Information," Otwell answered. "Do you know John Wallace?"

A tittering laugh came from a dark corner of the cabin. Miss Sally, Mayhayley's seventy-year-old sister, was sitting on the edge of a feather bed, looking like a very old, very frail child, in a long-sleeved, floor-length nightgown, a lace cap atop the waist-long hair that cascaded down her back.

"Go back to bed, Sally," Mayhayley commanded.

Miss Sally giggled again and got under the covers.

Otwell began again. "Do you know John Wallace?"

Mayhayley nodded her head.

"Has he been here to see you?"

Mayhayley nodded again and held up one bony finger, then two.

"He's been here twice?"

"Yes," Mayhayley said. "Once about a lost cow, once about a lost body."

Otwell and Hillin exchanged quick glances. "What did you tell him, Miss Mayhayley?"

"I told him where his cow was . . . in a pasture in Carrollton, taken there by a man named Turner."

"You told him *that?* How did you know?"

Mayhayley pulled the gypsy shawls closer around her shoulders. Her eyes narrowed with cunning. "I'm an oracle of the ages," she confided. "I was borned with this power."

Hillin leaned forward. "What did you tell him about the body, Miss Mayhayley?"

"That it would be found."

"Did he find it?"

"Yes."

"What did he do with it?"

Mayhayley held out her palm. "Money."

"How much?"

Mayhayley smiled her dark, toothless smile. "A dollar and a dime will buy the spirits' time."

Hillin took the money out of his pocket and laid it in her hand.

"Why a dollar and a dime?"

"A dollar for me, a dime for the dogs."

Holding the dollar bill up to the firelight, Mayhayley examined it, then wrapped it around the dime, lifted her ankle-length skirt, and stuffed it in the top of her high-button shoe.

From the corner of the fireplace she drew up a three-legged piano stool and placed it in front of her. Reaching inside the pocket of her

105

skirt, she brought out a deck of worn-out cards and set them square in the middle of the stool. Looking at Hillin with her one good eye, she said: "Cut the cards."

Hillin glanced at Otwell, Otwell nodded his head, and Hillin picked up half the deck. When he turned it over, the king of spades lay exposed on top.

Mayhayley threw up her frail arms. "Death!" she cried. "The king of spades means death!"

"What are you talking about, Miss Mayhayley?" Hillin asked. "Whose death?"

"Quiet!" Mayhayley silenced him with a look. "You'll scare the spirits away."

Otwell stirred uncomfortably.

"Now!" Mayhayley said crossly, "we'll have to use the hair from the hind leg of a possum."

From the mantelpiece she took a snuff can, opened it, and poured a few hairs into her hand. Drawing her chair closer to the hearth, she sat down, placed the hairs on the tip of her tongue, and spat into the fire. Hypnotically, she began to rock from side to side, her eyes fastened on the flames.

"Water . . . Fire . . . Water . . . Fire . . . Water . . . Fire."

She chanted the words to herself until her eyes closed and she lapsed into a long silence. Otwell thought she had gone to sleep.

"Hillin, let's get the hell outa here. That old fool's asleep."

Miss Sally tittered from her shadowed corner. "She ain't asleep. She's having a séance with the spirits."

Pulling aside a curtain beside her bed, Miss Sally looked out at the moon hanging high in the sky. "The moon looks right. She oughtn't to have any trouble tonight."

Suddenly, Mayhayley sat bolt upright in her chair, her eyes wide open and fixed on the fire in front of her. Her lips began to move, but made no sound. Gradually her voice became audible.

"I see a fire . . . a tremendous fire . . . a terrible fire . . . a holocaust!"

"Where's the body, Miss Mayhayley?" Hillin asked impatiently.

"Gone. Gone from its hiding place . . . men . . . horses . . . a truck . . . and fire . . . fire . . . fire . . ." Mayhayley slumped forward in her chair, her head hitting the piano stool in front of her, knocking the army cap off her head.

Miss Sally scurried from her shadowed corner to pick up the cap, replace it on Mayhayley's head, and settle her gently in the chair again. In her sweet voice Miss Sally said: "You'd better go now. She'll have to rest. Wrestling with the spirits is a very tiring job."

Back in the car, Otwell said: "That was the goddamnedest demonstration I *ever* saw."

"Do you think she knows what she's talking about?"

"Hell, no. I think she's nuts."

But an hour later, Sheriff Potts was listening intently to Otwell's description of their visit to Mayhayley.

"Well, Sheriff," he said as he finished, "what do you think of that?"

"I think you may have come on some good evidence."

"Aw, Sheriff! You don't mean it!"

"Why, sure. The very fact that Wallace went to Mayhayley trying to locate the body supports the conjecture that he had the body and wanted to conceal it. I talked to Solicitor Wyatt tonight after talking with you. He tells me he has used Mayhayley for years." Sheriff Potts was referring to the state prosecutor who would try the case should it come to trial.

"I can't believe Mr. Wyatt would use that old witch," Otwell said.

"Not for sorcery," Sheriff Potts smiled, "for information. She's a great favorite with criminals. As soon as they get in trouble with the law, they run to Mayhayley for help, tell her what they've done, where they've hidden stolen goods, and want to know if they'll be caught. Mayhayley is a very law-abiding old soul. When Solicitor Wyatt sends somebody over for information, she gives them a reading and spills the whole story. It's as simple as that."

"Well I'll be a bastard. Then we weren't just wasting time?"

"Not in the least," the sheriff said. "The evidence we've got so far shows that Wallace was both careless and confident that he wouldn't be caught. Maybe he figured if he couldn't find the body, we couldn't, either."

"Then we better find it before the preliminary hearing."

"We damned sure better. If we don't come up with Turner's body before Tuesday, the charges against Wallace and Sivell will be dismissed for lack of evidence."

Chapter Ten

A week had passed since the killing at Sunset. It was Tuesday, April 27, and Turner's body had not been found. The story, called "The Mystery of the Missing Body" by the metropolitan newspapers, had been front-page news ever since Wallace and Sivell had been arrested and locked up in the Coweta County jail.

At the commitment hearing today, the legal issue to be decided before Justices of the Peace J. O. Brown and C. S. Carswell was whether there was sufficient evidence against Wallace and Sivell to bind them over for a grand jury hearing. Since corpus delicti was a state requirement for trial and since no trace of a body had been found, Wallace and his attorneys were confident beyond a doubt that the charges would be dropped.

They were staunchly opposed in this view by State Legislator Myer Goldberg, a handsome, silver-haired criminal lawyer from Newnan who had been appointed special prosecutor for the commitment hearing by Solicitor Luther Wyatt. Rapier-sharp and quick, Goldberg shared Sheriff Potts's passion for justice.

All week long, rumors had been rampant. Some folks said that Wallace's friends had tried to buy off the witnesses. Some said they had tried to scare them off. Most folks from Meriwether said they wouldn't need any witnesses because the whole thing would be thrown out of court for lack of evidence. But Myer Goldberg was prepared.

Julia Turner had agreed to tell the court about the twenty gallons of liquor that had started the trouble between Wallace and her husband. Federal Agent Earl Lucas would testify that Wallace had reported Turner's moonshine activities and threatened to kill him if something wasn't done about it. Witnesses from Sunset would describe the killing and abduction.

On Tuesday morning, the courthouse in Newnan was filled with spectators from Coweta and Meriwether. Not wanting to miss a moment of the controversy, the old men on the courthouse square had come early that morning, finding seats for themselves on the brick wall outside so that they could see everyone who came and everything that happened. They saw Myer Goldberg escort a trembling Julia Turner into the courthouse, and watched the other witnesses arrive.

Out of the original eight from Sunset, only four would testify. Two had refused outright, frightened by the prospect of what might happen to them. Old Mr. Wilson, shattered by what he had seen from his garden fence, was bedridden and unable to be in court. Geneva Yaeger, the young waitress at Sunset, was willing to testify but Sheriff Potts felt the ordeal would be too much for her since she was only a schoolgirl.

The four remaining witnesses—Steve Smith, Merle Hannah, J. M. Phillips, and an insurance man named Keith—had come to court to point out the accused and tell what they had seen, despite rumors and threats.

Big, burly Steve Smith wanted to make sure everyone knew he was not afraid. "John Wallace or Jesus," he announced to anyone who would listen, "I ain't scared of nobody."

Merle Hannah, her eyes bright behind her glasses, had set her thin, pale lips in a resolute line. But her hands nervously twisted the strap on her handbag as she watched J. M. Phillips. Tall and thin as a rake handle, he sat in a corner of the witness room, his legs crossed and twined together like honeysuckle vines.

The sad-eyed, silent man had been eating dinner in the booth by the window next to the restaurant door when Wallace captured, beat, and killed Turner. At the time, he had been so thoroughly frightened by the violence that he had known nothing to do but to keep on eating. Profoundly affected by what he had done, Phillips had agreed to testify. Despite the fear he felt now, he was determined to keep his word.

Keeping his word was precisely what most troubled Keith, the blustery, big-talking insurance man. He had told everyone—his family, his friends, his customers—what he had seen and what he was going to do about it, delivering each time a speech on standing up to tyranny. This was before he learned that John Wallace was the man he would have to accuse. After he learned it, and much as he regretted the things he had said, there was no way to manfully get out of testifying. He waited now for court to convene, pacing back and forth, scouring his round, red face with a crumpled white handkerchief.

Sheriff Potts, leaning on a windowsill, was keeping an attentive eye on the witnesses as they felt the pressure of the waiting. Steve Smith, clearly impatient to get the job done, walked over to him. "Sheriff, I got a business to run. I can't be here at this courthouse all day."

"Now, just hold your horses, Steve," Sheriff Potts said in his soft, slow drawl. "Wallace and Sivell will be here shortly." Looking down at the street below, he said: "In fact, Otwell and J.H. are driving up with them now."

Hearing this, Keith wiped his face again with his handkerchief and continued walking back and forth with quick, short steps. "I just don't know if I'm up to it. I'm just not sure. I'm not a bit sure."

J. M. Phillips, who had watched Keith with increasing agitation, was himself having trouble with his Adam's apple, which was bobbing up and down like a yo-yo.

"H . . . h . . . hell, Keith," he managed to say, "you s . . . s . . . seen the same thing we did. All you got to d . . . d . . . do is be man enough to s . . . s . . . say so."

"I know, I know," Keith said, twisting his handkerchief into a rope, "but you got no idea . . . no idea atall . . . what those people are capable of. They're liable to kill us all and our families, too."

"Not with our sheriff here, they ain't," Merle Hannah said firmly, crossing her arms across her thin chest.

"Yeah, but what's to stop 'em in the dark when night comes?" Keith asked in a trembling voice.

Sheriff Potts had listened quietly as they worked off their anxieties, but now he became aware that Keith's mounting fear was beginning to erode the confidence of the other three. "What's the trouble, Keith?"

"Sheriff, I just don't know if I can go through with it. If I get too upset, I might faint."

"Nobody's holding you to testify, Keith," the sheriff said. "If it upsets you too much, go on home. Steve and Mrs. Hannah and Mr. Phillips can point out Wallace and Sivell."

The anguish in Keith's face lessened at the sheriff's words. Without looking at the others, he picked up his hat and walked out of the courthouse as fast as his fat legs could carry him.

The old men sitting on the courthouse wall saw Keith hurry out, his eyes directed on the sidewalk, looking neither left nor right.

"There goes one of 'em," one old man said.

110

Up in the crowded courtroom balcony, Sergeant Otwell and Hillin listened while the others gave their testimony. When Earl Lucas, Steve Smith, Merle Hannah, J. M. Phillips, and Mrs. Turner had finished, Otwell nudged Hillin and grinned. "How 'bout that?" Hillin grinned back. "Just like they weren't even scared."

"If it please the court . . ." Huddleston's voice had been bored, as if he had just endured a tedious recitation, "I would like to make an observation here."

"Yes, Mr. Huddleston."

"We've just heard an impressive array of witnesses, but I must remind the court that in capital cases in the State of Georgia, corpus delicti is a state requirement. Maybe I missed somethin' "—his tone was condescending and country-cracker—"but in all this testifyin' we've heard this mawning, I ain't heard nobody say nothin' about findin' the body of this so-called victim."

"Your Honor . . ."

"Yes, Mr. Goldberg."

"I would like to point out to my learned colleague that corpus delicti has been established on as little as bridgework or the charred rings belonging to the victim. According to Superior Judge Virlyn Moore, in the absence of this, trial can be held if it can be proved that the victim was dead the last time the witnesses saw him."

"You gotta be able to *prove* it."

"I don't think we'll have any trouble doing that," Myer Goldberg was confident.

"Gentlemen, gentlemen. This is a hearing, not a trial. If there are no more facts to be brought forth at this time, court is adjourned until a decision is reached."

The spectators stirred and the buzz of their voices reached Otwell in the balcony. He could see Sivell slouched down in his chair, and Wallace laughing and talking with his Meriwether friends, "like the whole thing was a big joke."

All at once the chatter in the courtroom stilled. The two justices of the peace had returned from chambers to make a pronouncement.

"It is the decision of this court that John Wallace and Herring Sivell, charged with the kidnapping and murder of Wilson Turner, be bound over for grand jury hearing and held without bail."

"*What!*" The scream of outrage came from John Wallace.

Judge Brown smashed his gavel down. "Court is adjourned."

Otwell went downstairs quickly to help J.H. take the prisoners back to jail before there was trouble.

In the courtroom below, Sheriff Potts was on his feet, ready for the

111

disturbance that seemed about to erupt. The spectators from Meriwether County were angry, outraged, and muttering threats. At sight of the sheriff standing before them, they turned instead, and began to leave.

When the courtroom had emptied, Sheriff Potts followed the angry Meriwether crowd down the stairs and out of the courthouse, watching from the steps until they were all in their automobiles and headed back toward Meriwether County. As he started back to his office, he saw the shadow of a man duck out of sight behind a courthouse column. Walking over to investigate, he asked: "What's your trouble, feller?"

The man, in his early twenties, shaggy-haired and shabby, flattened against the column. "I gotta find the sheriff."

"I'm the sheriff."

Suspicious eyes scanned Sheriff Potts . . . the white shirt, the gray trousers, the blue tie.

"Is this what you're looking for?" Sheriff Potts reached in his pocket for his badge.

The young man studied it a long time. Then, seeming to decide it was genuine, he said: "Sheriff, I gotta talk to you . . . private."

"We can go in my office."

Sheriff Potts led the way there, closed the door, and indicated a chair. "Now, what's your trouble?"

The man sat tensely on the edge of his chair, his rough hands gripping the sides. "I want you to arrest me," he said.

"What for?"

"Stealing cattle."

"Whose?"

"Them that belonged to John Wallace."

"What's your name?"

"Tommy Windham. Wilson Turner's my brother-in-law . . . married to my sister Julia. He took Wallace's cows 'cause Wallace ran him off his place and took his crops. Wilson figured he took what rightfully belonged to him. Wilson needed the money . . . bad. He asked me to help get the cows. I did. I was the lookout. Now, Wilson's done got hisself kilt and I'm scared I'm next and I want you to arrest me and lock me up so's they won't get me."

The words had poured out in a torrent, and when Tommy Windham had finished, he drew a deep breath and sat back in relief.

"Now, Tommy"—Sheriff Potts leaned back in his chair—"suppose you tell me a little more about this."

"You ain't gonna arrest me?"

112

"Sure, I'm going to arrest you, but I want to know how you got those cows and where you took them."

Tommy Windham then described how he, Turner, and Millard Rigsby had taken the cows from Wallace's pasture in Rigsby's truck.

"Where did you take the cows?" Sheriff Potts asked.

"We took one to Carrollton . . . that's the one they found, and the other we took to Turner's brother in Crawford County."

"Where in Crawford County?"

"Right outside of Roberta where Turner's family lives."

"What about Millard Rigsby?"

"Sheriff, he's scared slam to death. Been hidin' out ever since we found out what happened to Turner. I tried to get him to come with me today to turn hisself in, but he was too scart somebody would get him along the way. Them folks from Meriwether is out beatin' the bushes lookin' for any of us who was involved in this thing."

"Why is that?" Sheriff Potts asked, wanting to hear what Tommy Windham had to say.

The intensity returned to Tommy's face. " 'Cause we know this killin' was rigged up by John Wallace and Sheriff Collier and they don't want nobody talkin'. When Wilson never showed up that Sunday night, me and Millard went lookin' for him."

"This was Sunday, the eighteenth of April?"

Tommy nodded. "There was plenty of folks in Carrollton that seen Chief Threadgill bring Wilson to jail . . . they seen Wilson break and run when Wallace and Sivell come into town . . . and they heard Wilson hollering, 'Help, they're gonna kill me.' "

Tommy paused, his hands clenched. "When me and Millard got to Chief Threadgill, he tole us Collier had took Wilson back to Meriwether County . . . and when we went to Meriwether County, wouldn't nobody let us see or talk to Wilson . . . and we knowed then he was done for . . . and it wasn't no time fo' we heard what happened at Sunset."

"And since then you've been hiding out?" Sheriff Potts asked.

"Ever' minute."

"Where is Millard Rigsby?"

"Hid out in Carrollton."

"I'll call Chief Threadgill and have him picked up." Sheriff Potts reached for the phone.

When he had finished speaking to Threadgill, he called Sheriff O'Neal in Roberta, Georgia, explained the situation, and asked him to check the Turner pasture for the missing Guernsey cow.

"And if I find her?" Sheriff O'Neal asked.

"Contact Sheriff Collier in Meriwether County. They have jurisdiction."

Tommy Windham had leaned forward, listening intently to the conversation. "They gonna send the cow back to Meriwether County?"

Sheriff Potts nodded. "That's where she came from."

"How 'bout me?" Tommy asked, fear showing in his eyes again. "You ain't gonna send me to Meriwether, are you?"

"No, I'm taking you to the Coweta jail right now."

Tommy Windham got up and grinned. "I ain't never in my life been so glad to be arrested. I was afraid they'd get me fo' I got to jail."

"Nobody's going to get you in Coweta," Sheriff Potts told him. "Come along."

Before they got to the door, the telephone rang. The jailer, J. O. Peoples, was on the line. "Sheriff, could you come down to the jail right away?"

"I'm on my way now."

"I got something to show you. I think it's important."

Chapter Eleven

At the Coweta County jail J. O. Peoples was waiting for Sheriff Potts in the office. A slender Negro boy in his late teens fidgeted beside him.

"What's up?" Sheriff Potts asked.

The jailer hooked his thumb toward the boy. "This is Willie."

Willie embodied endless energy—twisting, twitching, turning his hands, head, or feet constantly, never standing at rest. His face looked familiar, but Sheriff Potts could not remember where he had seen him before.

"Willie brought me this," the jailer said, handing the sheriff a small, handwritten note. "Willie's the run-around-boy."

Run-around-boy was a position of trust given a deserving inmate serving his time. He was permitted the liberty of the jail, and his duties included delivering food trays from the kitchen to prisoners in their cells.

Sheriff Potts opened the note and read: *Remember Pat Brooks. Don't give me away. You owe me a lot. All of you do.*

"Where did you get this, Willie?"

The question set Willie in accelerated motion. Grinning and fidgeting, he said: "When I took the feed trays up from the kitchen, Mr. Wallace give me this and told me to take it to Mr. Sivell, but I brung it straight to Mr. Peoples."

"Good boy, Willie," Sheriff Potts said approvingly, "you did the right thing."

Willie's big black eyes were shining. "You see, Sheriff, I ain't forgot you."

Sheriff Potts frowned, trying to remember. "Didn't I put you in jail?"

"Yassuh, but that ain't whut I means."

115

Sheriff Potts waited.

"I mean about my ma."

"What about your ma?"

"Don't you remember, Sheriff?" Willie's face clouded with disappointment. "It was right at Christmastime. My ma sent me to town to buy Christmas and I gambled the money away and then went out and stole some more. That's when you catched me and put me in jail."

Sheriff Potts nodded. "I remember now."

Anxious to finish his story, Willie continued: "The money was gone and I was in jail and my ma didn't have no Christmas, and you said you wuzn't gonna have nobody you knew of go hungry on Christmas and you sent all the fixin's for Christmas out to my ma."

"I'd forgotten that."

"My ma ain't, and I ain't, either."

Knowing that despite his many charities, gratitude made Sheriff Potts uncomfortable, the jailer interrupted. "All right, Willie, better get back to your work now."

When Willie had gone he asked: "What do you think of that note, Sheriff?"

"I think it may be the first good break we've gotten."

"What did Wallace mean, 'Remember Pat Brooks'?"

"About eight years ago, Herring Sivell killed Pat Brooks in an argument over a poker game. Wallace helped get Sivell acquitted even though Pat Brooks was shot in the back and in front of witnesses."

"So now Wallace wants Sivell to be quiet about Turner."

"Exactly."

As they walked outside toward the sheriff's car, Joe Peoples asked: "Do you think he will?"

"Sivell will do whatever he has to do to save himself . . . he's that kind of feller."

"Then you think he'll give Wallace away?"

Sheriff Potts got in his car and looked back toward the jail where Sivell was silhouetted behind the bars. "Yeah, he'll give him away, it's just a matter of time."

With a nod and a wave, Sheriff Potts drove back to the courthouse. To J.H., who was standing on the sidewalk, he said: "Get all the deputies together. We're going back to Meriwether County this afternoon."

When J.H., Pete Bedenbaugh, Otwell, and Jim Hillin had gathered in his office, the sheriff showed them Wallace's note. "We've got a good chance here to break down Wallace's story," he said. "Sivell,

116

apparently, is about ready to talk, but he won't until someone else talks first."

J.H. pushed his battered hat back on his head. "Where we gonna find that 'someone else'?"

"We got to start looking for who, besides Sivell, helped Wallace chase Turner down. You remember Otwell learned from the road gang that there were two cars involved in the chase to Sunset. We want to know who was in that other car."

"What have you got in mind, Lamar?"

"I want you to go into Meriwether County this afternoon. Find and question everyone who performs services for Wallace or Sivell. Talk to the people they do their trading with. Find out where they buy their groceries, their gasoline, their farm supplies. With the results of the preliminary hearing fresh in their minds, they will be talking about what happened. Somebody may let something slip. Report back to me when you hear it."

In Meriwether County, J.H. and Otwell, who were working together, learned that Wallace's mechanic work was done by Broughton Myhand. They drove at once to his service station in Sivell's hometown of Chipley, and discovered that Myhand was literally a shade-tree mechanic. His service station was a small, white-frame store in the fork of the road, with two gas pumps, a shade tree, and a shed out back where he worked on cars.

When Otwell and J.H. drove up, he was working underneath a jacked-up automobile. Only his legs were visible. Otwell addressed himself to the pair of legs. "We're looking for Broughton Myhand."

Myhand, big and heavyset, rolled out from under the car and stood up facing Otwell and J.H. with unmistakable belligerence. "You're looking at him right now," he said, his hard, dark eyes roving over Otwell's uniform. From his back pocket he took a dirty rag and wiped the grease from his hands.

"I understand you do John Wallace's mechanic work for him," Otwell said.

Myland leaned back against the car he had been working on and spat off to the side. "I do a lot of people's mechanic work."

"Where were you last Tuesday morning, April the twentieth?"

"That's none of your damn business." Myhand shouldered his way between Otwell and J.H., heading back toward the store.

Otwell grabbed him by the collar and held him. "Don't you smart-ass off at me, buddy. You're talking to the law, not some

117

bought-off sheriff in Meriwether County. Now, suppose you tell me where you were last Tuesday."

Myhand wrenched away and snarled, "I ain't tellin' you a goddamn thing."

"J.H., let's throw his tail in that patrol car and take him back to Newnan."

"What in the hell for?" Myhand demanded as they hustled him into the back seat of the car.

"Questioning," Otwell replied. "'Maybe on the way up there you can think up better answers than you got now."

When they arrived in Newnan, Otwell and J.H. reported to Sheriff Potts and took Myhand to his office.

"Myhand," the sheriff said, "we know for a fact that a second car was involved in that chase to Sunset when Wallace and Sivell caught Turner. Were you in that car?"

The belligerence Myhand had shown Otwell and J.H. simmered down to sullenness before the sheriff. He looked down, kicked some imaginary spot on the floor, and refused to answer.

"Book him," Sheriff Potts told J.H.

"Hell, Sheriff," Myhand blurted out, "it wasn't me."

"Then who was it?"

Myhand looked down again and did not reply.

"Take him to jail, J.H."

J.H. snapped on the handcuffs and led the way toward the door. Myhand stopped. "It wasn't me. It was Henry Mobley."

"Where were you?"

Myhand hesitated. Sheriff Potts waited.

"I was supposed to go, but didn't."

"Why not?"

A strange look crossed Myhand's tough face, as though he had suddenly experienced a painful catch in his chest. He seemed to be having trouble in getting the answer out.

"Why not, man, why not?" Sheriff Potts demanded.

Broughton Myhand's wide shoulders slumped and he looked down at the floor. "My wife wouldn't let me."

"Holy God and Jesus Christ!" Otwell exclaimed. "If that don't beat all I ever heard. A big gorilla like that didn't get to go 'cause his *wife* wouldn't let him!"

Sheriff Potts silenced Otwell with a look. "Myhand," he said, "that just doesn't sound reasonable. What about John Wallace? Weren't you worried about not doing what he said?"

"Yeah, but it would've been worse if I had," Myhand mumbled. "My wife is a Carter, and them Carters is hell to tangle with. She got wind of what was going on, and when Tuesday came. . . ." His voice trailed off. His admission had robbed him of his toughness. Standing before the sheriff, he was now almost docile.

"All right, Myhand," Sheriff Potts said patiently, "if you weren't in that second car with Henry Mobley, then who was?"

The question stunned him. "Who said there was *two* people?"

"We've got witnesses who saw them."

Broughton Myhand shook his head, his face an agony of indecision. "I can't tell, Sheriff, I just can't tell. I'd rather go to jail."

"Why?" Sheriff Potts demanded.

"Because he'd kill me if I told."

"Lock him up, J.H."

After J.H. had left with Myhand, Sheriff Potts stood looking out of his office window in deep concentration. There was somebody out there they didn't know about . . . somebody Myhand feared more than Wallace.

"Wonder who the hell he's so scared of?" Otwell asked. "We got Wallace in jail. Who's tougher than Wallace in Meriwether County?"

"Can't tell yet," Sheriff Potts said, picking up his car keys. "Come on. Let's go."

"Where?"

"To pick up Henry Mobley."

Sheriff Potts and Otwell found Henry Mobley, that balding, middle-aged man, working in a feed store in Chipley not far from Broughton Myhand's service station. Mobley's brown eyes were friendly, and his reaction to questioning was completely different from that of the others. Wallace had been arrogant, Sivell sullen, Broughton Myhand belligerent. Henry Mobley was courteous, cooperative, and pleasant.

He readily admitted that he was Wallace's friend, that he had, at one time, lived on Wallace's farm, and that in addition to working at the feed store, he also dealt in livestock, sometimes helping John Wallace with his cattle. Beyond this, he declined to answer any question that was asked.

"No, sir, Sheriff," Mobley smiled pleasantly, "I don't know a thing."

"Look, Mobley, we already know you were driving the backup car. Who was the other man with you?"

A guarded look crossed Henry Mobley's face, and his eyes weren't

119

smiling anymore. "Like I told you, Sheriff, I don't know nothing. I got a nice wife and a twelve-year-old boy, and even if I was to know somethin', there ain't a way in the world you'd get me to say it."

"Okay, Mobley, you're under arrest."

"For what?"

"Accessory. You're allowed one phone call. You can contact your attorney if you like."

"I'd rather call my wife."

Sheriff Potts shrugged. "Suit yourself."

From the phone in the feed store, Henry Mobley made the call. "Louise? I been arrested . . . yeah . . . would you bring my pajamas to the Coweta County jail? Yeah. Soon as you can. Good-bye."

Henry Mobley smiled pleasantly as he walked with Sheriff Potts to his car. "I ain't never liked to sleep in my clothes," he said.

By Tuesday night, four suspects in the Turner murder were in the Coweta County jail, and people in Meriwether County had begun to talk—not about what *they* knew, but about what they had heard. From the information gathered by Sheriff Potts's deputies, four theories emerged as to the fate of Wilson Turner.

One theory was that he had been thrown into the wilderness of the Okefenokee Swamp, some two hundred miles away. Another was that his body had been burned in one of the old pits used for liquor stills on Wallace's two-thousand-acre estate. A third theory had it that a deep grave had been dug in a cornfield under cultivation, the body buried, the ground harrowed over, and seed planted to conceal the grave. The fourth and most favored theory was that the body had been split open so it wouldn't rise and had been sunk in the quicksand and mud of Wallace's forty-acre lake.

To explore all these possibilities, Sheriff Potts organized a mammoth manhunt for Wednesday morning. It would cover three counties . . . Meriwether, and neighboring Troup and Harris counties. Headquarters for the operation were set up at Mrs. Clyde Byrd's store in Durand, a country village in Meriwether County midway between Greenville and Chipley. At Sheriff Potts's request, the Atlanta radio stations broadcast appeals to all citizens in the area to join the search.

On Tuesday night, reporters from the national press services and the metropolitan dailies began arriving in Newnan to cover the story, among them, Hugh Park of the *Atlanta Journal* and Celestine Sibley of the *Atlanta Constitution*. Press headquarters had been arranged in the Virginia Hotel on the town square, an ancient two-story structure where longtime residents rocked in the chairs on the front porch.

Seeing the lights burning late in the sheriff's office, Hugh Park walked into the courthouse and found Sheriff Potts briefing the officers who were to help direct the posse the next morning. The three-county area had been broken down into segments, each with an officer in charge of volunteers.

"May I sit in on this?" Park asked. "I'm Hugh Park from the *Journal*."

Sheriff Potts looked up and smiled at the tall, gray-eyed reporter. "Sure, Hugh, come on in. I've been reading your reports."

Hugh Park smiled back. "I've been following your efforts."

Sheriff Potts laughed. "We hope to break this case soon. Elzie Hancock will join the search tomorrow."

"Who's he?"

"An Alcohol Tax Unit agent presently working out of Sheriff Howell's Muscogee County office in Columbus. I made a special request for him. Hancock is an expert in tracking and the greatest woodsman I've ever seen. If Turner's body is still out there, he'll find it."

"What do you mean by 'still out there'?"

"Well . . . it begins to appear that Turner's body may have been destroyed."

"What then?"

"We'll have to depend on a confession, but that might be hard to come by, scared as those people are down there."

Hugh Park frowned. "What about the five-hundred-dollar reward you offered? Did you get any response from that?"

"Not yet."

"Then what makes you think those people down there will talk now?"

"Since the commitment hearing this morning, people have begun to realize the seriousness of the situation. All this time . . . either out of fear or loyalty . . . they've obliged Wallace by not talking. Things have changed now. Wallace can't manipulate his way out of this. He's charged with *murder* . . . in jail without bond . . . waiting for a grand jury hearing. Loyalty doesn't last long when there's a murder charge involved."

"That's for damn sure," Hugh Park said. "You've made four arrests already."

"There'll be more," Sheriff Potts predicted. "We'll keep looking until we find Turner or what happened to him. Tomorrow's posse will be starting at dawn."

"I'll be there," Hugh Park said.

At daybreak, officers from the Georgia State Patrol, GBI, and State Alcohol Tax Unit, designated by the governor to assist Sheriff Potts in the search, began arriving. Earl Lucas and other agents from the Federal Alcohol Tax Unit, already involved in the surveillance of Wallace's illicit liquor making, also joined the citizens who had volunteered for the posse. These were independent, self-reliant, country people . . . farmers, firemen, small businessmen, clerks, and cattlemen . . . who had heard the appeal on the radio and left their fields and stores to aid Sheriff Potts in the search for Turner's body.

Special equipment teams arrived, and Sheriff Potts, standing on the porch of Mrs. Clyde Byrd's store, gave them instructions. When the grappling-hook crew came up for assignment, he told them: "There's a water-filled bauxite pit located near President Roosevelt's Little White House in Warm Springs. The pool formed by this pit is one hundred fifty by forty feet. You might have some trouble with the depth. It's estimated at thirty feet."

"If Turner's down there, we'll find him," the foreman said.

Other teams, equipped with well drags and ropes, were given designated areas. "Check *all* wells," the sheriff told them. "If a dry well looks like it recently caved in, dig down to make sure there's nothing underneath."

"What about John Wallace's forty-acre lake?" someone asked. "Are we gonna drag that, too?" Many of the men believed in the theory that the body had been sunk in the lake.

"It's not practical."

"Why not?" several men chorused.

"We've learned that when they built the lake, a bottom mat was made from logs and fallen trees before the water was let in. Grappling hooks would only snag on the logs. If we have to, we'll drain the lake. Meanwhile, we'll check out all creeks and ponds."

Men and equipment had already started moving out into the morning haze and the blue woods beyond when Elzie Hancock arrived from Columbus. "Sorry I'm late, Lamar," he said as they shook hands. "There are so many volunteers on the way out to help, I got held up in the traffic." Looking out at the crowd of men and cars lining both sides of the road, he added, "*They* sure as hell ought to be able to find Turner."

Sheriff Potts grinned. "I expect *you* to do that."

Behind his steel-rimmed glasses, Hancock's bright blue eyes twinkled. He relished the remark. A short, leathery man in his late fifties, Hancock had worked this area for the State and Federal

122

Alcohol Tax Units for nearly forty years. It was he who had shot and killed Wallace's outlaw uncle, John Strickland, years before.

Experience and determination had made him expert at uncovering whatever was concealed in the woods. He was the oldest man working in the field for that unit, but his drive and endurance outlasted that of men in their twenties. Because of all this, he had established a remarkable record, which he guarded with immeasurable pride.

"Well, now," he said, rubbing his hands together briskly, "what have we got to do here?"

While Sheriff Potts was briefing him, Otwell came up on the porch for a moment. "Elzie!" He clapped Hancock on the back. "What's an old man like you doin' out here today?"

Hancock grinned. "Want to have a footrace, young fellow?"

"Better not, Otwell," Sheriff Potts said. "I've seen this 'old man' raid a still, chase two bootleggers on foot four miles, catch one, handcuff him to a tree, and keep running till he caught the other."

"Aw, Sheriff, you're puttin' me on," Otwell teased, knowing the story to be true.

"Okay, now," Sheriff Potts got back to his maps. "Elzie, here's where we'll be working. Do you want an assignment?"

"No. I've got some ideas of my own."

"Do you need any help?"

"No, indeed. If I come on anything, I'll be in touch."

"Good. See you later."

After the last unit had been dispatched, Sheriff Potts still stood on the porch watching with satisfaction as men and equipment moved through the woods in every direction.

"That's quite an operation, Sheriff." Hugh Park had come up beside him. "How many men have you there, do you know?"

"Between four and five hundred." Sheriff Potts turned to Park. "I'm going to do some spot-checking now. Want to come along?"

"Sure."

In the sheriff's car, Hugh Park asked: "Did any of the officers from Meriwether County show up?"

"Not a soul."

Nor did the people of Meriwether County participate in the search. They watched behind curtained windows and waited. At noon, when Sheriff Potts and Hugh Park stopped by a country store in Meriwether County for a Coca-Cola, the proprietor, a staunch Wallace supporter named Williams, laid his hand on the Coke box and said: "We ain't got none."

123

"All right," Sheriff Potts said, "I'll take a package of Camel cigarettes."

"We're sold out."

Pointing to the rows of fresh cigarette packs on the shelf behind Williams, Sheriff Potts asked: "What's that?"

"Them's mine, and they ain't for sale."

Hugh Park stepped forward. "Could I use your phone to call my paper?"

Williams scowled. "It's outa order."

"Come on, Hugh," Sheriff Potts said. "This man's nearly out of business."

By midafternoon, when they stopped at the bauxite pit, the grappling-hook crew, working from a boat in the pool, had found nothing. "That fellow Turner just ain't in here," the foreman reported.

Bluford Jones, a seventeen-year-old textile worker, had told the investigators that he had seen a strange automobile traveling slowly down the old pit road on the day Turner disappeared. Now, tire tracks were discovered and men were sent to investigate, but again nothing was found.

Later, Sheriff Potts and Hugh Park arrived at a spot near Wallace's farm just as an abandoned well was discovered. John Cobb, the heavyset man who had found it, was lowered into the well. He had barely reached the bottom when he yelled up: "Get me a shovel. I think I've found something!"

The men crowded to the mouth of the well. A shovel was lowered.

"I got him!" Cobb cried. "I got him by the hair of the head! Get somebody down here to help."

Quickly another man was lowered.

"What have you got?" Sheriff Potts called.

A full minute passed, and the second man replied: "Not a goddamn thing. Let me back up."

They pulled him out. "What was it?"

"The damned tail off a dead mule that fell in the well and died."

The tension and tedium of the long day's work exploded into laughter. John Cobb emerged from the well red-faced and flustered. "How the hell could I tell?" he said. "It's dark down there."

By nightfall, the day's efforts had yielded only the debris of the woods and swamps: dead buzzards, dead animals, and rotted logs. At the office in the Coweta County courthouse, the deputies, tired and grimy from the search, gathered in a semicircle around the sheriff as he made plans for the following day.

"We have one new lead," he told them. "An unidentified caller said

124

if I met him alone at the train station in Harris City tonight at midnight, he would tell me something."

"That's Meriwether County!" J.H. exclaimed.

"Yeah."

"Hell," Otwell said. "I searched that area all day and there ain't much there but the train station. Might be a trap."

Sheriff Potts paused a moment before answering. "Possibly."

"Are you going?"

"Hell, yes."

Chapter Twelve

J.H. usually deferred to his brother's judgment and accepted his leadership without challenge, but Lamar's decision to meet the mysterious caller in Harris City at midnight aroused rare anger and argument from him. The planned rendezvous, J.H. felt, was plain, damned foolishness.

"I don't like it," he said. "I just, by God, don't like it. It's nothing but a trap. Why in the hell do you suppose they want you to come at midnight and why alone?"

The other three deputies watched silently, for J.H., being the sheriff's brother, was the only one at liberty to say what they all felt.

"Now, J.H.," Sheriff Potts began in a calm, even voice, "we don't know that it's a trap. There's a good possibility that someone is finally willing to talk. Harris City is only a village. If a man wanted to pass some information, the Harris City train station would be a reasonable place to pick. At that time of night the town is deserted. No one would know."

"You're damned right it's deserted, and you're damned right no one would know," J.H. shouted. "They could pick you off from a passing car, and next week we could be out beating the bushes, trying to find *you!*"

The sheriff smiled and shook his head. "J.H., if you keep carrying on, you'll have your blood pressure over two hundred again."

J.H. wiped the perspiration from his face with a crumpled handkerchief. "Look, Lamar," he said, turning from anger to appeal, "don't you know they'd like to get you out of the way? Don't you realize that if you were out of the picture, this whole thing would cool off and none of them would go to trial? Just do me a favor and don't go down there tonight. None of us feel you should."

126

The deputies' solemn faces reflected their concurrence, but Sheriff Potts replied, "I've made my decision."

J.H. picked up his hat, smashed it on his head, and stalked out of the office.

"J.H. just gets upset," Sheriff Potts explained to his still-silent deputies. "I don't expect any trouble down there tonight."

"Say, Sheriff," Otwell suggested, "how 'bout if we provide some cover for you when you meet this feller?"

"The conditions were that I come alone. Cover might scare him off."

Otwell nodded. There was no use arguing. "When are you leaving?"

Sheriff Potts took out his pocket watch. It was eleven thirty. "Right now. I'll see you when I get back."

"Good luck," said Otwell.

Despite his dismissal of J.H.'s anxieties, Sheriff Potts was well aware of the potentially dangerous situation. Only a fool would discount that. But there could be no stopping now. He didn't plan to take unnecessary risks, nor did he plan to take unnecessary precautions that would preclude a break in the case. He *had* to know what his caller had to say.

On the drive down the Federal Highway to Harris City, he watched the intersections and country sideroads. When he arrived in Harris City, he parked his car off the road and worked his way through the darkness to the unlighted train station.

Harris City was a short spur off the Federal Highway that ran through Greenville to Warm Springs. Barely a block long, it amounted to only a few village stores and a wood-frame station beside the railroad tracks. At midnight, the place was quiet and deserted. Waiting now in the darkness, it was hard for him to imagine who might come out of the shadows.

The muffled voice on the telephone had sounded sincere. Maybe the man who had called was an informer. Maybe he knew where Turner's body was hidden. Maybe . . . just maybe . . . he had something else in mind. Harris City *was* an isolated village. Harris City *was* in Meriwether County, and Meriwether County *was* hostile.

Years of assisting Federal officers on surprise raids of moonshiners and their stills had disciplined Sheriff Potts in moving soundlessly and waiting patiently. The moon moved across the midnight sky, shifting the shadows and glistening on the rails that disappeared on the dark horizon. Sheriff Potts listened intently for some sound, but there was

127

only the distant yowl of a cat and the responsive barking of a dog.

More than an hour passed before he heard the soft footsteps on the board platform of the station. Alert and ready to respond, he waited, but the padding steps belonged to a dog that paused for a moment to inspect him, then ambled off on his rounds.

A short time later, a car pulled into the street, passed slowly by the station, turned around, and drove out again. Sheriff Potts waited, but the car never returned. There was only the empty street, the deserted station, and the waning moon. At 2:00 A.M. he decided to return to Newnan.

J.H. was waiting for him in the courthouse. He jumped up when his brother entered. "What happened?"

"Nothing," Sheriff Potts said wearily, "absolutely nothing."

Before he could say more, the telephone rang. He picked it up. "Sheriff's office."

A voice on the other end of the line said: "Tom Strickland." Then the speaker hung up.

"What was that?" J.H. asked.

"The answer I've been looking for, I think. You know who Tom Strickland is, don't you?"

J.H. squinted, remembering. "Kin to John Wallace, isn't he?"

"Right. He's John's first cousin, the one whose wife was killed several years ago in Meriwether County."

J.H. snapped his fingers. "There was a coroner's inquest. A lot of talk."

"Yeah. The coroner ruled it suicide. I think Tom Strickland may be our man."

"You think he rode with Mobley in the backup car?"

Sheriff Potts nodded. "That would explain why Mobley and Myhand won't talk. Tom Strickland has the reputation of being a pretty tough character."

"What are you going to do?"

"Pick him up for questioning."

"When?"

"After I've talked to Hancock. He knows more about the Stricklands than anyone else."

The next day, when Sheriff Potts checked with him, Hancock said: "Tom's the meanest one in the Strickland bunch. If John Wallace shoots a man, he's usually got a reason. Tom figures he don't need a reason. The people in Meriwether County are scared to death of him. Seems like he just sets out to do all the meanest things he can think of just to prove how tough he is."

128

"How's that?"

"Well, you know his uncle, John Strickland, the one we got at the still that night, was his idol. Tom always did expect to inherit his place as head of the clan. When they chose John Wallace instead, it just stuck in his craw. After that, there wasn't no holding him. He figured he'd show everybody he was the toughest man in the territory."

"Is he?"

Hancock squinted one eye as though taking aim. "I always figured him for a coward. He talks tough and acts tough, but if it were ever to come to a showdown. . . ." Hancock's voice trailed off and he shook his head.

"We'll soon find out," Sheriff Potts said.

"When are you going for him?"

"Tonight."

"Mind you watch yourself," Hancock warned. "He's fast with a gun and he's reckless and don't care who he shoots."

Sheriff Potts grinned and draped an arm around Hancock's shoulders. It was rare for Hancock to stress caution. "Thanks, Elzie, but I don't figure on having any trouble."

"Don't be too sure," Hancock replied.

That night at eight o'clock, Sheriff Potts and Otwell drove to Meriwether County to pick up Tom Strickland. When they reached Greenville, the sheriff told Otwell they'd have to take somebody with them to find Strickland's house. "He lives somewhere down in their corner of the county," he said. "We damned sure don't want to go house to house and alert them. We'd never get him out of there."

Otwell pointed to a white-frame house adjacent to the courthouse. "There's a bailiff that lives just over there."

"Go in there and get him," Sheriff Potts said, "but don't tell him we're going after Tom Strickland. Just say we want him to ride around with us for a while."

When Otwell knocked at the house, the porch light came on and a rumpled-looking man in baggy pants opened the door. In a moment he went back inside and then came out, putting on his hat. Otwell opened the door to the back seat of the car and the man got in.

"This bailiff here says he'll ride with us," Otwell said, climbing in beside the sheriff.

"Good." Sheriff Potts looked back at the man's apprehensive face. "Have you lived here long?"

"All my life."

"I reckon you know most everybody in the county?"

"Down to the last nigger." The bailiff laughed nervously.

"That's good," Sheriff Potts said as they drove toward Warm Springs. "I want you to show us where Tom Strickland lives."

"Oh, my God!" the bailiff gasped. "Let me outa here."

Otwell turned to face him. "Now you rest easy, little feller." He tapped the bailiff on the knee with his finger. "You ain't got to do a thing in this world but show us where Tom Strickland lives."

"I . . . er . . . I . . . er . . . don't know where he lives," the bailiff stammered.

"He lives down there in what they call 'the Kingdom,' doesn't he?" Sheriff Potts asked. "Somewhere near John Wallace's place?"

"All the Stricklands live there. I can't be sure which house it is," the bailiff said.

"Then we'll just ride around till you remember."

As they drove through the dark toward their destination, the bailiff's uneasiness could be felt like a heartbeat. When the car turned onto the road that led toward the Kingdom, he bolted forward, his hands clutching the back of the front seat. "Wait! Stop here and let me find out for sure where Tom Strickland lives." He indicated a house, barely more than a shack, that sat on a hill beside the road. There was a light in the window.

"Some niggers live there," he said, "and you know how niggers are. They know everything."

Otwell looked at Sheriff Potts. Sheriff Potts nodded and said: "Go see what you can find out."

The bailiff sprang from the car and ran up the hill.

"Follow him, Otwell. He doesn't look like he intends to come back."

Otwell jumped out of the car, ran up the hill, and waited in the shadows of the yard. A Negro man in overalls answered the bailiff's knock on the door.

"You know where Mr. Tom Strickland lives?" the bailiff demanded in a tone intended to intimidate.

"Yassuh. Go down this here road 'bout fo' miles. Take the right fork, and Mr. Tawm lives in the curve. In that big white house with the pillars on the porch."

"You're sure?"

"Yassuh, I'se sure."

The bailiff turned away and went down the steps. The Negro closed the door. As he did, the bailiff looked around quickly and started to run behind the house.

"Wait a minute, little feller." Otwell stepped out of the shadows. "The car is back this way."

The bailiff's shoulders sagged like a punctured balloon. With Otwell behind him, he walked unwillingly down the hill to the car.

Following the Negro's directions, Sheriff Potts found Strickland's house. He turned out the car lights, pulled into the drive, and parked behind a willow tree in the side yard. As he and Otwell got out, the bailiff cowered in the corner of the back seat. "Stay where you are and you won't get hurt," the sheriff told him.

The house was dark except for a dim light in the center hall. "If Strickland comes to the door," Sheriff Potts said, "we mustn't let him go back inside. If he does, there'll be trouble."

Otwell nodded and moved to one side of the door as Sheriff Potts knocked. There was no answer. He knocked again. They waited. Still no reply. Sheriff Potts knocked once more, and they heard heavy footsteps coming toward them. Otwell flattened against the side of the house, and Sheriff Potts stepped away from the glass panes of the door.

The overhead porch light came on. The curtains over the door panes moved. A key was turned and a latch was lifted. The door opened and Tom Strickland stepped outside. Seeing Sheriff Potts and Otwell, he stood motionless, assessing the situation.

Strickland was tall, with long arms that hung loose from the shoulders. Although it was a warm evening, he wore a tattered tweed jacket over his shirt and khaki work pants. His matted and unkempt black hair hung in hanks around his ears, and there was a stubble of beard on his face.

"Strickland," Sheriff Potts said, moving toward him, "we want to talk to you."

For a moment, Strickland's pale eyes moved restlessly, as though searching for a means of escape. Finally he replied: "All right, let me get my hat."

With that, he whirled toward the open door, his hand going for the gun in the shoulder holster under his jacket. Before he could reach it, Sheriff Potts had drawn his own snub-nosed .38 and buried it in the soft diaphragm under Strickland's rib cage.

"Get your hands up!"

Strickland hesitated.

"Now!" Sheriff Potts shoved his .38 deeper.

Strickland raised his long arms over his head. Sheriff Potts reached inside the tweed jacket, took a .44-caliber pistol out of the holster, and handed it to Otwell. Through the handle of his own gun, he could feel Strickland's taut muscles ready to move.

"Check him out, Otwell."

Otwell removed a Bowie knife from Strickland's belt, and a small hand pistol from his trouser pocket. "He's clean now."

"Strickland," the sheriff said, "you're under arrest."

"What in the hell for?"

"Your part in the murder of Wilson Turner."

"The hell you say! I don't know nuthin' about Turner."

"Sure you do." Sheriff Potts's eyes were hard. "You rode in the backup car with Mobley when Turner was killed."

"What makes you say that?"

"Somebody talked."

With a sudden violent movement, Strickland hurled himself toward the porch steps. Sheriff Potts leaped forward, grabbed him by his trouser belt, swung him around, and held him. Face-to-face, each took the other's measure.

Strickland was stunned. He had never been caught undefended before. In this unaccustomed situation, he was wild-eyed and disoriented. Never having fought his own battles, he had no frame of reference. His retinue of hirelings, eager to ingratiate themselves, to share in the reflected power of the Strickland name, had always carried out his orders and prevented confrontations. Or John Wallace had. Tonight, Tom Strickland faced his challenge alone.

Sheriff Potts watched fear replace Strickland's anger, and he knew the contest was over. Hancock had been right. Tom Strickland, feared by so many, was a coward.

"You're coming with me, Strickland," he said.

Otwell followed them down the steps to the car. "Sit in back with Strickland," Sheriff Potts told him. "The bailiff can sit up front with me."

The frightened bailiff, however, had fled into the night.

Driving back to Newnan, Sheriff Potts decided to put Strickland in the city jail instead of in the county jail with the four other suspects. Deprived of their support, he might prove the weakest link in Wallace's chain. On the car radio he called J.H. at the sheriff's office.

"We're bringing Strickland in," he reported. "Call down to city jail and get a cell ready."

"*City* jail!" Strickland protested. "You got John and the rest of 'em in the county jail. Why the city jail for me?"

"We got a special place for you."

"I don't want nuthin' special," Strickland said, his voice filled with suspicion. "I want to be with my friends."

Despite his plea, a cell was waiting at the city jail in the new Municipal Building. When its iron door closed behind him, Tom

Strickland was like a wild animal suddenly caged. He grabbed the bars and shook them. He screamed, yelled, and cursed. He kicked the cell bunk furiously, threw the mattress on the floor, and battered the wall with his fists.

"There's no use carrying on like this, Strickland," Sheriff Potts said calmly. "When you're ready to talk sense, I'll be back."

The town clock was striking midnight as he left to go home. At 3:00 A.M., he was awakened by a telephone call from the jailer.

"Sheriff, could you come down here right away? That Strickland fellet has gone all to pieces. He's been carrying on like a madman for three hours. Now he says he's got something he wants to tell you."

Chapter Thirteen

Tom Strickland had never in all his fifty years known restraint. Confined in the city jail, he had become hysterical. Sheriff Potts found him crumpled on the floor, sobbing, his coarse hands hanging onto the bars.

"You've got something you want to say to me?" the sheriff asked.

Struggling to his knees, Strickland slowly looked up, his eyes moist with tears making little wet roadways through his stubble of beard.

"You gotta get me outa here, Sheriff. I can't stand being locked up. I gotta get out."

"I didn't come down here in the middle of the night to hear complaints. If this is all you have to tell me, I'll see you later in the morning." Sheriff Potts turned to leave.

Strickland shook the bars. "Wait! Wait! For the love of God, wait!" he screamed. "I do have something to say . . . about Turner."

"All right, let's have it."

Strickland pulled himself to his feet. "Turner wasn't nuthin' . . . nuthin' but pore white trash . . . not worth the powder to blow him to hell. All this lookin' and searchin' you been doin' has tore Meriwether County all to pieces . . . it ain't right. Turner wasn't nuthin' but a sorry little sonofabitch."

Sheriff Potts answered: "Turner was a human being."

Strickland looked surprised, then impatient. "He wasn't no human being. I told you! He was a low-life bastard that stole John's cows. He had no right. . . ."

"He had a right to his day in court," Sheriff Potts interrupted sharply. He made no effort to conceal his disgust.

Strickland sighed and pushed his hand through his matted hair.

134

"Sheriff, I'll say it plain out. Call off this search. Turner ain't worth it. You don't *understand*."

"Hell, no, I don't understand. I don't understand for one minute. No man sets himself up as judge and jury to decide . . . *on his own* . . . that another must die. I don't give a damn what he's done. The search for Turner will go on until he's found. Then, those who were involved will have *their* day in court, which is a damn sight more than he had." The sheriff turned and walked away.

Wild-eyed again, Strickland shrieked: "No! No! Wait! I gotta get outa here. I can't stand being locked up like this!"

"You got a long time to get used to it, Strickland. It's no telling how long it'll take us to find Turner."

As Potts turned to walk away, Strickland shouted, "Wait! I'll make a bargain with you."

Sheriff Potts stopped to listen.

"I'll tell you what happened to Turner, and you turn me loose."

Sheriff Potts shook his head. "No way. You tell me what happened to Turner and you'll make it easier on yourself, *but*"—his tone was emphatic—"you'll come to trial with the rest of them."

"I'll tell you where to find him," Strickland insisted, "but you gotta let me out."

"No bargains, Strickland," Sheriff Potts said. He walked to the jailer's office, sat down, and lit a cigarette.

Back in the corridor Strickland began again—shouting, beating the walls, and shaking the cell bars.

"What's with Strickland?" the jailer said.

"He's working himself up to a confession," Sheriff Potts replied. "He just needs a little more time."

Now Strickland was screaming: "Save me, Jesus! Save me! Lord have mercy, God! Save me! Get me outa here!"

"Sounds to me like he done got religion."

"That's usually the way," Sheriff Potts observed. "When all else fails, then they get religion . . . just long enough to get out of trouble."

For more than half an hour Strickland continued his tirade, crying, praying, calling on God to get him out. When this failed, he began to shout: "Get me the sheriff! Get the sheriff! I gotta see the sheriff!"

Sheriff Potts leaned back in his chair, propped his feet on the office desk, and lit another cigarette. "Go down and see what he wants," he told the jailer.

In a moment the jailer returned. "Says he's ready to talk, and I

135

hope to hell he does. Ain't nobody in this jail had any sleep atall tonight."

Sheriff Potts nodded. "These things take time. With a little patience a feller like that talks *himself* into talking. He doesn't need any convincing."

"Well, I sure as hell hope he hurries," the jailer said wearily.

Sheriff Potts finished his cigarette and walked slowly back to Strickland's cell. "You ready to talk, Strickland?"

Strickland was exhausted. Leaning the full weight of his body against the cell door, he lifted his ravaged face to Sheriff Potts.

"It wasn't none of my idea to go after Turner," Strickland began. "John made me."

"*Made* you? How could he do that?"

"Same way he always does. He gets you beholden. Then when he calls back the favors he's done, there ain't no way out, no matter *what* he says do."

Strickland paused. Sheriff Potts waited.

"He told me Turner had stole two of his purebred cows, and he was gonna get him. John done me a favor awhile back when I had some trouble, so I *had* to help him."

"How?"

"John figured to trap Turner when he left the Meriwether County jail. John and Herring Sivell were to block one exit from town, Henry Mobley and me was to seal off the other. John planned to get Turner right there in Greenville and say he broke jail."

"What happened?"

"Mrs. Matthews and the Negro trusty screwed things up," Strickland said, and he proceeded to describe the series of errors that had occurred that Tuesday morning in the Meriwether County jail. "So Turner got a head start," he concluded, "and John didn't catch him till he got clear to Sunset. You know what happened then."

"I want to know what happened *after* you left Sunset," Sheriff Potts said.

"Me and Mobley never got to Sunset," Strickland said quickly. "When Turner wheeled in there, John signaled for us to fall back and wait. After they got him, we followed Sivell's car for about a mile to where he turned off on a dirt road. Sivell's car had a flat tire. Then they transferred Turner from Sivell's car to ours."

Strickland stopped. As the explanation approached *his* actions, he began to have misgivings. Grasping the bars, he pressed his forehead against them.

"What did you do with Turner after that?" Sheriff Potts asked.

136

"I didn't do nuthin' with him," Strickland replied. "John did. He took Turner off down in the woods."

"Where?"

"On his place."

"What did he do with him?"

"I dunno. He took Turner out of the car. I went with him into the woods partway, then he told me he could handle it from there. He sent me back to his house to get some clean clothes."

"Clean clothes?"

"Yeah, his were all bloody from carrying Turner over his shoulder."

"What about Henry Mobley?"

"Mobley drove me back to John's house for the clothes. When we got back, John was waitin' there alone."

"Where is this place that John took Turner?"

"Down there in the swamp about two or three miles from his house."

"What did John do with him?"

The frightened look returned to Strickland's eyes, and again tears rolled down his cheeks.

"What did John do with Turner?"

Strickland began to sob uncontrollably and sank to the floor.

Sheriff Potts motioned to the jailer who had been standing behind him, listening to Strickland's confession. "Go down to the kitchen and have the cook make some strong coffee. This man needs it."

He left the city jail and drove across town to the county jail. There he spoke to the sleepy jailer dozing behind the desk. "I want to talk to John Wallace."

"Startin' work kinda early, ain't you, Sheriff?" the jailer said, handing him the key to the cell. "It's four o'clock in the morning."

Sheriff Potts smiled. "I'm still finishing up last night's work."

Wallace was asleep on the top bunk in his cell. When Sheriff Potts spoke to him, he pounced down with animal alertness. He squinted against the brightness as the lights came on, but he was as cool and composed as though he had been waiting for this moment.

"We have Tom Strickland in jail," Sheriff Potts informed him. "He's told us what happened."

Wallace's face registered no reaction. "Did he now?"

"We know that you planned to trap Turner, that you ran him down, caught him, and took him off to the woods on your place."

Wallace's smile was icy. "He told you all that, did he?"

Sheriff Potts nodded.

137

"Well, there's something else you ought to know, Sheriff. Tom's the family fool. This thing's got him all upset. He never could stand up to stress. Goes all to pieces." Wallace dismissed Strickland's story as if it were village gossip. "You can't believe a thing he says."

Sheriff Potts held him with a long look. "You're saying that Tom Strickland's version isn't true?"

"Not a word of it."

"You want to give me *your* version?"

Wallace's lip curled as though he had been asked an absurdity. "I know nothing at all about Turner. You can look from now till Doomsday and you won't find a thing." He was a cement buttress . . . cold, unyielding, emotionless.

"Don't count on that," Sheriff Potts said. He locked the cell door and returned to the jailer's office.

"Any luck?" the jailer asked.

"Not yet, but I want you to do something for me. See to it that the word gets around in the jail this morning that Tom Strickland broke last night."

Dawn was beginning to streak pastels across the sky as Sheriff Potts left the county jail and drove toward the courthouse. The round, lighted face on the dome of its clock glowed gold against the still-dark sky. Birds had begun to stir and start their chatter as dawn moved toward morning.

In his office Sheriff Potts took out the detailed relief maps of Meriwether County and spread them out on his desk. With Tom Strickland's account of what had happened, the posse's search could now be limited to a small area on Wallace's farm. Marking it, he made his plans for the coming day.

As the courthouse clock struck six, J.H. walked in, huffing: "Lamar, where in the world have you been? I just called your house and Catherine said you left last night around three."

Sheriff Potts looked up from his maps, his face showing his fatigue. "Tom Strickland broke last night."

"That tough bird!"

"Went all to pieces," Sheriff Potts said, and he told J.H. what had happened during the night. "According to Strickland, Turner's body is in the woods within a radius of two or three miles from Wallace's house. I want that area searched today foot by foot. I don't want a leaf left unturned or a squirrel's nest overlooked. I want you to organize that for me. I'm going home to a shower and a shave."

J.H. nodded. "I'll call the boys and get started."

138

The spring morning was just beginning to awaken the residents on the quiet, tree-lined street where Sheriff Potts lived. As he drove toward home, lights were on in kitchen windows and busy mothers were preparing breakfast for children who would soon be on their way to school. Here the dark events of the night seemed a world away. Reality was here where the sun was painting his two-story white house with a rosy glow, where crepe myrtle and mimosa shared the lawn with boxwood, and flower beds still glistened from last night's dew.

At the back door two bicycles waited. The smaller, red one belonged to his ten-year-old son Bubber. The larger, blue one with the wire basket, to his sixteen-year-old daughter Harriet. Inside, he found them both at the breakfast table, his trim, attractive wife pouring their orange juice.

"I was beginning to worry about you, Lamar," she said.

"Now, Catherine." Sheriff Potts kissed her cheek. "You know you don't have to worry about me."

"Hey, Dad, you shoulda been at the ball game last night," Bubber said. "We won and I pitched."

Sheriff Potts scruffed his son's head with his hand. "Good goin'."

Sitting down at the table beside his daughter, he tugged at one long lock. "Whose eye are you trying to catch with that red ribbon in your hair?"

"Oh, *Daddy!*"

Sheriff Potts grinned, and Harriet, looking up, grinned back.

"Say, Dad," Bubber began, "have you found that guy yet?"

Catherine Potts silenced her son with a quick look of reproof from her calm blue eyes. "Lamar, are you ready for breakfast?"

"I only have time for coffee."

"You aren't gonna eat your bananas and cornflakes?" Bubber exclaimed. "You *always* eat your bananas and cornflakes."

The telephone rang and Catherine got up from the table. Returning, she said: "J.H. wants to talk to you, Lamar."

Concern crossed Sheriff Potts's face as he answered the phone. The county jail had just reported that Herring Sivell wanted to talk to him immediately.

"All right, J.H.," he said. "I'll meet you there in fifteen minutes." He picked up his hat to leave.

"Lamar, aren't you even going to finish your coffee?" Catherine asked. "You really should have something to eat."

"Not now," Sheriff Potts replied, kissing her again and waving to the children. "Behave yourselves in school today," he said, and enjoyed their mock exasperation.

Driving back toward town, he felt refreshed by having touched the routine of a normal day. He was not so tired anymore, even though there had not been time for a shave, shower, or breakfast.

When he got to the county jail, J.H. was waiting for him, and he sent at once for Herring Sivell.

Presently, they heard the uneven tread of Sivell's footsteps on the stairs with the jailer. Bigger than John Wallace and younger by thirteen years, Sivell, however, did not have Wallace's strength or fitness. He lumbered into the office, running his hand through the stubble of his graying red crew cut. His eyes, small, green, and restless, brushed past Sheriff Potts's steady gaze and darted about the room, settling in turn on the desk, the window, the curtains, the chairs, and J.H.

"I won't talk to nobody but the sheriff," Sivell announced.

"J.H. is my deputy," Sheriff Potts said.

"He's your brother, ain't he?"

Sheriff Potts nodded. Sivell stopped to consider, his eyes searching the room again. "All right," he agreed, "but not him." He indicated the jailer, who backed out of the room and closed the door.

Sheriff Potts said: "What is it you want to tell me?"

"I heard Tom Strickland threw his guts all over the floor last night."

"He talked."

Sivell shifted restlessly, sliding his hands into his back pockets. "I made up my mind," he said, "to tell you what happened before it gets all screwed up and I get accused of somethin' I didn't do."

"Go ahead."

"John was out to get Turner on two counts . . . liquor and cows. They'd had a falling out, and John was worried that Turner would spill his guts to the government boys about the moonshine and get him in trouble. That was bad enough, but when Turner stole John's prize cows, John set out to get him.

"What I never could figure," Sivell said, interrupting himself with a perplexed look on his face, "was why Turner was fool enough to take John's cows. John's the kind of man who'll give you most anything you need, but you take something from him and he'll kill you for it. Turner knew that, and still. . . ."

His voice trailed off. Then, by way of explanation, he added: "Of course, Turner was a sorry devil . . . not worth killin' . . . and *damn sure* not worth going to jail for."

"Just how do you decide whether a man's worth killing or not?" Sheriff Potts asked.

"You can just look at him and tell," Sivell said casually, as though he were discussing livestock. "Like Turner. He was nuthin' but a sawed-off little sonofabitch with an empty belly and a hot hankerin' for cash. If he would have done what he was told and stayed in his place, things wouldn't have never come to this."

"You were going to tell me what happened," Sheriff Potts reminded him.

"John set Turner up."

"How?"

Sivell then recounted the same story that Strickland had told about the events in Greenville—before the abduction. "John had instructed Collier to drain Turner's pickup of all but enough gas to get started," he went on, "but when Turner saw us and took off for Coweta, we couldn't catch him. He was driving like somebody gone crazy. John kept hanging out the window, trying to shoot him, but he never could make a hit. John was just too mad to shoot straight."

Sivell sighed and continued: "When Turner got to Sunset he jumped out screaming . . . that yellow-bellied little coward. A whole bunch of people came pouring out of the restaurant, and me and John dragged him to the car. When he wouldn't get in, John whopped him over the head with his sawed-off shotgun. Turner fell forward into the car, and John crawled in on top of him, still beating him. He was so mad he couldn't seem to quit."

"What happened then?"

"We took off for Meriwether and hadn't gone a mile from Sunset when my car had a flat tire. I pulled off on a dirt sideroad, and Mobley and Strickland, who were riding backup, pulled off, too. Just as I stopped, John said he thought he saw Turner move and took the car jack and cracked him across the head again. If John didn't get Turner that first time, he damned sure did the second time. The back seat was full of blood."

"You were still in Coweta County?"

"Hell, yes, and John was in a hurry to get outa there. He loaded Turner into Henry Mobley's car and they took off for Meriwether and left me to fix the flat." Sivell stopped and looked at Sheriff Potts a moment to gauge his reaction. "That's the last I had to do with it."

"Do you know where they took Turner?"

"No, I didn't go with them."

"Tom Strickland said Wallace took him to the woods about two or three miles from his house."

Sivell considered this for a moment, shifting his weight off his lame foot. "I think I could find it."

"Is that an offer?"

"Hell, yes, it's an offer. When John first told me he had a job to do, I said I'd help, but I never bargained for nuthin' like this."

"Why did you agree to go in the first place?"

"I was obliged to," Sivell said, looking down at the floor. "I got in a bind sometime back, and John helped me out."

"What kind of bind?"

"They had me accused of killing Pat Brooks. John did what he could for me then, but John don't never do nuthin' for free." Sivell stopped to think about this, then continued: "I'm paid up now, and I ain't havin' no more of it. If you want me to go with you to find that place, I will. I got a pretty good idea where it's at."

"All right," the sheriff said, "but I'll have to check with Solicitor Wyatt before I can take you out of jail."

"How soon will you know?"

"About an hour."

Sheriff Potts summoned the jailer to take Sivell back to his cell, then left the jail and drove to the courthouse. In his own office he telephoned Luther Wyatt in LaGrange about Sivell's proposal.

"You'll be taking one helluva chance to take him back down there to Meriwether County," Wyatt said. "He'll be seen, and there's every chance that they'll try to ambush you."

"Then they'll have to ambush the whole damn posse."

"They could do it and take you for hostage."

"Hell, Luther, if we sit here thinking about all the things that could go wrong, we won't get a damn thing done. Right now . . . this minute . . . Herring Sivell is ready to sell out. We better take our chance while we've got it."

"I don't know," Luther hesitated. "I think I'd better check with Judge Boykin. I'll call you back."

Samuel Boykin was the circuit court judge who would try the case. His twelve years on the bench had gained him the reputation of being able to make difficult decisions and being willing to cut through red tape to get the job done.

When Luther Wyatt called back, he said: "Lamar, you got the green light. The judge said if you had guts enough to do it, he had guts enough to let you try."

Sheriff Potts laughed. "That's what I like to hear."

"When are you going?"

"Just as soon as I hang up this phone."

"Good luck."

"Thanks, Luther."

In the courthouse square, J.H. had the posse lined up and ready to roll. They picked Herring Sivell up at the county jail and drove through Meriwether County to Wallace's farm. For five hours, following Sivell's directions and under heavy guard, they searched the area described by Tom Strickland. Nothing was found.

Overhearing an angry and impatient comment, Sivell protested. "I swear to God, Sheriff, I thought I could find the place, but you can see what a jungle this swamp is. You can be standing in one place, walk off a hundred yards, and not be able to find it again."

During the five-hour search, Sheriff Potts had watched Sivell's mounting anxiety reach near panic. Having made his decision to break with John Wallace, he was desperate for some solid evidence against him. His hopes of finding Turner now gone, Sivell said: "I want to cut loose from this thing with John Wallace. I don't want no part of it."

"What do you propose to do?"

"If you'll take me to my house in Chipley so my wife can hear firsthand, I'll make a written confession."

The suggestion surprised Sheriff Potts. Sivell didn't strike him as a concerned family man. Sivell's only concern was to save himself.

"Why is it so important for your wife to hear?" he asked.

"She hasn't believed a word I've told her about what happened. I think this would convince her."

As Sheriff Potts considered Sivell's proposal, J.H. was quick to voice his disapproval. "It could be dangerous, Lamar." Otwell and Pete Bedenbaugh agreed, but Sheriff Potts said:

"If it is, we'll leave, but we won't know till we try. Otwell, get me your best deputies. We'll take two cars." It was another calculated risk that he knew he had to take. A written confession would be something solid to go on.

When he drew up before Sivell's pleasant brick bungalow in Chipley, they found the yard full of cars and the porch and steps crowded with big, muscular men.

"What's this?" Sheriff Potts asked.

"Those are my relatives," Sivell replied.

The men watched their arrival with grim, tense faces. The atmosphere was charged, ready to ignite. Without taking a head count, Sheriff Potts figured they were outnumbered by about three to one.

Sivell, who had been cooperative and compliant until now, was suddenly taking charge of the situation. "I'll go in the house and speak to my wife first," he announced.

143

At this moment a young boy darted from the barn toward the house. The men on the porch tensed up, waiting.

"You'll do no such damn thing." Sheriff Potts snapped the handcuffs back on Sivell's wrists. "We'll go back to Newnan and take the confession there."

"You said I could go in and tell my wife."

"That was before I found all your relatives waiting on the porch."

"In that case," Sivell said, "I've changed my mind."

"Suit yourself," Sheriff Potts replied, knowing that Sivell would follow his survival instincts and confess.

On the drive back to Coweta County jail, Sivell writhed and wrestled with his decision. Finally, as they reached the outskirts of Newnan, he said: "I've changed my mind."

"You're ready to give a written confession?"

"Yes."

"Then we'll go to my office and take it down."

As they walked into the courthouse Sheriff Potts saw an old colleague on the steps. Pierre Howard, who had been an assistant United States district attorney, had worked with him many times.

"Pierre! Good to see you," he said as they shook hands. "What brings you down here?"

"Business," Pierre replied.

"I'll be with you shortly. We have a confession to take."

"That's why I'm here. I've been retained to represent Mr. Sivell."

Pierre's father, Old Man Schley (pronounced "Sly"), was considered one of the most effective criminal lawyers in the state. Pierre, in partnership with him, was following in his footsteps. "After you left Chipley," he explained, "Mr. Sivell's father called and asked me to represent him. I'd like to talk with him."

"Certainly," the sheriff said.

After a whispered conference on the courthouse steps, Pierre Howard reported: "Mr. Sivell repudiates everything he said."

The disheartened deputies watched wearily as Sivell was taken back to jail. It had taken eight days of hard, continuous search and perseverance to reach this point. Expectations of solving the case had risen with Sivell's decision to confess. Now, under advice of counsel, he refused to say another word about the Turner affair.

Tom Strickland, having regained his composure, steadfastly denied the accounts that the Atlanta papers carried about his confession.

Added to these demoralizing developments was the fact that Elzie Hancock had been ill. Determined to make a quick discovery, he had worked with such unrelenting fervor that first day in the swamp that he had come down with a fever and had been bedridden for two days. On Friday night, however, he called to say he would return to the search on Saturday morning.

"I want to talk with you before going out again," Hancock told Sheriff Potts.

"Anything new?"

"I think so."

Chapter Fourteen

Late on Wednesday, before coming down with a fever, Elzie Hancock had found a set of very strange and intriguing tracks in the swamp . . . footprints and horse tracks, side by side. He was sure this was what he had been searching for, but he had told no one about it for fear the trail would be disturbed and the telltale signs destroyed.

After his years of experience, Hancock could follow a trail and tell how old the tracks were, approximately what time of the day or night they had been made, and why the person who made them had gone into the woods. Every broken twig and blade of bruised grass said something to him. Dust blown over a track or small pieces of caved-in bank told him things that others were not aware of. Weather conditions helped him determine the time and age of a track. A footprint made in the evening dew looked nothing like one made in the hot sun of midday. The tracks he had found were just about the right age. Their purpose in the woods was still a mystery.

The delay, brought on by his illness, had been almost unbearable for Hancock. For more than a week, ever since Wilson Turner's disappearance, the weather had been clear and cloudless. A sudden rain could destroy all the secrets that the woods held.

On Saturday morning, May 1, Hancock put on what he called his "raiding clothes," gray cotton twill pants and shirt, a softball cap, and high-top boots with composition soles. These clothes, essential in his job of raiding stills, were of special advantage in tracking, for even the sound of a briar scratching a harder cotton fabric could alert a woodsman to his approach. Moreover, the boots' composition soles gave him firm footing on the slick pine needles that covered the ground under the dense growth of trees.

Checking in with Sheriff Potts at the courthouse, Hancock told him

146

that he had found a trail that he thought was "some of Wallace's doings."

"Do you want any help?"

"Not yet."

Heading for the place where he had worked before, Hancock drove down the red clay road that ran through the Strickland "Kingdom," past the tenant houses, and on to the woodland beyond. Parking his car on the side of the road, he climbed the embankment and went into the woods where he again located the tracks. Kneeling down, he studied them.

There were two separate sets of man-sized footprints and two separate sets of horse tracks. The men apparently were wearing brogans. Their tracks, made when the mud was soft, clearly showed the nails in the sole and the Cat's Paw brand of rubber heel.

The hoofprints differed in that only one horse was shod. The shod horse had the smaller foot of a riding horse. The wide, unshod foot of the other, indicated a workhorse.

Following the trail, Hancock noted that the riding horse had led the way and the workhorse apparently had been led by one man and followed by another. Both men seemed to have the same shoe size, but the one who led the workhorse was heavier, for his footprints sank deeper in the mud.

The curious thing was the damage done to the brush and the saplings where the workhorse had walked. The leaves and tender twigs were broken for some three or four feet on either side of his hoof-prints. The trail wound crazily up and down the bank alongside the creek, the foliage damaged all along the way. It was obvious to Hancock that the workhorse had carried some burden that was too wide to get unobstructed through the dense woods.

That night when he told Sheriff Potts what he had found, Hancock said: "I'm 'most sure that Wallace moved the body."

The sheriff agreed. "That would account for our not finding Turner in the area Strickland described and where Sivell tried to locate it. The question now is where he took it, who helped him, and what they did with it."

"I can tell you this much. There were three of them down in those woods. Someone was riding that lead horse."

"Could you tell where the tracks were headed?"

"Not yet."

Sunday morning, Hancock was back in the woods, following the trail. His theory that Wallace had hauled the body to another location was reinforced by what he found. The sapling leaves were damaged

147

approximately five feet from the ground, just about the right height for a horse carrying a pack on his back. Some of the limbs were broken, and pieces of lint hung from their jagged edges.

Carefully removing the fiber from the limbs, Hancock examined it, rolling it between his fingers and sniffing it. It was unquestionably burlap. This discovery was one more piece to fit into the puzzle. Wherever the body had been moved, it had first been wrapped in burlap.

Intent on finding the end of the trail, Hancock followed the tracks down the creek bank until they entered the water. Here, the muddy red stream obscured the trail, but he still could follow it by watching for the marks of feet and sliding hooves on the slime-slick rocks. Trailing through the water, he came at last to a deep, wide pool in the creek bed. Here, the tracks stopped.

Hancock felt sure that this was where Turner's body was concealed. From his pack he took a small set of grappling hooks, tied them to the end of a long rope, and dragged the bottom of the muddy pool. Over and over again he did this, but he came up with only one rotted log. Finally he decided he would ask Sheriff Potts to call in a grappling-hook crew.

For the moment, his aim would be to reestablish the trail; to find out where the horses had gone after leaving the pool. Finding no tracks on either side of the bank, he concluded they must have backtracked through the water. He studied the moss-green rocks scarred by the hoofprints, but it was impossible to determine their direction; he only knew that they had been there.

Searching both sides of the bank, Hancock finally found a place where the riding horse had left the creek bed, gone up the bank to the top of a hill, and returned again to the water. Puzzled by this, he tried to figure a purpose; finding none, he went on until he located a spot where both men and horses had left the creek and climbed the hill of an embankment. On reaching the top, Hancock was astonished to see below him the dirt road that angled through the Strickland property and led to John Wallace's house. But now the tracks went down the embankment to the road, where countless cars had driven back and forth in their search for Wilson Turner. There was not a trace of a footprint or a horse track left. The trail that he had followed ended at the roadside.

Hancock flagged down the first patrol car that came by and asked to be taken to Sheriff Potts. Finding him with part of the posse, he described what he had discovered. "I figure Wallace weighted the

148

body down," he said, "dumped it in the pool, and returned to his farm down that dirt road."

Sheriff Potts at once got hold of a grappling-hook crew, and Hancock led the way to the pool, careful to avoid the trail he had found, in order to keep the tracks there undisturbed. Standing on the creek bank with Sheriff Potts, he watched the efforts of the grappling-hook crew. Nothing was found.

"It doesn't make sense," Hancock said. "Why would they go back down the road to Wallace's place if they still had the body? By rights, it *ought* to be in that water."

"I'm satisfied it's not," Sheriff Potts replied.

Hancock pushed his ball cap forward, scratching the back of his head. "Those tracks haven't told me all I need to know. I'm going to track the trail back to its point of origin. If I can find out where those men started from, maybe I can figure out where they went."

"Sounds like a good idea, Elzie."

Back on the trail again, Hancock slowly and meticulously traced it backward, in the direction from which the tracks had come. For more than a mile he traced the winding path of footprints and horse tracks until he came again to the top of the embankment overlooking the road—this time, closer to Wallace's house.

At this spot there was no longer a trail but a great many tracks concentrated in one area. Hancock knew at once that something had happened here. He found a stripped sapling pole and a pile of recently cut branches. Beneath their curling dead leaves, he discovered that the wild plants that grew in profusion in the woods had been mashed. Something had rested in this spot, something that likely had been covered over with the cut branches.

As Hancock searched further, the clues became confusing. Three sets of footprints came out of the woods to the right, two sets of hoofprints came up the embankment to the left. Two men seemed to have sat and smoked on this grassy knoll. The cigarette butts were still on the ground. It was apparent to Hancock that the men and horses had met here. The question now was, Where in the deep woods had the men come from and why?

Immersed in the excitement of near discovery, Hancock had lost all sense of time and was surprised to see darkness closing in on him. He knew then he would have to wait until daylight to continue his search in the woods.

As he returned to his car, he met Felder Spivey, a fellow worker from his Columbus office who had volunteered to help the posse in the search for Wilson Turner.

"How's it going, Elzie?" Spivey asked.

"Pretty good."

"Found anything?"

"I think so."

"What?"

"Can't say just yet."

Hancock thought no more about this casual encounter and drove on to Newnan to report his findings to Sheriff Potts. At the courthouse, sitting at his desk, the sheriff listened intently.

"That's good news, Elzie, but we've got bad news, too. There's a storm out of the Gulf headed our way."

"Hell!" Hancock frowned. "If it rains, every clue will be washed away."

"That's why we've *got* to find Turner tomorrow."

"First thing in the morning, I'll go back to that knoll. Beginning there, I'll track the three men's trail to their starting place in the woods."

Sheriff Potts nodded. "While you're doing that, I'm going to check out the woods on the other side of the road."

The suggestion surprised Hancock. "The *other* side?"

Sheriff Potts pushed back in his chair. "You know, Elzie, we may have figured this thing wrong."

"How's that?"

"Down there by the creek that we dragged today, we *assumed* that the three men and two horses returned toward Wallace's house after leaving the woods. Maybe they didn't. Maybe they *crossed* the road and went into the woods on the other side."

Hancock's eyes snapped with alertness. "Could be." Getting up to leave, he said: "With you on one side of the road and me on the other, we oughta come up with something."

"We got to."

"I'll be there first thing in the morning."

"You'll be staying in Newnan tonight?"

"No, I'm going back home to Columbus. I haven't seen my wife in a couple of days and I want to check by the office."

Hancock's decision to return home that night altered the course of what was to happen. On arrival in Columbus he learned that his co-worker, Felder Spivey, had reported his mention of a discovery to Sheriff Howell. And since Hancock worked out of Sheriff Howell's Muscogee County office, he was called in and questioned about what he had found.

150

Sheriff Howell, ambitious and up for reelection, had been quick to see the political advantage of sharing the spotlight with Hancock when Turner's body was discovered. Satisfied that the mystery that had claimed state and nationwide interest was about to be solved, he decided to join Hancock on his search the next day. Not, however, until court adjourned on Monday morning, because that was important to him, too . . . to be seen at court.

Hancock protested this delay, pointing out that the weather bureau was predicting heavy rains, which would wash away all clues. But Howell scoffed at the bureau's accuracy and insisted that they wait for him to finish court. Reluctantly Hancock agreed.

It was important to Hancock, who was approaching retirement age, to be the one who found Turner's body. It was also important to him to share the attendant publicity with Sheriff Howell. The newspapers had carried accounts of his expertise. Predictions had been made about his expected success. He had a reputation to maintain. Having Sheriff Howell and his co-workers along when the discovery was made would serve to enhance his image. He decided to gamble on the predicted rain and wait for Sheriff Howell to finish court before going back to the swamp.

By Monday morning everyone in the posse knew that Hancock was "on to something," and they waited expectantly for him to arrive. When he didn't show up at the appointed time, Sheriff Potts, thinking that Hancock in his enthusiasm had begun his search earlier, carried on with the plan he had outlined the night before.

After dispatching the posse teams to assigned search areas, he drove his car to the spot described to him by Hancock where the horses and men had come out of the creek bed and entered the road that ran through the Strickland property. Alone, he went into the woods on the opposite side. Working his way up and down the tree line, he finally picked up the footprints and horse tracks again. Following them carefully toward the swamp in the forest, he soon found himself in dense woods. There was a cool, musty smell of damp, fallen leaves that never got dry and a silence so deep that every movement echoed through the trees.

The tracks were exactly as Hancock had described them . . . two men, two horses. He followed them along until the forest grew denser and the trail split, the horses going off in one direction, the men in another. Here, Sheriff Potts stooped down to examine more carefully what had happened. As he did so, the silence was broken.

"Sheriff Potts?"

He wheeled around. Behind him, standing beside a tree, was a big, broad-shouldered woodsman holding a long-handled ax with a gleaming blade at his side.

"I'm Sheriff Potts," he said, rising to face the man.

"You don't know me, Sheriff, but I talked to you before . . . on the phone."

Sheriff Potts was certain he had never seen the man before. He wore a plaid work shirt, khaki work pants, and heavy boots laced up the front. He had obviously been cutting wood. His face was sweating and bits of bark and wood had stuck on his face.

"Remember the call about the meeting at midnight in Harris City at the train station?"

Sheriff Potts nodded.

"That was me."

"What happened? You never showed up."

"I got down there, all right, but I saw two of John Wallace's friends cruising around in a car. I got scared and left. Later I called you again. All I said was 'Tom Strickland.' Remember?"

"Yes," Sheriff Potts replied. "That was very helpful. We picked him up."

"Well," the woodsman began, looking down at the toe of his boot with a sudden awkwardness, "I come to ask you something."

"What's that?"

"Are you still offering that five-hundred-dollar reward to find Turner's body?"

"Yes."

"Can you guarantee won't nobody know who told?"

"I can guarantee it."

The woodsman looked down again and studied the ax he had propped at his side. Leaning on the handle, he squiggled the ax head back and forth, staring at the half-moons it made in the dirt.

Sheriff Potts waited.

"If I tell, you won't *never* tell nobody I told?"

"I give you my word," Sheriff Potts said solemnly.

The woodsman drew in his breath. "You ain't gonna find Wilson Turner. They done burnt him up."

"Burned him up!" The startling words had the ring of truth. And Sheriff Potts remembered that one of the theories advanced in Meriwether County was that Turner's body had been burned in a liquor-still pit. At the time, the idea seemed too bizarre to be so. "Who burned him up?" he asked.

"John Wallace and two of his nigger hired hands."

152

"How?"

"Wallace first had hid Turner's body in a well. When he learned you were after him, he took the two niggers, loaded Turner's body on horseback, and took him to an old liquor-still pit. That's where he burned him up."

"Where is the pit?"

"About a half a mile from here, straight through them woods."

"Who are the Negroes who helped?"

"Albert Brooks and Robert Lee Gates."

Sheriff Potts took his notebook from his shirt pocket and jotted down both names. Then, searching the man's face, he asked: "How do you *know* they burned Turner up?"

"Everybody down here knows. Most of us heard the explosion when the gasoline ignited. We even saw the fire down in the swamp that evening."

"Did you go down to see what it was?"

"No, sir! We all figured it was some of John Wallace's doings, and don't nobody around here mess in his business. At first we thought that one of his stills had blowed up. Later we found out what *really* happened."

"How did you manage that?"

"What Wallace made them niggers do nearly scared them both to death. Robert Lee told his wife. She couldn't keep a secret no better than he could, and pretty soon everybody knew."

Sheriff Potts nodded. "I'm just surprised that no one down here has told before now."

"Plenty of people wanted to, but all of 'em were scared. They figured if they talked and Wallace were to get out of that jail, they'd be next."

"How did you happen to find me down here?"

"I been watchin' for a chance to talk to you ever since that night at Harris City. I never could get to you 'cause you were always surrounded by the posse. When I saw you start to the swamp by yourself this morning, I figured this was my chance."

"How can I get the reward money to you?"

The woodsman gave directions to a relative's house in another county. "Leave it there. They'll get it to me."

"Now tell me, where can I find Albert Brooks and Robert Lee Gates?"

"Robert Lee lives on that road up yonder in one of them tenant houses. Albert Brooks lives a little further on."

Sheriff Potts shook hands with his informant. "I'm much obliged to you."

Hanging on to the handclasp a moment, the man said once more: "For sure, no one will know?"

"You have my word."

"I'll depend on it."

"You can."

Sheriff Potts turned and hurried back toward the road from which he had come. The first job was to locate Albert Brooks and Robert Lee Gates, have them lead the way to the liquor-still pit where Turner's body had been burned, and gather what evidence could be found.

Looking up through the dark leaves, he could not tell whether or not the sun was still out. He only knew it was not raining . . . yet. Turning in the direction of the tenant houses, he reached the road and found the sky still a cloudless blue. Although this was a relief, it was no assurance. Spring storms came on suddenly.

When he found the right house, Robert Lee's wife, holding a baby and accompanied by two small, curious children, came to the door and told him: "Robert Lee ain't come home for dinner yet. He's still in the back field, plowin' the garden."

It was almost noon when he found Robert Lee, the plow lines draped around his neck, pushing the plow that his mule pulled through the red, sun-baked soil. Seen there at his task, he looked nothing like a man who had helped burn up another. Absorbed in his plowing, he did not notice the sheriff until he heard his name called.

"Robert Lee?"

Robert Lee drew his head back against the reins, pulling his mule to a stop. "Whoa."

"Are you Robert Lee Gates?"

"Yassuh." Robert Lee recognized the Coweta sheriff, whom everyone in Meriwether now knew by sight.

"Are you ready to tell me about burning that man up?"

Robert Lee looked down at his plow, retreating from Sheriff Potts's penetrating gaze. Sweat bathed his thin, black, uncomplicated face. He made no effort to escape or deny. There was just a great weariness from waiting.

"Yassuh, Sheriff, I'm ready."

Picture Gallery

Sheriff Lamar Potts inspects
the small box holding all
that remained of murdered
Wilson [William] Turner.
Photo: Atlanta *Journal*

The Newnan courtroom is filled
to capacity as the jury
is drawn for the Turner
murder trial, June 14, 1948.
In the center foreground are Henry Mobley (left)
and John Wallace.

Photo: Atlanta *Journal*

John Wallace sits with Sheriff
Lamar Potts (left) and defense
lawyer Fred New (right) in the
Newnan courtroom, June 18, 1948,
after hearing the verdict.

Photo: Atlanta *Journal*

Sheriff Lamar Potts and Albert
Brooks, twenty years after the
trial of John Wallace. This
photo was taken in the Newnan
courthouse when the author was
interviewing them while
gathering material for this book.
Photo: Joe Norman

Johnny Cash as Sheriff Lamar Potts in the CBS-TV movie, *Murder in Coweta County*, produced by Telecom Entertainment, Inc./TIPS.
Atlanta Journal/Constitution
Photo by Nick Arroyo

June Carter Cash (center) as the mystic, Mayhayley Lancaster, ushered into the courthouse by Johnny Cash as Sheriff Potts, pauses for a prediction.

Watergate attorney James Neal (right foreground) as defense attorney, A.L. Henson, demands acquittal for John Wallace at the 1948 trial.

Andy Griffith, as John Wallace, moments before his 1950

The Investigation

Chapter Fifteen

Robert Lee Gates admitted that he and Albert Brooks were the ones who had helped Wallace burn Turner at the still pit in the swamp. The agony of the admission left him trembling, and as he sat in the sheriff's car, his eyes rolled from side to side in his dread of what lay ahead.

"There's no need to be nervous, Robert Lee," Sheriff Potts said. "Nobody's going to harm you."

Robert Lee clasped his quivering knees with his long, thin hands. "I ain't nervous, Sheriff, I'se scart."

"No need for that, either. We'll get Albert Brooks, and both of you can show us where the pit is."

Picking up the microphone on his car radio, Sheriff Potts called J.H., who had been manning communications all day. "J.H., what's the latest word on the weather?"

"Heavy rains tonight or tomorrow. They haven't pinned down yet how fast that storm out of the Gulf is moving our way."

"There's been a break in the case."

"Wilson Turner's been found?"

"We know what happened to him."

"Hallelujah, Jesus!" J.H. shouted.

"We've got to move fast before the rain comes. Have Otwell and Pete Bedenbaugh pick up a Negro named Albert Brooks in one of Wallace's tenant houses. Then call the posse in. Meet me at section sixteen-Y on the map. I'll be waiting."

"Roger."

Otwell and Pete Bedenbaugh found Albert Brooks sitting at his kitchen table, drinking a pint of moonshine liquor. Ever since the night when they had burned Wilson Turner, Albert had been drinking

157

heavily, returning to his house several times a day to burn the anxiety out of his guts with another shot of moonshine. After the arrests of Wallace, Sivell, Myhand, Mobley, and Tom Strickland, Albert knew they would get him, too. He just didn't know when.

When Otwell told him, "The sheriff wants you," Albert replied: "I been expectin' that." Picking up his hat, he followed Otwell and Pete Bedenbaugh to the patrol car.

While Sheriff Potts waited on the road for the posse, Hancock drove up with Sheriff Howell and two Muscogee County deputies in his car and jumped out at once. Running his eyes over Hancock's clean clothes and spotless boots, the sheriff realized that he had not been in the swamp at all, but was only now arriving for his search.

"Elzie, where in the hell have you been?"

Hancock glanced sheepishly over his shoulder at Sheriff Howell and the others who were just getting out of the car. "Sheriff Howell wanted to come with me today, and I had to wait till he got out of court."

"You picked one helluva time to do that." Taking Hancock off to the side, Sheriff Potts told him briefly about the informant and Robert Lee's admission. "I'm waiting for the posse now."

Hancock's face was filled with disappointment. "I'm really sorry about this, Lamar. . . ."

"Forget it, I need your help on something else." In order to protect his informant, Sheriff Potts wanted Hancock to provide the cover story. " 'Most everybody knew you were onto something. They're going to assume that you were the one who found out what happened to Turner."

"What must I tell them?"

"Anything you like about tracking and finding the pit. My only requirement is that my informant remain unknown and protected."

Hancock's face brightened with the prospect of receiving the acclaim he so coveted, but as he thought about it, he said: "You know, Lamar, it's not right that I should get the credit when you cracked the case."

Sheriff Potts clapped Hancock on the back. "Hell, Elzie, you know me better than that. The only thing that matters is getting the job done, not who gets credit for it. Now let's get on with it before the rain catches us."

The posse had begun to gather now, and as Sheriff Potts and Hancock made their way through the crowd, several of the men came up to congratulate the agent. "Hancock, you old devil!" one said. "I heard you were onto something. How'd you do it?"

158

Hancock smiled a thin, modest smile. "Just lucky, I guess."

A red dust cloud rolled down the road as Otwell and Pete Bedenbaugh drove up with Albert Brooks. "This is the one you asked for, Sheriff," Otwell said.

Sheriff Potts looked at the big, yellow-skinned Negro in the back of the patrol car. "Are you the other one that helped Mr. Wallace burn that man up?"

"Yassuh, it wuz me," Albert admitted, his face taut with anxiety.

"Pete, go get Robert Lee Gates out of my car. They're going to show where this burning took place."

The road was full of men and cars. In pairs and in groups they moved toward the woods where Albert Brooks and Robert Lee Gates waited with Otwell and Pete Bedenbaugh. Albert slid his hands in the back pockets of his overalls and kept them there as though he were trying to hold himself together. Robert Lee was misery in motion. His too-big overalls hung from his thin shoulders like the apparel of a scarecrow. He stood first on one foot, then the other, crossed them, uncrossed them, wrung his hands, and looked toward heaven.

Seeing their misery, Sheriff Potts spoke to them in a calm, authoritative tone. "Albert, I want you and Robert Lee to lead the way down to the pit and show us where you burned that fellow up."

Albert and Robert Lee nodded in unison and started off toward the swamp. Sheriff Potts, Hancock, Sheriff Howell, and the deputies followed close behind.

The swamp became heavier as they walked deeper into the woods. Thick brambles and bushes crowded in between the trunks of the tremendously tall virgin trees. Tangled vines fell from overhead. Coarse swamp grass grew thigh-high in the soft, sucking mud. After struggling through this for more than half a mile, they came to a clearing where the jungle-green swamp turned to gutted black ash. The trees surrounding the area were burned and charred to a height of sixty feet, their mutilated limbs exposed to tell their grim story. The forest floor was black, the wild green growing things all swept away by the holocaust that had blazed there. In the midst of this ashen devastation they saw the liquor-still pit. Scraped clean and tidy, it stood out in contrast to the ruin that surrounded it.

"Is this the place?" Sheriff Potts asked the two Negroes.

"Yassuh, this is h'it."

"All right. You boys sit over there." He indicated the ledge of the pit. "Start from the beginning and tell us what happened."

Finding a place on the ledge, Albert and Robert Lee sat side by side, their feet dangling. The deputies circled around the pit and waited. Sheriff Potts took his notebook from his pocket, propped his foot on a log, and began taking notes as Robert Lee started to tell what happened.

Beginning with the Wednesday night after Turner's murder on Tuesday, April 20, Robert Lee recounted how Wallace had taken them to the swamp to search for a package, their fruitless all-night search, their return the next morning, and Wallace's learning of the well's location from old Wilson Wood. As he described finding Turner's body, pulling it out with well drags, wrapping it in burlap, and carrying it on a sapling pole through the swamp to the grassy knoll overlooking the road, Hancock nodded his head, for what he had found on the trail confirmed what was being told.

The mystery of the creek pool cleared up when Robert Lee told how they had backtracked through the water until a suitable place had been found to cross the road to the other side. He continued, describing their trek to the liquor-still pit with the body, until Sheriff Potts asked: "When did you burn Turner up?"

Robert Lee's voice faltered. When he seemed unable to go on, Albert took up the story, telling the posse about the cordwood and gasoline Wallace had brought to the swamp on Mr. Mozart's truck.

"Is that Mr. Mozart Strickland you're talking about?" Sheriff Potts asked. "Mr. Wallace's uncle?"

"Yassuh."

Sheriff Potts jotted the name down in his notebook. "What happened then, Albert?"

Aware of the faces ringed around him, reluctant to tell the last part of his story, Albert turned to Robert Lee. But Robert Lee had closed his eyes and lowered his grief-stricken face.

"We brung the wood to Mr. Wallace, and when he was done rackin' it up, he told me and Robert Lee to put Mr. Turner on the pile. . . ." Albert's voice broke. He leaned forward and grasped his trembling knees, squeezing them with clasped hands.

Seeing him relive his anguish, Sheriff Potts said: "Albert, what made you do that? You didn't have to help burn a man up."

Albert hung his head, but Robert Lee spoke up: "Mr. Wallace made us. He was wearin' that big fawty-fo' pistol of his'n on his hip. If we hadna did whut he said, he'da shot us both. So we done whut he said."

Albert nodded his head. "We laid Mr. Turner up on the rack," he continued. "Then Mr. Wallace poured on the gasoline and throwed on the match."

160

"What happened then?"

"A big boom and fire sprung out all over. Me and Robert Lee run for the ditch, but Mr. Wallace just stood there a-lookin'."

His listeners' eyes traveled to the charred treetops and back again to the Negroes who sat on the ledge of the pit where the burning had taken place. Experienced as they were in criminal work, the men of the posse, most of them law officers, were appalled by what they had heard.

Squirming under their scrutiny, Robert Lee wrung his hands while Albert described how they had cleaned out the pit the next morning, put the ashes in feed bags, and dumped the debris in a nearby stream. Surprised by this disclosure, Sheriff Potts said: "Hold it right there, Albert. You say you dumped the ashes in a nearby stream?"

"Yassuh."

"What stream?"

"Down yonder about forty yards," Albert pointed.

"I want you to show me . . . exactly the way you went."

Albert and Robert Lee both slipped off the ledge of the pit. Sheriff Potts motioned to Hancock and told the others to stay where they were. "We don't want to destroy any tracks," he said.

Sheriff Howell started to follow anyway, but J.H. caught him by the sleeve. "Lamar said to stay where you are." Howell jerked away from J.H.'s grasp, glaring at him angrily. Propping both hands on his hips, J.H. glared back. Howell remained where he was.

Sheriff Potts and Hancock followed Albert and Robert Lee down the bank toward a winding stream that worked its way over tree roots and rippled over rocks. As they walked along, Sheriff Potts noticed a thin, wavering line of something on the ground. It was so fine as to be almost indiscernible. Bending down he said: "Elzie, take a look at this. Looks to me like ashes."

"Damn if it don't!" Hancock was beside him, pinching some of the substance between his fingers, rubbing them together.

"Albert," Sheriff Potts said, calling him back, "what did you tell me you carried those ashes in?"

"Burlap sacks."

"Did you notice if they had any holes in them before you used them?"

Albert thought for a minute and shook his head. "I couldn't rightly say. Me and Robert Lee was so nerved up, ain't likely we'da noticed much of anythin'."

"Mighta been some of them ashes coulda burnt a hole in one of

161

'em sacks," Robert Lee broke in. "I told Albert when we wuz shovelin' 'em up that them coals near the bottom of the pit wuz still hot." Robert Lee turned an I-told-you-so look on Albert.

While the other three were talking, Hancock, alert and intense again, had followed the telltale line of ashes farther on toward the stream. "Looks like we got more than ashes!" he called. "Take a look, Lamar, I believe we got some charred bone fragments here."

Hurrying over to him, Sheriff Potts examined the small white chips in Hancock's palm.

"By God, Elzie, I believe you're right."

Hancock shook his head from side to side, amazed at what he held. "That's what you call the Sure Hand of Fate."

"The only way we can be certain is to have them tested by Dr. Jones at the Crime Lab." The sheriff searched his pockets. "Here. I've got a metal cartridge box. We'll put them in this for safekeeping." Emptying the cartridges into another pocket, he carefully placed the bone fragments in the box and motioned to Albert to go on to the stream.

Albert stopped at the bank. "Here's where we dumped the ashes in the water."

"Yassuh," Robert Lee volunteered. "We put 'em right here."

As they pointed to the spot, Sheriff Potts's eye caught a small black mass trapped in a bend of the stream. Taking his handkerchief from his back pocket, he slid it underneath the debris and brought it out of the water.

"Elzie," he said, "you can call it the Sure Hand of Fate if you want to, but somebody up there's looking after us."

"Bless God! These are some of the ashes they dumped in the stream."

"We'll know for sure when Dr. Jones takes a look," Sheriff Potts said, tying the corners of the handkerchief together.

When they had returned to the pit, he told the posse: "Men, it looks like we've found what we've been looking for . . . charred bone chips down by the stream and ashes dumped in the water."

A cheer went up from the weary men, and J.H. jumped up and shouted: "Hot damn! We got corpus delicti!"

Throughout the account told by the Negroes, Sheriff Potts had made notations in his notebook. Going back over the list now, he had Albert and Robert Lee describe where each item they had used was hidden. When they finished, he ripped the pages out and handed them to J.H.

"This is a list of the corroborating evidence," he told the deputies

162

and members of the posse. "I want you to find it, label it, date it, and bring it to my office. It's critical that we get it all and get it before it rains. J.H. will be in charge. Find the well first, J.H. Albert and Robert Lee can tell you how to get there."

"Why don't you leave Hancock here to show us the way?"

"I need him with me," Sheriff Potts said without explanation. "And I want to get those Negroes to Newnan before anything happens to them. As soon as the word gets out that they've talked, their lives won't be worth a nickel."

Leaving the swamp, they all followed the trail to the edge of the woods where the cordwood and gasoline had been thrown off. Hancock, anxious to add to the discoveries that would give his story credence, found the tire tracks made by Mozart Strickland's truck.

"The impressions are deep and clear, Lamar. Dr. Jones shouldn't have any trouble making casts."

"We'll get him down here tomorrow. Better get my raincoat out of my car. Cover the tire tracks and pile some pine needles over them so the water will run off in case it rains."

When they reached the road, Hancock watched forlornly as J.H., Otwell, and Pete Bedenbaugh led the posse across it and into the woods toward the well.

"I sure as hell wish I was going with them," he said.

"You've got another job to do."

"What's that?"

"Give the story to the press . . . remember, you're my cover."

Hancock's spirits visibly rose as he remembered this. "When're we going to do that?"

"As soon as we have these Negroes safely put away," Sheriff Potts said.

On the drive back to Newnan, he began assessing the difficulties that lay ahead. The first problem was to preserve the integrity of Albert's and Robert Lee's confessions. In a criminal trial of this sort, where the defendant was not only a white man accused by his Negro hired hands, but a wealthy, influential white man, the defense attorney would likely attempt to discredit the evidence by claiming the Negroes' admissions had been beaten from them.

To forestall any charge of police brutality, Sheriff Potts decided to take Albert and Robert Lee to Special Prosecutor Myer Goldberg's office on the courthouse square and have a written confession taken in front of witnesses . . . witnesses whose word was unimpeachable. For this he chose Roy Brown, the town's most respected businessman, and Preacher Faulkner, the area's most revered minister. Calling them from Myer Goldberg's office, Sheriff Potts explained the situation and requested their help. Both men readily agreed.

"You know, Lamar," Preacher Faulkner said, "my regard for your integrity is such that if you say the confession is freely given, I'll certify it's so without having to hear it."

"I appreciate your confidence," Sheriff Potts replied, "but it will go better in court if you did, in fact, hear it."

"In that case, I'll come right down."

In Myer Goldberg's office, Roy Brown and Preacher Faulkner listened as Albert Brooks and Robert Lee Gates told their story and the secretary wrote it down.

When this had been done, Hancock asked Sheriff Potts if he was ready to call in the press.

"Not until Albert and Robert Lee are safe," the sheriff answered.

He knew that Wallace's staunch supporters would resort to whatever desperate measures were necessary to silence the Negroes' damning evidence. To protect them from being killed or taken out of jail, he would have to hide them somewhere until time for the trial. As they left Myer Goldberg's office, he said, "Elzie, I've decided we'll take Albert and Robert Lee to Columbus. No one will think of looking for them there."

Ninety miles away at the Muscogee County jail, Sheriff Potts booked Albert and Robert Lee under fictitious names and put them in a cell together. Seeing their worried looks as he started to leave, he assured them: "You'll be safe here. Nothing will happen to you."

"Ain't me I'se worried 'bout," Albert said. "It's my fambly. Ain't no tellin' what they might do to Lola Mae and the kids when they finds out whut I tolt."

Sheriff Potts considered this for a moment. "How many kids you got, Albert?"

"Nine."

"How many you got, Robert Lee?"

"Four."

Sheriff Potts knew their fears were well founded. The families would be even more vulnerable than the men. "I'll send trucks down to Meriwether County and move them out."

"Where you gonna take 'em to?" Albert asked.

"Where they'll be safe. There are farms in Coweta County that will take them in."

"Safe, fo' sure?" Robert Lee said, his lips trembling.

"For sure," Sheriff Potts replied, turning to leave.

"Sheriff Potts . . ." Albert began. Gulping down a lump in his

164

throat, he said hoarsely, "Lola Mae will be much obliged, an' I'll be much obliged, too. You know, it's purty turrible when a man ain't got no way to pertect his fambly."

There was a bond of understanding between them. "I know that, Albert," Sheriff Potts said. "We'll see to it that nothing happens to them."

Satisfied that the two men were safe, he returned to the jailer's office. There he found Hancock sitting behind the desk with a newspaper in his hands.

"Our job is finished here," the sheriff said. "We can give the story to the press now."

"Too late, Lamar," Hancock said wryly, tossing the folded front page across the desk for Sheriff Potts to see. "Sheriff Howell beat you to it."

Beneath front-page headlines, the morning edition of the *Columbus Enquirer* announced: "A burned and buried body, identified as that of a missing twenty-six-year-old sharecropper was found late Monday on the 2,000-acre farm of one of four men accused of murdering him, Sheriff E. F. Howell reported."

The story continued with Howell's account of his own efforts and of how Hancock's skilled detection had led to the pit where Turner was burned.

"I knew Howell was running hard for election," Hancock said bitterly, "but he didn't have to run that damned hard."

"Elzie, I'm sorry you didn't get to give the story out yourself," Sheriff Potts said, "I know it meant something to you."

"It's not me I'm mad about," Hancock said, trying to minimize his disappointment. "By rights, the announcement should have come from you. Howell must have come straight from the pit to the newspaper office. Talk about grabbing someone else's glory! That beats all I ever heard! You been down there looking for Turner for two weeks, and to hear him tell it, he did it all."

Sheriff Potts smiled at Hancock's concern. "That doesn't matter to me, Elzie, as long as you get credit for discovery."

Hancock's anger was unrelieved, his blue eyes snapping with indignation. "Damnedest thing I ever saw!"

"I got one more job for you," Sheriff Potts said.

"What's that?"

"I want you to pick up that five-hundred-dollar reward money and deliver it for me. I'll give you the address. The people there will know who it's for and how to get it to him."

"Not even a name?" Hancock looked up in surprise.

"His identity will never be known. I gave him my word."

Hancock shrugged. "Whatever you say."

Sheriff Potts looked at his watch. It was 2:30 A.M. "I've got to get back to Newnan to see what the posse found. I'll see you tomorrow."

The dark night was ending when Sheriff Potts arrived at the outskirts of Newnan. Driving in from the west, he saw the courthouse keeping its sentinel watch over the still-sleeping town, its dome silhouetted by the sunrise against a rose-and-lavender sky. The square was ablaze with lights. Cars were parked in the street in front of his office. Men were hurrying up and down the steps. The posse had returned.

Chapter Sixteen

Sheriff Potts sensed the excitement as soon as he stepped out of his car. Deputies and members of the posse, carrying boxes, packages, and bundles, hurried up and down the wide granite steps of the courthouse, bringing in the evidence that had been found in the swamp.

J.H., tired, tattered, and muddy, stood in the doorway checking each item as it was brought in, making certain that it had been labeled and dated. At sight of his brother, his face lit up with triumph. "We got it all, Lamar! Down to the last scrub pine! We brought back everything but the horse they carried the body on."

"I knew I could depend on you." This was an accolade, and J.H. grinned.

"Let me show you." J.H. led him into the office. With a sweep of his hand he said: "There it is . . . the milk cans Wallace carried the gasoline in, the well drags, the bloody sapling pole . . . we even dug up the stump it was cut from."

It was all there . . . the branches, the brush, the ropes, the ax, the knife . . . everything that had been used to take Wilson Turner from the well and remove all trace of him.

"J.H., I never saw a better job," the sheriff said.

"That's not the half of it. Wait." J.H. hurried out and in a moment was back again with Otwell and Pete Bedenbaugh.

"Did you find the well?" the sheriff asked.

The fatigue of the twelve-day search had taken its toll on Otwell, too, but his weary face glowed with success. "Yes, sir, we found the well, but you can't hardly believe what we found in it. . . . Go get 'em, Pete."

Pete Bedenbaugh wheeled out the door and came back with two

small tin buckets and a large rock. Handing the buckets to Sheriff Potts, he said: "Take a look at that."

In the smaller bucket were two large lumps of coagulated blood; in the larger bucket, an unmistakable mass of ruptured brains.

"God Almighty! Where did you get *this*?"

"From the bottom of the well," Otwell said. "We found the place just like Albert and Robert Lee described it. The ground was tore up around it and we could tell something had happened there, so we got a rope, I went down, and that's what I found."

"In the bottom of the well!"

"Yes, sir, and there was this fifty-pound rock that's got blood and brains all over it. From the way it looked, Wallace threw Turner in the well, then throwed the rock down on top of him. I figured that's what busted his brains out so bad."

Examining the bloodstained rock, Sheriff Potts said: "It looks like Wallace just couldn't quit killing Turner. He knocked off the back of his head, threw him in a well, dropped a rock on top of him, dragged him back out, burned him up, and threw his ashes away."

"You haven't seen it all yet," Otwell said, handing him three white cigarette papers that were folded in the middle. "Look at this."

"What is it?"

"A note. Read it."

J.H., Otwell, and Pete had a look of high expectancy as they watched Sheriff Potts open the folded papers. Scrawled in pencil across them was the message that Turner had written in jail:

"James, I am asking you to go to Carrollton and go to Rigsby Bros. mule barn and ask Frank Shack if he will take you to my house and James let Julia have 10 dollars if you will and when I get out I will pay you back and she are at your Mama and will be more than glad to pay you for your trouble. James, she do not have any money and then she can the truck and get Tom to drive it to come here so I can get out. I am in jail, I hate to say."

The note was signed: "Always, Wilson Turner." Under the signature was a postscript: "James, I left out part of it. If she is not at home, go to your Mama and tell her and I will promise you that I will never bother you again in jail."

It was an incredible piece of evidence, a pathetic, penciled plea, scrawled in a childish hand, that had gone unheard. *"Where* did you find this?"

"That came out of the bottom of the well, too," Otwell answered. "The way we figured it, Wallace threw Turner in the well headfirst, and this note fell from his pocket."

168

"Who is this James that the note is addressed to?"

"We found out he's James Windham, one of Julia Turner's brothers."

The evidence dovetailed with the story the Negroes had told, and formed a flawless picture of what Wallace had done.

"Well, Lamar," J.H. said, "what do you think of that?"

Sheriff Potts was not given to superlatives. His accustomed way was a word or a look of recognition, and those who worked for him knew when he was pleased. His eye traveled from J.H. to Otwell to Pete and back to the evidence before him. "I think that's the most remarkable job of collecting evidence I ever saw."

Otwell grinned and nudged Pete in the ribs. "See there, Pete, I told you he was gonna be tickled plumb to death."

"What's next, Lamar?"

"We got to get Albert and Robert Lee's families out of Meriwether County. I want you to get a cattle truck and two more trucks for hauling. Get some men to help you. Go down there and load up everything . . . furniture, kids, cattle, dogs . . . whatever belongs to them . . . and bring them back to Coweta."

"What in the name of the Lord are you gonna do with them then?"

"I'll find a farm that will take them in. I got a couple of places around here in mind."

J.H. swept off his battered straw hat and flapped it against his leg. "Whew! You sure as hell aren't gonna do anything halfway! Anything else?"

"I've got to get ahold of Dr. Jones and get him down to the pit to get the impressions of these tire tracks. By the way, whatever happened to that rain we were running so hard from?"

"I think we'll get it today," J.H. predicted. "There've been spot tornadoes in Alabama."

The courthouse clock struck six. "We can't put it off any longer. I'll have to call Dr. Jones at home."

He picked up the telephone and gave the number. Then, apologizing to Dr. Jones for the early hour, he explained the urgency of the situation.

An hour later Dr. Jones and his assistant, George Cornett, arrived in a pickup truck that carried moulage equipment for making casts. George Cornett was an experienced, accredited photographer with the Fulton County Police Department, and an expert in ballistics. Dr. Jones, himself a precise scientist, had the finely cut features of a patrician and the formal manner of speech reminiscent of an earlier time.

169

"We are prepared to get under way," he informed Sheriff Potts.

Hurrying to beat the gathering rain clouds, the sheriff took them at once to the woods near the liquor-still pit. Dr. Jones rode with him, and George Cornett followed in the Crime Lab's truck. At the edge of the woods he stopped to uncover the tire tracks so that George Cornett could begin making casts while he and Dr. Jones went on to the still pit.

Dr. Jones silently surveyed the charred trees and the pit where the cremation had taken place. "In all my years in criminal work," he said at last, "I don't believe there has been a more barbarous act nor a more bizarre crime."

"Or a more calculated one," Sheriff Potts added.

Working meticulously, Dr. Jones took samples, sifted ashes, and examined the debris. Down by the stream he found a few more bone chips. "We'll add these to the ones you found yesterday," he said.

The tire casts completed, George Cornett arrived to take photographs of the charred trees, the pit, the stream, and the surrounding area, all of these to be used as state exhibits at the trial. When he had finished, Sheriff Potts, following J.H.'s directions, led both men to the well. After the area had been examined and photographed, the job was finished.

They were packing up Cornett's equipment in the truck when darkness suddenly overtook them. "I didn't realize it was getting so late," Dr. Jones said, looking at his watch. "Why, it's only midafternoon. . . ."

Before he finished his sentence, large raindrops began to fall and thunder rolled across the sky. The expected storm had begun. The sheriff and Dr. Jones reached the car just as the downpour started. Lightning flashed and cracked in angry bolts across the slate-gray sky. Rain poured down the barren clay hills, gushing red in the gutters.

"How do you account for that?" Dr. Jones remarked, drying his glasses. "The weather bureau has been predicting this storm for days. Uncanny that it waited until the very moment we finished our work to begin."

"Hancock said something like that when we found the bone chips," the sheriff said. "He called it the Sure Hand of Fate."

Dr. Jones replaced his glasses, adjusting them to their correct position. "I'd call it an Act of God."

"I couldn't agree more. Efficient as Wallace was in covering up his crime, it's as though a force greater than his was working against him. In the end, God gave up all his secrets."

Dr. Jones nodded. "Despite all he could do."

The ferocity of the storm was at its height, bending trees, washing clean the woods and hills and all the things hidden there. Turning on the headlights to see through the driving rain, Sheriff Potts started back toward Newnan. As they approached John Wallace's house on the left, they saw a Negro woman under a pink parasol frantically waving a white tea towel. Recognizing Wallace's cook, Sheriff Potts stopped the car and rolled down the window.

"Is dat you in there, Sheriff Potts? Miss Josephine say she be obliged if you come speak wid her."

"All right." He turned into the driveway and Cornett turned in behind him to wait. "Josephine is John Wallace's wife," he explained to Dr. Jones. "Come in with me, I'd like you to meet her."

The cook held open the door as they ran through the rain to the house. Josephine, dressed in black velvet slacks and a long-sleeved white blouse, was waiting in the living room. Her pale face was sad, and there were dark circles under her eyes.

"I heard that you had found Wilson Turner," she said.

"We found a few remains."

"Will John still be in jail?"

Dr. Jones, who had never met Josephine, was obviously surprised by her question.

"I'm afraid so," Sheriff Potts said.

Tears filled Josephine's eyes and she looked away. "I think John is staying there just to keep away from me."

"I can assure you that isn't the case at all."

Taking a lace-edged handkerchief from her pocket, Josephine dried her eyes and regained her composure. "He's been gone two weeks now. He doesn't even know the flowers in the front yard are blooming."

She walked quickly across the room and picked up a crudely crayoned picture of a house with flowers in bright, primary colors. "I made this picture for him. Do you think he will like it?"

"I'm sure he will."

"Would you give it to him for me?"

"I'd be glad to." Sheriff Potts took the picture she held out to him. "If there's anything else I can do, please feel free to call on me."

"I will," Josephine smiled, "and thank you for coming by, Sheriff." Holding out her hand for Dr. Jones to shake, she said: "It was nice meeting you, Dr. Jones."

Dr. Jones bowed slightly. "My pleasure."

As they started through the doorway, Josephine asked: "When do you think John will be home?"

Sheriff Potts hesitated. "It might be a very long time," he said gently.

On the way back to Newnan, Dr. Jones remarked: "That's a real tragedy . . . a beautiful, well-bred woman like that."

"She's been under a strain for a long time."

"There's something pathetic in this effort to reach her husband." Dr. Jones was looking at the crayon drawing. "I wonder what Wallace will say."

"Likely the same he's said before. Whenever anyone from there comes to Coweta, she'll send a drawing she's made or a poem she's written . . . sometimes a flower. Wallace always reacts the same . . . wads them up and throws them out the window."

"Why?"

The sheriff shrugged, "I'm told he has someone else who suits him better."

The rain continued to beat against the windshield, making it difficult to clearly see the road ahead. On the radio, the weatherman was calling it a torrential downpour, damaging to crops and destructive to property.

By the time Sheriff Potts, Dr. Jones and George Cornett reached Newnan, however, the storm had let up for the moment. Glancing at the blackness overhead, Dr. Jones remarked that he'd like to be on his way as quickly as possible.

"There's quite a bit more evidence for testing," Sheriff Potts told him, "but it looks like a number of the deputies are here. It won't take them long to load it."

Not only deputies were there, but also a great many of the interested and curious. They had come upon hearing that the mystery that had gripped the county had been solved, and that the remains of Wilson Turner had been found. The latest rumor from Meriwether County was that an effort would be made to seize and destroy the evidence.

Aware of the tension and not knowing friend from foe, Dr. Jones stood beside the Crime Lab's truck as it was loaded. Concealed in his pocket he held a gun, ready to protect the evidence being put in his custody.

When the last item had been loaded and covered over with a tarpaulin, Sheriff Potts went up to his office safe and brought down the small box containing the bone chips.

"What is this?" Dr. Jones asked.

"This," Sheriff Potts said, "is Wilson Turner."

It was a poignant moment. The remains of a human being—trans-

172

ferred from one man's hand to another—in a container no larger than a penny matchbox.

"Awesome," Dr. Jones said.

"Awesome, indeed," Sheriff Potts replied.

"You've done a masterful job in solving this crime."

Dr. Jones had said he would need the tires on Mozart Strickland's truck to match to the casts Cornett had made. Late on Tuesday afternoon, therefore, Sheriff Potts and Otwell returned to Meriwether County with a warrant charging complicity in the murder of Wilson Turner, and served it on the white-haired patriarch of the Strickland clan.

Tall and straight, eighty-year-old Mozart Strickland had a gruff dignity that he used to intimidate those who confronted him.

"What do you mean, suh, I'm under arrest?" he demanded of Sheriff Potts. "What is the nature of the charge?"

Sheriff Potts remained unperturbed. "Complicity," he replied.

"Complicity, indeed! I know nothing about this wretched affair or what happened to that troublesome Turner."

"Your truck and your cordwood were implicated in the disposition of Wilson Turner's body. I'm here to take both you and your truck back to the county jail in Newnan."

Mozart Strickland looked down his long, thin nose at Sheriff Potts. "See here, young feller," he said condescendingly, "do you realize that I was a personal friend of the late President Roosevelt? That I was many times a guest at the barbecues at the Little White House in Warm Springs?"

"I wasn't aware of that, Mr. Mozart," Sheriff Potts said matter-of-factly, "but under the present circumstances, it won't do you a bit of good."

"In that case," Mozart said indignantly, "I'll surrender in custody of my attorney."

Picking up the telephone, he called his nephew, Kiser Whatley, the young, redheaded lawyer who was the junior member of John Wallace's defense team. "Kiser? I've been arrested . . . some damn-fool thing about that tenant named Turner. I want you to take me in in your custody. *Now!* Immediately!"

Complying with this request, Kiser arrived to drive his uncle to the Coweta County jail. The truck, which Otwell drove to Newnan, was turned over to Pete Bedenbaugh to deliver to Dr. Jones at the Crime Lab.

That night, when the run-around-boy brought his dinner to him, Mr. Mozart, sitting rigidly on the edge of his bunk, took one indignant look at the tray of food and said: "I demand to have my meals brought down from the hotel in town." At the boy's shocked expression, he added: "At my expense, of course." Because of Mr. Mozart's age and failing digestive tract, Sheriff Potts agreed to the request. Mr. Mozart's meals were brought in from the Virginia Hotel and duly charged to his account.

By Wednesday, May 5, eight arrests had been made in connection with the murder of Wilson Turner. Seven, including Mr. Mozart, remained in jail. Only Broughton Myhand, arrested as a material witness, had been released. Albert Brooks and Robert Lee Gates were still in the Columbus jail. John Wallace, Herring Sivell, Henry Mobley, Tom Strickland, and Mr. Mozart were being held without bail in Coweta.

When newspaper reporters arrived to interview the prisoners, only Mr. Mozart consented to talk. Enraged by his arrest, he told them that he had been in jail before, for making illegal liquor, a penalty he considered absurd.

"All I ever wanted to do," Mr. Mozart said, "was grow enough corn to feed my stock and make a little liquor for me and my friends. Aye, God! They put me in jail for it."

His pale parchment skin stiffened with fury. "This time I haven't even done that! I don't know *why* I'm here. There's no justice! Absolutely no justice for a peace-lovin', law-abidin' man who's just tryin' to mind his own business."

Later, talking to Sheriff Potts, the reporters asked for a comment on the possible outcome of the case. With the seven suspects in jail, the confessions of the two Negroes, and all the corroborating evidence collected, he told them he was satisfied that the case against John Wallace was "clinched."

Reading this report in the newspapers the next day brought a measure of relief to the citizens of Meriwether County. Wallace was in jail and apparently he would stay there. But the unrest remained. No one in Meriwether County *really* believed that John Wallace would come to trial. He had always had a Houdini's skill for getting himself out of a tight spot. They expected Wallace would get himself out of this one, too . . . somehow.

They had not long to wait. Two days later, the most startling development of the entire case exploded in black headlines across the morning edition of the *Atlanta Constitution*.

Chapter Seventeen

Wilson Turner was alive!

The shocking news reported by the *Atlanta Constitution* on Thursday morning, May 6, had come from Crawford County Sheriff L. R. O'Neal in the small town of Roberta, Georgia, eighty miles east of Greenville. O'Neal claimed that he had held Wilson Turner in the Crawford County jail on a cattle-theft charge until Wednesday, May 5.

After reading the *Constitution*'s account, Sheriff Potts tried to contact Sheriff O'Neal by phone for confirmation of the story. Unable to reach him, he called GBI agent Jim Hillin and requested that he go to Roberta to investigate.

Reporting back, Hillin said: "It's true. There's been a mix-up."

Wilson Turner, he explained, was the dead man's brother. He lived on the family farm in Roberta. The murdered Turner was William. The brothers looked alike, and the identity mix-up had begun when William Turner deserted the army in wartime and stole his idiot brother's 4-F draft card. Assuming the alias of Wilson, he had moved to Carrollton and married Julia Windham. Neither his wife of four years nor his family knew he had changed his name.

"How is it, then," Sheriff Potts asked Hillin, "that the idiot brother, Wilson, was in the Crawford County jail charged with cattle theft?"

"Well, it's pretty involved," Hillin said. "William Turner was the one who worked for Wallace and stole his two registered cows. He took one of them to Roberta to his brother, the real Wilson, for safekeeping."

"That's the cow I called Sheriff O'Neal about," Potts interrupted. "When Tommy Windham turned himself in, he told me what happened to Wallace's cows and I asked O'Neal to check on it."

"He did. That's how he happened to have Wilson Turner in jail. He went looking for the cow and found her in the Turner family pasture with her head cut off."

"With her head cut off!"

"Yeah. When all this trouble came up between William and Wallace, brother Wilson was left with a 'hot' cow on his hands. He couldn't figure out what to do about it because all the auctions were being watched, so he cut her head off. That's when Sheriff O'Neal caught and arrested Wilson and put him in the Crawford County jail."

"Where is he now?"

"O'Neal told me he turned him loose yesterday after some relative came and posted bond. He claims he doesn't know where he is now."

The answers didn't add up. "I've got one question," Sheriff Potts said. "Why did O'Neal wait until now to announce that all that time he'd had Wilson Turner in his jail?"

"He says he reported Wilson's arrest to Sheriff Collier since Meriwether County had jurisdiction. He even took the cow's chain down there. Collier told him to hold Wilson in jail and charge him with malicious conduct."

"It strikes me as damn peculiar that for two weeks we've been tearing up hell and half of Georgia looking for Wilson Turner and no one bothered to say a word until now."

"I'm with you."

"In fact, I would say the whole thing was engineered and comes damn close to collusion."

In following up its story about the mixed identities, the *Atlanta Constitution* located John Turner, father of William and Wilson. When Mr. Turner, a work-worn sharecropper, had learned of William's mysterious disappearance, he had come from his home in Roberta to stay with his daughter in Macon, Georgia. It was in her home that he confirmed the report that William, not Wilson, was the murdered man.

Not until she read the newspaper account did Julia Turner realize that she was technically married to her husband's brother. Celestine Sibley, the *Constitution* staff writer who had been reporting the Wallace story from the beginning, discovered Julia living with relatives in Bowdon, Georgia. Miss Sibley, a skillful reporter, soft-voiced and with an easy manner, found Mrs. Turner very willing to talk about her bewildering situation.

"Now I know why Wilson . . . I'll always think of him by that name . . . insisted on naming our baby John William," Julia Turner

176

said. "I knew he said John was for his father, but he wouldn't tell me the truth about why he wanted to call the baby William.

"Sometimes he'd say it was for his brother, and sometimes he'd say it was for mine. Then again, he'd just grin and say, 'Maybe someday you'll know, honey.' " Julia Turner's crossed eyes filled with tears. "Now I know."

She had been working for the cotton mill in Carrollton when she met William Turner. He was working there, too, and helping Millard Rigsby haul cows and hogs besides. They had known each other only ten days when they decided to get married.

"He never mentioned any army service," Julia Turner said. "At first he said he had no relatives. When we moved on John Wallace's place and the trouble with the liquor business began, he told me to get in touch with his sister in Macon if anything happened. I never dreamed it would end like this!"

John Wallace's friends rejoiced when they learned of the confusion in identity. It seemed—and they took for granted—that a technicality would prevent his ever coming to trial.

"By God, we knew all the time ole John was gonna get off some way. We just didn't know how," they said. "Ain't a way in the world they can charge him with murdering a man who's still alive."

The jubilation, however, was short-lived. The fiery special prosecutor, Myer Goldberg, had other plans. After consulting with Sheriff Potts he said: "Wallace may *think* he's going to get off on a technicality, but we will amend the charge to read 'for the murder of William, alias Wilson, Turner.' " Solicitor Luther Wyatt and Circuit Court Judge Samuel Boykin, who would hear the case, approved the amendment when it was presented to them. The murder charge against Wallace and Sivell stood as amended.

Reaction to this in the Wallace camp was immediate. "The only thing Coweta County has got to go on is a bunch of bones and the confessions of two niggers . . . and who ever believed anything a nigger ever said? John ain't got a thing to worry about."

On the day after the *Atlanta Constitution*'s startling report, Friday, May 7, Dr. Herman Jones completed the laboratory tests on the first evidence Sheriff Potts had sent him—the bloody pants and shirt found in John Wallace's house on the day of his arrest.

"We have definite proof," Dr. Jones reported from the Crime Lab in Atlanta, "that the blood on Wallace's clothing is human blood."

Wallace's friends were quick to rally. "That don't mean nothing," they claimed. "John himself said the bloodstains came from briar scratches he got while riding his horse in the pasture."

177

But the photograph Sheriff Potts had had taken of the minor scratches on Wallace's hand, the day he made the claim, was already a matter of record and had been entered among the exhibits the state would use in the trial. To strengthen Dr. Jones's findings, however, Sheriff Potts now requested William Turner's blood type from the War Department.

The next day, Saturday, May 8, another charge was brought against John Wallace. This time "for conspiracy to violate the Internal Revenue Laws." Federal agents of the Alcohol Tax Unit, who had assisted Sheriff Potts in finding William Turner's body, had uncovered overwhelming evidence of Wallace's illegal liquor making during the twelve-day search of his two-thousand-acre farm. Their investigation, begun six months before Wallace had requested Federal Agent Earl Lucas to apprehend and arrest William Turner for making liquor on his land, was now completed. They called the operation on Wallace's farm "one of the biggest liquor rings in the state." Warrants for Wallace and ten other men were issued. Among those charged was Cecil Perkerson, who had twice warned Sheriff Potts to stay out of Meriwether County.

Following his trial for the murder of William Turner, Wallace would then answer Federal charges, authorities said. Therefore, to protect himself from paying back taxes and penalties on the illegal liquor, he had his young cousin, Kiser Whatley, transfer all his property to a mail carrier named Pope Davis, an old friend he knew he could trust. Kiser worked throughout the night, drawing deeds. By morning, John Wallace was practically penniless, his only assets the cattle and equipment left on his farm.

While Kiser worked on Wallace's deeds, Judge Boykin held a meeting with Solicitor Luther Wyatt, Special Prosecutor Myer Goldberg, and Sheriff Potts in Newnan. The next regular session of the Superior Court was not scheduled until September, and as the charges against John Wallace grew, the emotional climate between Meriwether and Coweta counties was intensifying into an ugly mood.

"Justice will not be served by delay," Judge Boykin said.

His decision to call the grand jury into special session on May 31 was agreed to by the other three. If indictments were returned against the seven man charged, trial would be set for June 14.

"Our job," Solicitor Wyatt told Goldberg and Sheriff Potts, "will be to untangle the intrigues and involvements of this case so that what happened will be unmistakably clear to the judge, jury, and the public."

178

The task was a challenge. Witnesses would have to be found, depositions taken, briefs prepared, and the trial was only six weeks away. As the investigation progressed and evidence piled up, it became increasingly clear to Sheriff Potts that there was one accomplice to the murder of William Turner who had not yet been charged and arrested. This accomplice was Meriwether County's sheriff, Hardy Collier.

Collier had aided John Wallace in taking Turner from the Carrollton jail without a warrant to Meriwether County, where he was held incommunicado and denied even a phone call from or to his family. Later, when Wallace was arrested, the warrant had been obtained from a blind justice of the peace who relied on his secretary to tell him what he was signing.

These obstructions of justice were minor, the sheriff learned, compared to Collier's active participation in Wallace's scheme to trap and kill Turner. Obeying Wallace's instructions, Collier had arranged Turner's release at the appointed hour, drained his pickup truck of most of its gas, denied any knowledge of Turner or his truck when Sheriff Potts called from Sunset, then claimed Wallace was having dinner with him at the time of the abduction.

Sheriff Potts swore out a warrant charging Sheriff Collier as an accessory to murder. Then he called the Meriwether County jail and asked for Sheriff Collier.

"Sheriff Collier's in bed," Mrs. Matthews told him. "He ain't feelin' too good. His heart's actin' up on him again."

"Then tell him I'll be down to see him."

J.H. and Otwell were both off interviewing witnesses, and only Pete Bedenbaugh was in the sheriff's office. Taking Pete along with him, Sheriff Potts arrived at the Meriwether County jail in the late afternoon. Ninety-degree shafts of heat ricocheted off the red-brick walls of the jail as they waited for Mrs. Matthews to answer their knock.

When she came to the door, Sheriff Potts said: "Please tell Sheriff Collier I'm here."

Mrs. Matthews seemed nervous and uncertain, her face apprehensive. "Sheriff Collier said he'd see you upstairs in his apartment."

Pete shot a warning glance at Sheriff Potts, but he took no notice. He walked up the stairs two at a time, Pete behind him. Opening the bedroom door, he found Collier lying in bed with a wool blanket pulled up to his chin. The darkened room was hot and sultry.

"Sheriff Collier . . ." Sheriff Potts began. He did not finish.

Collier's face had a strangled look, the veins protruding darkly. His eyes were fever-bright and anxious. Under the blanket, his chest visibly rose and fell.

Instantly, Sheriff Potts drew his gun and aimed it straight at Collier's chest. "Don't move, Collier, or you'll be in hell for breakfast."

Collier went rigid under the blanket, his eyes dilating, his pale lips trembling. Holding the gun on him, Sheriff Potts snatched back the blanket. Fully clothed, Collier lay with both arms alongside him, a .44 pistol clutched in each hand.

"Now, raise your hands very slowly," Sheriff Potts said, "or I'll fill you so full of lead they won't be able to lift you off that bed."

Slowly, Collier loosened his grip on the pistols and raised his arms until they rested on the pillows under his head. "You aren't gonna haul me in like I was some common criminal," Collier blurted out, his face twisting with anguish. "I'm a *sheriff.*"

"You're a sorry goddamn excuse for a sheriff," Sheriff Potts snapped angrily, picking up the pistols and handing them to Bedenbaugh. "You and your kind, Collier, tarnish the name of every good lawman. Now get the hell out of that bed before I wrap your guts around that bedpost."

Frightened now, the bluster and tough talk gone, Collier blinked rapidly. His lips moved without making a sound. "I can't," he finally managed to say. "It's my heart. I got to stay in bed for my heart." He picked up a bottle of pills from the bedside table. "See, I gotta take pills for my heart. I gotta stay in bed. The doctor said so."

Sheriff Potts paused a moment. "Make damn sure you do." Pulling a paper from his back pocket, he handed it to Collier. "I'm serving you with a warrant charging you as an accessory to murder. Don't try to leave, Collier . . . there's no place so far that I won't find you."

With that, he left the room, walked down the steps, out the door, and into his car. Pete, carrying Collier's pistols, ran along behind.

"Goddamn!" Pete exclaimed, getting in the car beside him, "I ain't never seen you so mad. I thought you might pistol-whip him."

"By God, I'd like to." Sheriff Potts pulled down his hat brim and headed the car toward Newnan. "It's bad enough when an ordinary citizen breaks the law, but a *sheriff*! . . . hired to uphold the law! It takes a long time to build confidence, but to *rebuild* it. . . ." His voice trailed off. Anger was overridden by melancholy. Collier's actions only contributed to the collective myth that all Southern sheriffs were corrupt.

180

"How the hell did you figure he was lying there with two pistols ready to shoot?" Pete asked.

"It was too hot to be under that blanket. Pulled up to his chin that way, it just didn't look natural. Then his face gave him away. Did you notice how excited he was when we came in . . . like he was trying to brace himself for something?"

"It's a good thing *you* noticed, else you might've got yourself shot."

"Not likely."

"Mrs. Matthews was standing outside the room crying," Pete told him. "She said Collier had told her if you tried to take him, he was going to take you with him."

"He hasn't got the guts," Sheriff Potts said evenly, his eyes on the road ahead.

The following week, on May 20, Dr. Jones finished the laboratory tests on the burned bone chips found at the still pit. All along, Wallace's friends had scoffed at the contention that they were human bones. "Those bones are likely dog bones or possum bones," they said. "With all the things Sheriff Potts and his posse dug out of that swamp, they might even be baboon bones."

Laboratory tests, however, proved that the bone chips found at the pit *were* human bones. Like the blood on Wallace's clothing, the blood and brains, found at the bottom of the well, were human blood and brains. Responding to reporters' questions, Dr. Jones told them that he had not been able to identify William Turner's blood type in the blood found in the well because of its decomposition. All the other items of evidence that Sheriff Potts had turned over to him had been tested and checked out "proof positive."

"The job done by Sheriff Potts in this case," Dr. Jones told the press, "is one of the best examples of crime detection I have ever seen. A perfect chain of evidence has been formed."

After the grand jury's special session on Monday, May 31, indictments for murder were returned against John Wallace, Herring Sivell, Henry Mobley, and Tom Strickland. Albert Brooks, Robert Lee Gates, Mozart Strickland, and Sheriff Hardy Collier were indicted as accessories to murder. Trial was set for Monday, June 14. Sheriff Collier, charged as an accessory before the fact, was released on $10,000 bond with his trial scheduled for the regular session of Superior Court in September.

On Friday, June 4, Judge Boykin announced that he would hear pleas of the accused on the following Monday. If any of the accused

181

wanted to plead guilty, he would sentence them immediately. If the defense had any new motions to make, they could be brought up at this time.

The talk in Meriwether County had been that Wallace's lawyers would file for change of venue to Meriwether County where preferential treatment of the accused could be expected. This would require a statement saying that Turner had died in Meriwether, not Coweta. From the beginning, at the preliminary hearing, and before the grand jury, Wallace had stoutly denied any knowledge of Turner's death. He continued to maintain this contention and refused to allow his lawyers to petition for a change of venue.

"Meriwether County," Gus Huddleston told Wallace, "is your only chance. No jury would convict you."

"No jury in Coweta is going to convict me, either."

"I wouldn't count on that."

In Coweta County there was no way of telling what a jury might do or what might happen. Huddleston knew the people there to be an independent lot. They believed in giving a man a chance but not an advantage. Wallace, relying heavily on political power and personal prestige, expected the jury to consider who he *was,* not what he had done. Outraged at being arrested and held in jail without bond, he wanted to go to court and show in public what he could do. It was not enough just to win the case, he wanted to win it in his own way. He intended, he told Gus Huddleston, "to beat the whole rap, hands down."

"It would have never come to this," Gus Huddleston replied, "if you had followed my advice in the beginning. If you had had Collier arrest you when this Turner affair began, the whole thing could have been handled in Meriwether County. Very likely the case would have been thrown out of court and never come to trial."

"That didn't seem necessary then," Wallace replied acidly, "and it doesn't seem necessary now."

Dissatisfied with Gus Huddleston's handling of the case, disgusted with the indictment by the grand jury, and unwilling to petition for a venue change, Wallace hired A. L. Henson, a politically influential Atlanta attorney, as his chief counsel. Henson agreed with Wallace that a change of venue was not necessary. Vain, self-confident, and cunning, Henson was certain he could make short work of a county sheriff and a country jury.

Pierre Howard, attorney for Herring Sivell and Henry Mobley, did not share Henson's assurance. He considered the situation very grave. He knew that Solicitor Luther Wyatt had prepared the state's case

182

against the defendants with meticulous care. Sheriff Potts had obtained sworn statements from thirty-eight witnesses who would tell the story of how William Turner was murdered. This would be supported by forty-three pieces of physical evidence tested in the Crime Lab and confirmed by Dr. Jones. The chain of evidence was overwhelming.

Pierre Howard decided to petition for a plea of severance so that Sivell and Mobley could be tried after Wallace. Tom Strickland's attorney, Jack Allen, agreed with Howard and moved to have his client's trial separate from Wallace's also.

Undaunted in his supreme self-confidence, Henson made no effort in preparing his defense to contact or interview any of the witnesses listed on the indictment. He had a plan, a plan to have the whole case thrown out of court, and he was sure it would work.

Chapter Eighteen

Precedent was heavily in John Wallace's favor. Although Solicitor Luther Wyatt was satisfied that every possible effort had been made in the preparation of the case, conviction was by no means certain. No white man—especially a man of Wallace's prominence and position— had ever before been accused by Negro hired hands and convicted of a capital crime in a Georgia court.

In addition, Wallace's friends in Meriwether County had continued their campaign to harass and intimidate not only the key witnesses who had seen the killing at Sunset Tourist Camp but all the others who would provide links in the chain of evidence. So far, no one had backed down, but the question in everyone's mind the night before the trial began was this: Would their courage last when it came time to take the witness stand and face John Wallace?

The outcome of the trial was further complicated by the fact that Judge Revel, native of Meriwether County, owner of the Greenville newspaper, and friend of John Wallace, was court reporter for the Coweta Circuit. Entrenched in local politics, he had been court reporter for nearly fifty years, and was notorious for his inaccuracies. Almost deaf, he took down in shorthand what he heard of courtroom testimony, later deciphering his own system of squiggles to a secretary, who typed up the transcript of the trial for the official record. Solicitor Wyatt and Sheriff Potts agreed that Judge Revel's reporting could not be relied upon in a case so important as the one against Wallace. He would have to be replaced, a move certain to cause repercussions and retaliatory action in Meriwether County.

Rumors that Wallace's friends would try to seize and destroy the collected evidence were still being reported on the night before the

184

trial when Dr. Jones returned all the items that had been tested in the laboratory, the report for each one signed and dated.

"That's everything but the blood and brains found in the bottom of the well," he told Sheriff Potts. "Because of their state of decomposition, I assumed you would want to keep them at the laboratory until the day you enter them as evidence."

"What do you have them in . . . formaldehyde?"

"Certainly not! The defense would charge me with tampering with the evidence. I have them in my refrigerator at the laboratory at a temperature just above freezing."

Because of the importance of the chain of custody, Sheriff Potts set up a cot in his office so that he could personally protect the evidence against any last, desperate attempt by Wallace's friends. In the darkened courthouse, with his shotgun across his lap, he took up his long vigil, trying to relax against the tensions of the coming day.

It was a time of quiet reflection. Tomorrow the courthouse would throb with explosive emotions, unspent anger, rising hopes, blinding hurts, failing courage, and steadfast conviction. But now, this moment of peace was one in which to gather strength.

Several times during the night, cars circled the square. Sheriff Potts listened, waited, ready for whatever might happen, but no one stopped and no one came.

The courthouse clock struck off the hours toward daylight, and dawn arrived with an apricot sun that colored the sky with ribbons of lavendar, red and rose. The day had begun. The courthouse stood in readiness, the stone corridors scrubbed clean and smelling faintly of the antiseptic soap used by the cleaning women the night before, the brass spittoons polished to a golden glow.

At six o'clock, J.H. and Otwell arrived, J.H. mopping the perspiration from his forehead with a fresh handkerchief. Early though it was, there was no cool in the morning air. Already, it was heavy, still, and hot. The leaves on the magnolia trees that bordered the four corners of the square drooped listlessly, the grass beneath was limp, unrefreshed by the morning dew.

"Man, it's gonna be a hot one today," J.H. predicted.

"In more ways than one," Otwell added. "By this afternoon tempers and temperature both will be hotter'n a three-dollar pistol."

"That's the very thing we've got to avoid," Sheriff Potts told them. "I want you to arrange to have State Patrolmen at all four doors of the courthouse. I want them there all day and I want them to make certain that nobody carries a gun into that courtroom."

185

"Not even the *officers*?" J.H. asked.

"*Nobody*," Sheriff Potts said emphatically, "and I mean *nobody* gets in that courtroom with a weapon of any kind. Search them if you have to."

"They ain't gonna like that."

"Then they can stay outside. J.H., I want you to work out some system of checking guns and weapons. They can leave them at the door when they come in and have them back when they leave."

"Anything else?" Otwell asked.

Sheriff Potts looked at the checklist in his notebook. "Yes, I want a State Patrol escort for Judge Boykin. Pick a man who can stand his ground. I expect the judge will raise hell about this, but it's twenty-two miles from here to his home in Carrollton. Most of the way is through rural, deserted areas. Anything could happen."

Leaving J.H. and Otwell in charge, the sheriff drove home for breakfast and returned an hour later to find Hancock waiting for him.

"By God, Elzie," he said smiling, "you're dressed up like a big-city undertaker."

Hancock shifted self-consciously in his light-gray suit and fingered his black silk tie. "Well, with a big trial like this one, I figured I ought to wear something besides my raiding clothes."

"Did you have any trouble delivering that reward money?"

"No. I took it to the address you gave me and turned it over to the woman who answered the door. She seemed to know what it was all about and said she would see to it that the proper person received it."

"I'm satisfied she did. I appreciate your taking it over."

Hancock nodded, looked down at the floor, then away through the windows as though he had something to say but could not find words to say it. Finally he asked: "Is there anything I can do for you now, Lamar?"

From Hancock's tone and the tight, tense spots on his cheekbones, Sheriff Potts knew that missing the discovery by waiting for Sheriff Howell that morning was still a private grief for him.

"Thank you, no, Elzie. I don't believe so. Is there something I can do for *you*?"

Pushing his white straw hat to the back of his head with his thumb, Hancock crossed his arms over his chest. "No, I don't reckon so." He paused, his lips stiff. "I just feel sort of out of it."

"What do you mean?"

"Well . . . not being called as a witness. Everybody . . . including Mayhayley Lancaster . . . has been asked to testify. I wasn't."

Sheriff Potts looked him straight in the eye. "You *know* we can't afford to put you on that stand, Elzie. The very first question about how you discovered the pit, and we're dead. We're going to protect our informant, but not by perjury."

"How the hell *are* you going to explain how the pit was found?"

"We're going to explain *what* we found, not *how* we found it."

"How are you going to do that?"

"The way Luther Wyatt has it laid out, witnesses will tell what Wallace's declared intentions were, how he and his friends waited on the courthouse square, the chase to Sunset, and the beating and abduction that took place there. Then Robert Lee Gates and Albert Brooks will describe how Wallace destroyed Turner's body, identifying the corroborating evidence, piece by piece. Dr. Jones will verify the evidence with his lab findings, and the deputies will tell where it was found, confirming the story that Robert Lee and Albert have told. At no point will the prosecution touch on *how* it was found, and you can damn well count on the defense not calling anybody who can."

Hancock listened intently, squinting through his glasses and nodding agreement. "Sounds to me like you've got a conviction."

"Well," Sheriff Potts said slowly, "that's our plan. There's no telling what the defense might do."

Otwell stuck his head inside the door. "Hey, Sheriff, look who's coming up the courthouse steps!"

Sheriff Potts and Hancock both turned toward the window.

"For the love of God! It's Miss Mayhayley!" Hancock exclaimed. "That's the first time I ever saw her without her army cap and her long skirt!"

Looking as if she was wrapped in flag bunting, Miss Mayhayley wore a siren-red dress patterned with black dragons, and a discarded Shriner's hat with glittering glass beads pinned across the front. The beads dangled down and bounced with each bob of her head. Moving beside her like a dark cloud was a figure completely clothed in black.

"Who in the hell is that with her?" Hancock asked.

The frail figure trailing alongside Mayhayley wore a black dress that swept the ground, black gloves that overlapped the long sleeves, and a broad-brimmed black hat so heavily veiled that the wearer's face could not be seen.

Sheriff Potts shook his head. "I have no idea."

At the door, the patrolman stopped Miss Mayhayley and her companion. When J.H. asked if she was carrying any weapons, Miss Mayhayley replied: "Only my hatpin," indicating the five-inch pin with the red jeweled knob stuck through the back of her Shriner's hat.

"Well, as long as you leave it in your hat and don't use it on anybody, I reckon it's all right," J.H. grinned.

Miss Mayhayley's lips stretched into a thin smile. "If I feel the need of that, I'll just put a curse on them."

Walking into the sheriff's office, she nodded to Otwell and Hancock and held out her hand to Sheriff Potts. Taking it in his, Sheriff Potts said: "Miss Mayhayley, I appreciate your coming down to testify."

"Just doin' my duty, Sheriff."

"Who is this you have with you?"

"Why, that's my sister," Mayhayley said, surprised he did not know who she was.

Turning to the black-clad figure, Sheriff Potts apologized. "Miss Sally, I didn't recognize you."

Miss Sally raised the end of her black veil so that no more than the tip of her chin was exposed. "Hello, Sheriff," she said in a whisper. After this quick exposure, she lowered the veil again so that it hung down over her frail chest.

"She's shy about people lookin' at her," Miss Mayhayley explained. "Besides, she ain't been feelin' well."

"I'm sorry to hear that," Sheriff Potts replied.

"The only thing I've been able to keep on my stomach," Miss Sally confided, "is some parched corn and a little whiskey."

Otwell's eyes were exploding with laughter, and Sheriff Potts gave him a warning glance. "I gotta go help J.H.," Otwell said. He backed out of the office and Hancock followed him.

As they left, they passed Solicitor Wyatt and Myer Goldberg coming in. Wyatt, a big man with a bulging waistline, carried his jacket over his arm and had rolled the sleeves of his white shirt to the elbow.

"Miss Mayhayley!" he said warmly, shaking her hand. "You look mighty handsome in that red dress."

Mayhayley's ancient eyes gave a responsive flutter.

"We appreciate your coming to the courthouse today," Myer Goldberg said, stepping forward to shake hands with her, too.

"Just doin' my duty," Miss Mayhayley repeated.

"How do things look to you?" Wyatt asked her.

Mayhayley gave him a measured look. "Are you payin' or pryin'?"

He reached for his wallet, but Mayhayley held up her hand to stop him. Her craggy face was suddenly serious. "The courthouse clock struck doom the day John Wallace waited for Turner," she said. It was a pronouncement.

188

"Do you mean . . ." Wyatt began.

J.H. came to the door. "Excuse me," he said, addressing himself to his brother. "Judge Revel is here, Lamar. He says he, by God, *will* be court reporter for this trial, and nobody's going to stop him."

"Be goddamned if that's so!" Luther Wyatt said, wheeling around to face J.H. "Where is he?"

"He's already gone upstairs to the courtroom."

Sheriff Potts's eyes were on Luther Wyatt, whose glasses steamed with his rising anger.

"It won't do to have Judge Revel as court reporter," he said dispassionately. "If John Wallace beats this rap, he's going to do it fair and square and not because the court reporter couldn't hear and got the testimony down wrong."

"Damn right," Luther Wyatt said, "we're going to settle this right now. He can either drop out or I'll challenge him in court."

"Then you'd better get to it. Court starts in an hour."

"Come on." Wyatt motioned to Myer Goldberg. Together they moved toward the staircase to the courtroom.

Mayhayley had listened to the conversation with her mouth pursed into a wrinkled circle. She made no comment, only shook her head. "We got to be goin', too," she said to her sister, who had receded into a corner of the room. Miss Sally patted her heavy black veil into place and moved as silently as smoke toward the door.

"By the way, Sheriff," Mayhayley paused to say, "you won't mind if I do a little business, will you?"

Sheriff Potts smiled. Mayhayley, at seventy-two, was a rich woman with land, timber, and untold cash sewn into her mattress, yet she never missed an opportunity to turn a dollar. "So long as you don't set up shop in the courthouse," he said.

Mayhayley's good eye glittered. "I got plenty of customers outside."

The courthouse square was now filled with people who had come from Meriwether and Coweta to attend the trial of John Wallace. Down the four streets that led from the center of town, cars were parked along the curb as far as the eye could see. Farther out, mules and wagons driven to town by farmers who had come to see if justice would be done, were tied up to trees that lined the streets. In the back of the wagons were gallon jars of buttermilk, kept cool in brown paper bags, and shoeboxes filled with ham-and-biscuit sandwiches.

A murmur rose from the crowd clustered on the courthouse steps when Miss Mayhayley walked out. Several men surged forward, their money in their hands, pleading with her for a reading.

A man from Meriwether County, wearing a straw hat and red galluses, thrust past the others and pressed his dollar and dime into Mayhayley's hand. "I just bet three hundred twenty dollars that John Wallace wouldn't even come to trial today," he said breathlessly.

Mayhayley curled her talonlike fingers around the money, reached down the bosom of her dress, and drew out a cloth tobacco sack with a drawstring. Opening the sack, she deposited the money and hooked the string around her little finger. She fixed her eyes on the inquirer. "Why three hundred twenty dollars?"

"That's all the money I had." Looking expectantly at Mayhayley, he asked: "Well, what d'you say?"

"A fool's way is a fool's pay," Mayhayley replied loftily, and moved on to the next customer.

Inside the courthouse Myer Goldberg hurried into the sheriff's office. "I need to use your phone," he said. "Judge Revel is raising hell upstairs and Luther wants me to get a court reporter with a steno machine from Atlanta before the trial begins."

"Where is Luther?"

"Upstairs."

Making his way through the crowd of spectators that jammed the central corridor and lined the stairs, Sheriff Potts got to the second-floor courtroom just as Judge Revel stomped away, sputtering indignantly. "An outrage, suh! An outrage." His three-hundred-pound mountain of flesh quivered as he stormed through the courtroom, his stiff white hair, brushed into a ducktail, switched with each short, quick step.

Luther Wyatt, standing at the prosecution's table in front of the judge's bench, shuffled his papers, trying hard to control the anger that shook his heavy jowls.

"Pretty bad, huh?" Sheriff Potts said inquiringly.

"I got a grandstand speech on his honor being impugned."

"Couldn't be helped."

"I know."

Spectators now packed every space in the courtroom, and the overflow filled the upstairs balcony. Those who could not find a seat stood in the back along the sides of the room by the ornate, oak-framed, two-story windows. Already, the air was hot and still from the capacity crowd and the morning sun blazing through the east windows. Making his way downstairs again, the sheriff found Otwell. "Admit no one else but jury members," he said. "The courtroom is packed."

190

J.H. leaned out of the office and motioned to him. "Judge Boykin is on the line. Mad as hell."

Taking the telephone, Sheriff Potts was ready for the volley. "Yes, sir?"

"Why is this patrolman at my house?" Judge Boykin demanded.

"Safety precaution."

"I have my own driver, and he's perfectly capable of getting me there."

"I know, but under the circumstances I felt that this was necessary."

"I'd feel like a damn fool arriving with a police escort."

"I'd feel like a damn fool if you had an accident before you got here. I'd consider it a favor. . . ."

"Favor!" Judge Boykin thundered, "that's no favor, that's a damned indulgence!"

"I'd appreciate it. . . ."

"All right!" Judge Boykin snapped, slamming down the phone.

Outside, reporters from the wire services and the metropolitan dailies, waiting for Wallace's arrival, were interviewing some of the crowd on the courthouse steps. When Henson, Huddleston, and Kiser Whatley arrived, the reporters hurried over to ask Wallace's lawyers what plans they had for the first day of trial.

Kiser Whatley drew his mouth into a hard, straight line and said nothing; Huddleston assumed a look of lofty dignity; but Henson preened himself. Almost a head shorter than Huddleston, he arched his thin, dark brows, pursed his small, red mouth, posed for photographers, and talked confidently to reporters.

"What are my plans?" he asked, repeating the reporters' question: "To lead the witnesses into confusion and the judge into error." When the reporters tried to pursue this reply, Henson held his hand up, smiled cunningly, and said: "No more for now."

Thirty minutes before court convened, Sheriff Potts and J.H. went to the jail to get Wallace and the others. There, the jailer told them that Mrs. Wallace and her father, Mr. Leath, had visited Wallace earlier. There had been angry words, the jailer reported, but he had not been close enough to hear what was said.

Despite this, Sheriff Potts found Wallace in a jovial mood, laughing and joking and talking with an animation he had never shown during his eight weeks in jail. At the courthouse he smiled and waved gaily to everyone in the crowd from Meriwether County. In the courtroom, he shook hands with Solicitor Wyatt and Myer Goldberg, greeting them like old friends. His attitude was that of a host at an enormous party

191

and he gave every appearance of thoroughly enjoying the occasion.

By way of contrast, Herring Sivell, rumpled and gloomy, sat quietly beside his attorney, Pierre Howard, who was watching Wallace's posturing with grim amusement. The moment court began, he would make a plea of severance for his clients.

Henry Mobley, anxious about how the trial would affect his twelve-year-old son, talked seriously with his pretty young wife, holding her hand and trying to comfort her.

Tom Strickland, so silent and withdrawn that his friends hardly recognized him, sat staring straight ahead. Still smarting from the disgrace of his emotional breakdown the night of his arrest and Wallace's disdain, he spoke to no one.

The clock was moving toward ten when Josephine Wallace arrived with her father, a thin, wasted man of seventy-two with sunken brown eyes. Wallace willingly posed for photographers with his wife and father-in-law, and jokingly scolded reporters for having called him "bull-necked" in their news stories.

Josephine submitted to the picture taking, but said nothing, her beautiful face full of silent pain. She wore a soft, sleeveless summer dress, a single strand of pearls, and a fresh blue bruise on her arm that she tried to keep covered with her hand.

When her father was asked how he thought the trial might go, he replied: "I've been a judge in Calhoun County, Florida, seven terms. I always like to hear the evidence first."

Irritated by this answer, Wallace turned away to talk with the friends who pressed around the defense table. Laughing and chatting with them, he inquired after their health, their cows, and the condition of their crops. While he talked, his eyes restlessly searched the rows of spectators in the balcony and came to rest at last on a pretty, dark-haired young woman with intense, hyacinth-blue eyes. The young woman, so slender she seemed frail, smiled down at him. Wallace's eyes held hers for a long moment, then slid away.

Josephine, seeing the exchange, stiffened and looked down to hide the tears that filled her eyes. Her fingers crushed the lace handkerchief she held in her lap. She looked at the gold watch on her wrist. It was time for the trial to begin.

The Trial

Chapter Nineteen

The courthouse clock struck ten. The solemn tone rumbled through the courthouse, stilling the chatter of the spectators. The festive mood was gone and tension rose like heat from the floor.

The bailiff announced: "Superior Court of Coweta County is now in session. The Honorable Samuel J. Boykin presiding."

Judge Boykin, a small man with thinning, black, curly hair and intense dark eyes, swept into the courtroom, his black robe swirling around him. He stood for a moment looking hard at the rows of spectators below him. Throughout the Coweta Circuit he was known as a tough, fair jurist who ran a tight court. His message was clear: *There would be no misconduct in his courtroom.*

Smashing down his gavel, he said: "Court is now in session."

Immediately, Pierre Howard came forward and petitioned for a plea of severance for Herring Sivell and Henry Mobley. "I do not believe my clients' best interests can be served by being tried jointly with the defendant," he told the judge.

Jack Allen, representing Tom Strickland, made a similar plea for his client. Judge Boykin granted both requests and the bailiff returned Sivell, Mobley, and Strickland to jail. Pierre Howard remained in the courtroom to observe the conduct of the case that Henson was so certain he could have dismissed.

Now there was a stir among the spectators. Solicitor Wyatt was calling Case No. 446: the State versus John Wallace, charged with murder. Judge Boykin turned to Wallace's lawyers. "What say you about the defendant?"

Exuding confidence, Henson stood up and delicately balanced his fingertips on the table in front of him. "We announce ready, if Your Honor please."

"The State is ready," Luther Wyatt said.

Henson then approached the bench and informed Judge Boykin that irregularities in obtaining the indictment and drawing and summoning the jury had been brought to light. "I am convinced that neither the grand jury, which returned the indictment, nor the panel of jurors drawn to try the case, was legally constituted.

"Moreover," he said, "a reward was paid in this case by the sheriff, making him a party-at-interest. As such, he was disqualified to summon the jury, to have custody of the jury, and to serve as a member of the court. Therefore, I have prepared a plea in abatement to have the indictments dismissed."

Judge Boykin looked at Sheriff Potts, who sat beside the jury box. "Has any reward been paid?"

"Yes, sir," Sheriff Potts replied. "I paid it myself."

Again there was a stir in the courtroom, and Henson edged closer to the bench to say: "I prefer that this be investigated in chambers."

Judge Boykin agreed. "We'll take a ten-minute recess."

The intended ten minutes lasted for more than an hour. Henson contended that Sheriff Potts had acted as prosecutor in the case by offering a reward, that contributions had been solicited. He maintained that this constituted prejudicial interest and that the entire list of a hundred jurors called by the sheriff should be struck.

Under oath, in chambers before Judge Boykin, Sheriff Potts testified about the reward. "Here is what I offered: five hundred dollars reward for anyone who would give information as to the location of Turner's body. Mr. E. J. Hancock is the man to whom I paid the reward."

"Did you pay that personally?" Henson asked.

"Yes."

"Did you ask any contributions at all?"

"No."

"Was the reward paid before or after the commitment trial?"

"After."

"These defendants were bound over without bond for murder before you paid any reward?"

"That is right."

Judge Boykin leaned forward. "Sheriff Potts, do you have any personal interest in this case outside of seeing that it is prosecuted from the standpoint of your duty as sheriff?"

"That is all," Sheriff Potts replied solemnly.

Henson then presented a challenge to the array of jurors on the ground that no summons had been issued to them as provided by law.

196

"A postal card, signed by the sheriff and mailed by the clerk of court, Wallace Gray, notified jurors of service. This is not a process issuing from the court," Henson claimed. "Therefore, the hundred jurors who appeared for duty this morning were not officially called and should be struck."

"This method of jury call has been used in Coweta County for over twenty years," Solicitor Wyatt pointed out.

"No *personal* service on jurors has been effected," Henson insisted.

Having listened to the arguments, Judge Boykin adjourned the hearing in chambers and recessed court until after lunch.

At one o'clock the afternoon session began, and he announced that he had overruled Henson's objections, citing two Supreme Court rulings as the basis for his decision.

This was a blow for Henson. During the two weeks since he had been made Wallace's chief counsel, he had made no effort to prepare for the trial, certain of being granted the plea in abatement and having the indictments dismissed. Unprepared, he now had the task of defending his client against the testimony of the State's thirty-eight witnesses, supported by forty-three pieces of physical evidence.

Gus Huddleston, opposed to Henson's plan from the beginning, angered by his miscalculation, demanded: "All right, Henson, what now?"

"Like I said, I plan to lead the witnesses into confusion and the judge into error."

The spirited skirmishing for jurors that the courtroom spectators had anticipated did not develop. Within forty-five minutes a panel of twelve men—eight farmers, a service station operator, a lumberman, an oil distributor, and a textile worker—had been chosen to serve. Three panels had been called, the defense challenging seventeen men, the prosecution six. One man, opposed to capital punishment, was excused for cause.

Judge Boykin instructed the jury, and trial began with Solicitor Wyatt's opening statement: "The defendant, John Wallace, did on April 20, 1948, willfully, feloniously, and with malice aforethought, kill and murder William, alias Wilson, Turner. Witnesses will tell you of Wallace's declared intention, they will describe his act of murder, and you will see the subsequent results."

To settle the dispute on the name mixup of William and Wilson, Solicitor Wyatt called Turner's wife, Julia, as the first witness.

Thin, pale, nervously fingering the skirt of her cheap print dress, Julia Turner took the oath.

"What was your husband's real name?"

"His real name was William H. Turner, but he told me his name was Wilson."

Under questioning, Julia Turner then told the jury that her husband had worked as a tenant on John Wallace's farm for two and one-half years. During that time, she testified, Wallace and Turner had made liquor together.

"Why did your husband leave Mr. Wallace's farm?"

"They had a fallin' out over twenty gallons of liquor. Mr. Wallace told Wilson to get off his land and if he ever saw him again, he'd . . . kill him. . . ." Julia Turner's thin body crumpled in the witness chair, her last words lost in a sob.

Luther Wyatt touched her shoulder to steady her and gave her a moment to recover. "Would you repeat your last statement for the jury?"

Struggling to regain her composure, Julia Turner straightened her back and lifted her chin. "Mr. Wallace said he would kill him."

"Thank you, Mrs. Turner." He turned to Henson. "Your witness."

Henson, who seemed annoyed by the emotional outburst, directed his reply to Judge Boykin: "I do not care to question this witness at this time."

When Julia Turner stepped down, Earl Lucas, investigator for the Internal Revenue Department's Alcohol Tax Unit, was called to explain the circumstances under which his department had come into the Wallace case.

"Last October," Lucas said, "the Alcohol Tax Unit in Atlanta received a request from Mr. Wallace through his attorney, Gus Huddleston, asking that an agent be sent down to stop the liquor making on his property. I was the agent sent in response to Mr. Wallace's request.

"Mr. Wallace told me that his tenant, Wilson Turner, was making liquor on his land. He was worried about this because he said he had already done time twice in the penitentiary for making liquor himself, and he was afraid Turner's activities would involve him and cause him to be sent to prison again. He wanted Wilson Turner caught. Turner had caused him so much trouble, Wallace said, he had thought several times of killing him."

"Thought several times of killing him?" Solicitor Wyatt repeated.

"Yes, sir. On one occasion, Mr. Wallace said he met Turner on the road out there on his place. He said he would have killed him then, but he had his wife and baby with him."

A hush fell over the courtroom, and the eyes of the spectators traveled from the witness stand to the table where John Wallace sat between his attorneys. Wallace, absorbed in writing on a yellow legal pad, gave no indication that he had heard Lucas testify.

Luther Wyatt looked over his glasses and nodded at Henson. "Your witness, Mr. Henson."

Obviously displeased with the tenor of the testimony, Henson marched over to the witness stand and raked Lucas with angry eyes.

"You *knew* John Wallace wanted the liquor business on his land broken up, didn't you?"

"He wanted Wilson Turner caught," Lucas replied evenly. "I'm convinced of that."

"Well, you *knew* Turner was making liquor over there!"

"We knew somebody was making liquor over there."

"You *knew* it was not Wallace."

"No, I did *not* know it was not Wallace."

"It was after this thing happened to Turner in Meriwether County," Henson said, shaking an accusing finger at Lucas, "that your department went back and developed a conspiracy case against Wallace. *Why?* Who was it that got you in motion to make this case?"

"Wait a minute!" Judge Boykin interrupted. "What had *that* got to do with the case being tried now? Anything that transpired *after* Mr. Wallace was charged with this crime, I rule out."

Solicitor Wyatt had listened quietly, pleased to have Henson's accusations answered under oath. Now he stood up and told Judge Boykin: "We have no objection to the defense going into that."

"We'll be here for about a month if he does," the judge scowled. "Get on with the questioning."

Thwarted in his attempt to show calculated prejudice in the development of the conspiracy case, Henson let his mouth curl into an angry curve. "Step down, Mr. Witness," he said to Lucas. Turning his back, he walked away.

The next witness, E. R. Threadgill, chief of the Carrollton police, was asked to describe the events leading to Turner's arrest in Carrollton on Sunday night, April 18. He began by telling how he had found Wallace's cow in a Carrollton pasture, had caught and arrested Turner and locked him up in the Carrollton jail. "At three thirty in the morning," he went on, "Mr. Wallace phoned me at home and said Sheriff Collier was at the jail to take Turner. I asked if he had a warrant. Mr. Wallace replied, 'I suppose so. I told him to get one.' "

"Did you ever see the warrant?" Solicitor Wyatt asked.

"No, sir."

"That's all for now, Mr. Threadgill."

Threadgill was a tall, angular man with bulging eyes. Nothing

199

seemed to escape their notice. As he waited for Henson's approach, they roved around the courtroom and came to rest on Sheriff Potts, whom he had known and worked with for a long time. Potts well knew that Rader Threadgill was not one to be intimidated or talked out of proceeding toward prosecution once he was convinced a crime had been committed. Before the trial, Wallace's friends had paid him a visit and tried persuasion on him, but he had refused to alter the testimony he intended to give.

"Right is right and wrong is wrong," he had told them, "and there wasn't no damn sense in killing that boy over stealing a cow."

Henson walked toward the witness stand with his head down, studying the oak boards in the floor. It was important to Wallace's defense to prove that no malice was intended in transferring Turner from the jail in Carrollton to the jail in Meriwether County, that, indeed, there *had* been a warrant. Appearing deep in thought, he clasped his hands behind his back, pacing back and forth in front of Threadgill. Suddenly he wheeled around, faced the witness, and demanded: "The sheriff of Meriwether County *did* come and get Turner with a warrant for stealing cows, didn't he, Mr. Threadgill?"

Unimpressed with this attempt to startle an admission from him, Threadgill gave Henson a bored look, blinked his eyes slowly, and drawled: "I never saw no warrant."

"He *told* you he had it."

"Mr. Wallace said he did, but I never saw it."

Seeking to establish that if Turner had been let go from the Meriwether jail, there must have been a warrant, Henson reviewed his release to Sheriff Collier step by step, over and over, until the spectators grew weary and the jury grew restless. Finally, unable to break Threadgill's steadfast stand, he took out his white linen handkerchief, fastidiously blotted the beads of perspiration from his brow, and released the witness.

Returning for cross-examination, Solicitor Wyatt asked Threadgill to tell the court what had happened on the afternoon of the murder, Tuesday, April 20.

Shortly after five o'clock, Threadgill reported, Wallace and Sheriff Collier had come to his office in Carrollton. "We just came by to tell you what happened to Turner," Wallace had said. "We turned him loose. Sheriff Collier checked with the solicitor. He said we didn't have enough evidence to hold Turner on that cattle-theft charge."

Threadgill knew Wallace was lying. He had already heard what had happened to Turner at Sunset Tourist Camp. He knew Wallace's visit was an effort to establish an alibi.

200

"I told Sheriff Collier then," Threadgill testified, "that he should have brought Turner back to Carrollton. As much evidence as we had on him for cattle theft, there wasn't a jury in Carroll County that would have turned him loose."

"Now, Mr. Threadgill," Solicitor Wyatt said, turning to the jury and firmly establishing the date and the duplicity. "That was on Tuesday, April the twentieth."

"Yes, sir, at five o'clock in the afternoon."

"Thank you, Mr. Threadgill. That will be all."

It was now midafternoon. The temperature in the courtroom, having risen steadily throughout the day, stood at a merciless 97 degrees. The giant propeller blades of the ceiling fans only stirred the stifling air, but in no way dispelled the heat. Despite the sweltering discomfort, no spectator left his seat. They sat transfixed by the story unfolding before them.

Archie Hodges, an itinerant cotton mill worker, was the next witness to be called. His ravaged face, aged beyond his years, had the lint-colored look of his trade; perspiration plastered his ash-gray hair to his head. Shambling up to the witness stand, he took the oath and sank into the chair in a heap. Conscious of the patched knee on his frayed brown pants, he carefully crossed his legs to cover it. Archie had been in the Carrollton County jail the night Wilson Turner was locked up. He testified that from his adjoining cell he had overheard Turner tell Wallace that if he didn't let him out of jail by the next morning, he was going to tell about that big liquor still on Wallace's place.

"What did Wallace say to that?"

Archie glanced quickly at Wallace and saw that he was still taking no notice of the testimony. "Mr. Wallace said he was going to take Turner back to Meriwether County, but Turner said he was scared to go. Said they'd gang up on him and kill him. About three thirty in the morning, the sheriff from Meriwether come and took him away. Turner screamed he didn't want to go. He said they were going to kill him." Archie hesitated, then added in a half-whisper: "But they took him away."

Archie Hodges was the kind of witness Henson had been waiting for. Until now, the testimony had been very damaging, and he had been able to do nothing to set it aside. With Archie, it was different. Ignorant, easily intimidated, with sins of his own to hide, he was, in fact, so easy a target that Henson found him contemptible. Aware of this, Archie, trapped in the witness chair, hunched his shoulders as though to ward off a physical blow.

201

Standing some distance away, as if closer contact would contaminate him, Henson asked: "Archie, what were you in jail for?"

A burst of laughter ripped through the quiet courtroom. Judge Boykin's gavel brought silence. "Don't let that happen again," he warned.

But the spectators found it hard not to smile. In every county they knew about Archie. A chronic drunk, he moved from place to place, cotton-milling long enough to buy himself a bottle and get himself in trouble. When he was drunk, any woman, no matter how old or ugly, looked good to Archie. His intentions never materialized, and he was considered a harmless nuisance who had to be jailed until he sobered up and came to his senses. His latest arrest concerned a fat, willing, fifteen-year-old girl whose angry mama had had him thrown in jail and charged with attempting to persuade underaged children.

"What were you in jail for, Archie?" Henson repeated.

"That don't concern this case."

"Don't you want these gentlemen in the jury to know what you were charged with?" Henson asked, his lip curling with amusement at Archie's discomfiture.

"No. I wouldn't care about them knowin'."

"I'm afraid you'll *have* to tell them. What was it?"

Archie bowed his head and studied his heavy brogans. "They had me accused of persuading underaged children out of the county," he admitted.

"*Persuading . . . underaged . . . children!*" In Henson's mouth, the words became evil. The deed that had amused the court minutes before now seemed depraved. Henson ran his eye down the line of jurymen sitting in the box, giving them time to consider the sinister act. Archie shriveled under the humiliation of public exposure.

"Did you know Turner before you met him in jail?" Henson asked.

"Yes, sir."

"Are you kin to those Turners?"

"I'm a little kin to his wife in a way," Archie answered. "Turner's wife's mother is my wife's sister."

"Well!" Henson exploded, as though the truth had finally been revealed. "*That* is the reason you came up here to swear in this case."

"No, sir, it wasn't," Archie protested. "I come to tell what Turner said."

Henson's face wore the mocking grin of a man who has caught another in a lie. "Step down, Mr. Witness." Still smiling, he returned to the defense table, his chest ballooned with self-confidence, satisfied that Archie's worth as a witness for the State had been utterly destroyed. Across the room, the members of the jury did not seem to share his assessment. Courtroom conduct was one thing, but shaming a man like Henson had done . . . that was something else.

When Archie had crept away, Willie Page Pucket, a truck driver for Purina Feed, testified that he had been delivering supplies to Greenville on the day Turner was killed. Shortly after noon, he had met a pickup truck speeding toward Sunset Tourist Camp and followed by two cars. Herring Sivell was the driver of the first car, Henry Mobley, the driver of the second.

"How long have you known Herring Sivell?" Solicitor Wyatt asked.

"Twenty-five years," Willie Page replied.

"Henry Mobley?"

"Eighteen years."

Henson chose not to cross-examine, and a recess was called.

There was a crush as the spectators, relieved at leaving the heat of the courtroom, went down the stairs to the water fountain. Julia Turner, among the first to have left, was returning when she met John Wallace face-to-face on the stairway. Clutching her eighteen-month-old son to her thin chest, she edged away. Wallace, who was escorted by Sheriff Potts and his attorneys, smiled expansively. Patting little John William on the head, he told Julia Turner: "You don't have a thing to worry about, Mrs. Turner. As soon as this trial's over, you can pick out any place on my land and live there as long as you like."

Frightened, Julia Turner fled up the stairs. Wallace followed her flight with hooded eyes. Behind him, Kiser Whatley nudged his shoulder impatiently. "Come on, John. This is no time for grandstand gestures."

Kiser's comment was lost on Wallace. He was busy enjoying the astonished faces of the people who pressed around him, busy exhibiting a puzzled look as though Julia Turner's reaction was beyond his comprehension.

When court reconvened, the bailiff called the last witness of the day: Mayhayley Lancaster. Except for the whirr of the fans, the courtroom was silent. Spectators edged forward in their seats. In the balcony people leaned over the rail.

Mayhayley was both feared and respected, for there was an eerie accuracy in her predictions. There were those who believed implicitly in what she said and there were others who claimed they didn't. But no one could completely dismiss her utterances for fear they might be so. In the audience that afternoon were a mother, a banker, and a businessman, all beneficiaries of her expertise. The mother's son, reported killed in action during the war, returned from behind enemy lines six weeks later as Mayhayley had predicted he would. The banker recovered a lost packet of money when Mayhayley told him he would find it in a wastepaper basket where a careless clerk had dropped it. The businessman found a missing pair of heirloom cuff links when Mayhayley directed him to look under the paper lining in his bureau drawer.

On the witness stand, Mayhayley told the court that John Wallace had been to see her twice—once about a lost cow, once about a lost body. One of the cows, she told him, would be found in a Carrollton pasture, taken there by a man named Turner. Wallace said when he caught Turner he would kill him.

"I warned him then," Mayhayley said in a voice that sent chills through the courtroom, "not to kill Turner."

Later, Wallace had returned, saying that he had lost a body. "I told him the body was in a well with green flies flying around. He asked would it be found. I told him it would."

Henson had listened to Mayhayley's testimony with great irritation and impatience. The superstitious country people hereabouts might be taken in by such nonsense, but he planned to establish clearly and unequivocally that Mayhayley was both a fool and a fraud. As he strode across the courtroom, his face was set with ill-concealed scorn. "I didn't get your name awhile ago," he said.

Mayhayley crossed her broomstick legs and trained her one good eye on Henson, her expression just short of disdain. She had seen the nonbelievers and the blasphemers before, and a slick city lawyer with a buttoned-up suit held no challenge for her. As though talking to a backward child, she began spelling. "It's Miss M-a-y-h-a-y-l-e-y L-a-n-c-a-s-t-e-r."

"You're what folks call a fortune-teller."

"*I* am an oracle of the ages."

Henson smiled indulgently. "Well, now, just how does the mind of an oracle of the ages work?"

"The wise foreseeth and hideth himself."

"Is that what an oracle of the ages does?"

A smile hovered around Mayhayley's thin mouth. "I do many things. I buy oxen and mules."

A muffled sound of strangled laughter came from the spectators.

Sheriff Potts, sitting in the chair beside the witness stand, looked down at the hat he held. If Henson had done his homework, he would have known about Mayhayley. Verbal assaults in court only made her incorrigible. Before it was over, she would make a monkey out of him.

"Being an oracle," Henson persisted, "you don't have to see

anything to know it, do you? You say you saw a man's body in the well with green flies flying around. Did you see the flies with your natural eyes? The ones you are looking at me with?"

"I have an artificial left eye," Mayhayley announced.

Henson looked stunned. "*How* did you see, then?"

"Astrology is a science that treats the stars."

"Tell the jury how it got to you through the stars!"

"The jury is examining a murder case," Mayhayley reminded him, "not the stars."

Angered by the reply, Henson snapped: "Do you know what it is to take an oath to tell the truth?"

"I've been sworn a good many times."

"Just answer yes or no."

"I am *not* going to tell this court or anybody else that I saw them flies with my natural eyes."

"Have you got another pair of eyes that you can see them things with?" Henson asked, deliberately ungrammatical.

"Crawfishes' eyes are in their tail. Mine are in my head."

Without looking, Henson knew the spectators, the judge, and the jury were laughing, not openly, but inside where it counted. He stiffened his back and attempted a knowing smile, as though he were about to share a confidence. "Now, Mr. Wallace was just joking about killing somebody that was taking his cattle, wasn't he?"

"No!" Mayhayley said firmly. "He said he was going to do it."

Henson turned his back on Mayhayley and looked out over the courtroom, inviting everyone to share his joke. "You can tell what's going to happen in the future, can't you?"

Mayhayley nodded.

"Wel-l-l-l . . ." Henson purred derisively, "I'd like to know what is going to happen to me in the future."

Mayhayley fixed him with a hard, unyielding look. In a voice as ominous as thunder she announced: "*You* may get what Turner got!"

There was a gasp from the spectators. Judge Boykin's black eyes flashed in annoyance, and he brought his gavel down and ordered: "Go on to something else!"

Henson, wearied with the verbal haggling and lack of progress, glared at Mayhayley. "Go down," he said, and swung away, leaving her enthroned on the witness stand.

Judge Boykin turned to Luther Wyatt. "Anything else?"

"That is all," Wyatt said.

Judge Boykin instructed the jury, and court was adjourned until morning. Members of the press swarmed around the table where John

Wallace sat with his defense team. His festive mood gone, Wallace now was cold and unresponsive. In reply to reporters' questions, he gave a terse: "No comment."

Henson was visibly shaken by the day's defeats. In answer to a reporter's request for his assessment of this first day, he snapped: "Not since the seventeenth century has the testimony of a witch been allowed in a court of law."

Asked to respond to this charge, Luther Wyatt said: "Miss Mayhayley's testimony has neither been disputed nor disproved. It stands as a matter of record."

Wallace's friends pressed forward to have a word with him, but sensing his changed mood, shook his hand silently and moved on. Josephine, separated from her husband by well-wishers, tried in vain to get through the press of people. Weakened by the overpowering heat and the long day's emotional strain, she turned to her father beside her and said: "Let's wait and go by the jail to see him."

Mr. Leath agreed. Taking his daughter's arm, he guided her through the departing crowd. In the car, Josephine unconsciously wrung her handkerchief in a wad. "It went very badly for John today, didn't it, Poppa?"

Mr. Leath's eyes showed the strain and weariness he felt. "I'm afraid so, Pet. The evidence was very damaging."

Josephine twisted the handkerchief around and around her fingers. "Please take me to the florist. I'll get a flower to cheer him up."

Mr. Leath frowned, knowing the gesture would not set too well with Wallace. "Now, Pet . . ."

"Please, Poppa."

Her eyes were anguished, and he did not have the heart to deny her anything. Not now.

Keheley Florist was located two blocks beyond the Coweta County jail. On her visits to the jail before the trial, Josephine had often gone there to buy John a flower. Kathryne Barnes, a pretty, dark-eyed woman behind the counter, recognized her at once.

"Hello, Mrs. Wallace," she said in her gentle voice, "what can I get for you today?"

"I want something brave and beautiful . . . something red."

"A carnation or a rose?"

"A rose! A rose is brave and beautiful," Josephine said softly, "and a rose is for love."

As Kathryne turned to get the flower, Josephine added: "Would you put it in a little glass vial? The jail has no flower vases! Imagine!"

In the car, where Mr. Leath had waited, Josephine held out the flower like a pleased child. "See, Poppa? I know John will like it."

"I hope so," Mr. Leath said listlessly.

They drove to the jail and together they walked to Wallace's cell. But then Mr. Leath tactfully stepped back. John's young friend with the hyacinth-blue eyes was standing outside his cell, her pale hands clinging to the bars, his hands covering hers, their faces close together. Aware of the wife's arrival, the woman turned on her heels, and without a word, brushed past Josephine and went out the door of the corridor.

Wallace was enraged by the interruption. His face reddened with anger he could no longer control, his eyes blazing with hostility.

"*Jo-se-phine!*" he said through clenched teeth. "Get the hell out of here and go home. Don't you ever come here or to the trial again. *Do you hear?*"

Josephine, standing in the other's place, raised her stunned face. "Why, John? Why?"

"Because I don't want to see you anymore. Ever! Is that clear? Can you understand that?"

Josephine did not reply. With trembling fingers she handed the rose in the glass vial to him through the bars. "I brought you this."

Wallace took the slender rose in his fist and smashed it against the wall. The glass vial shattered. "And," he shouted, "don't send me any more of these silly, goddamn flowers nor any more silly, goddamn pictures."

Josephine, with a cry of pain, fled through the door into her father's waiting arms. He was too old and weak to defend her, all he could do was comfort her and take her home.

The Coweta County jail was small, and everyone there had heard Wallace's angry words. Sheriff Potts, in the jailer's office upstairs, heard them, too, and saw Josephine rush out on her way to the car. He followed to offer some word of comfort or assistance, but by then the car was pulling away from the curb, Josephine sobbing beside her father.

Watching them disappear over the hill, Sheriff Potts felt a gut-deep sadness. Turner was not Wallace's only victim. The list of damaged lives was endless, concentrically increasing like the ever-widening circles from a pebble thrown into a pond.

Chapter Twenty

John Wallace's intention of killing William Turner had been clearly established on the first day of trial. On the second day, Tuesday, the State planned to show how he did it.

Twenty-two witnesses, many of them from Meriwether County, all of whom had signed sworn statements, had been called to testify. Most of them were nervous, some of them fearful, now that the moment had come to accuse John Wallace in court.

Henson, angered by his failure to have the case thrown out and infuriated by the *Columbus Inquirer* headline: DEFENSE LOSES FIRST ROUND, had vowed to tear their testimony to pieces. The threat was unsettling to all the witnesses, but particularly to Albert Brooks and Robert Lee Gates, who had been brought from Columbus to the Coweta County jail for the trial. On Tuesday, Robert Lee would tell his story, which would be followed on Wednesday by Albert's identification of the evidence.

When Wallace learned on Monday night that the two Negroes had been brought back and locked up in the cell below him, he called down to them from his window: "Hey, boys, what they got you all in here for? You ain't done nothing."

Hearing Wallace's voice again frightened Robert Lee into panic. Albert clapped his hand over Robert Lee's mouth and replied: "I dunno."

"Are they treating you all right?" Wallace asked solicitously. "Are you getting enough to eat?"

"Yassuh, we'ze doin' all right."

"Tell you what. I'll get Young Missy to bring you something good to eat tomorrow."

Albert and Robert Lee exchanged suspicious glances. Young Missy was the name Wallace gave his hyacinth-eyed mistress.

"We'ze much obliged to you, Mr. Wallace," Albert said, "but us is gettin' plenty."

"Young Missy won't mind," Wallace insisted. "She'll bring something tomorrow."

Albert took his hand from Robert Lee's mouth.

"Ain't no tellin' whut he's up to now, Albert," Robert Lee said. "You better say yo' piece tomorrow, too, else you might not be here to say it the next day."

"Sheriff Potts done said he was goin' to pertect us, and that's whut he's gwine to do, so shet yo' mouth and rest easy."

Robert Lee curled into a cocoon on his cot and moaned, "Oh, Lawd, I'se liable to see Jesus tomorrow."

When trial resumed the next day, Solicitor Wyatt recalled Julia Turner to the stand to identify a photograph of her husband, thereby unequivocally establishing that the man the witnesses had seen, known to them as Wilson Turner, was her husband. She described her unsuccessful efforts to get in touch with her husband after learning of his arrest in Carrollton and his transfer to the Meriwether County jail. Mrs. Matthews, the assistant jailer, had refused to let her see him on Monday or to allow her to talk with him on the phone on Tuesday.

"That was Tuesday, April the twentieth?" Solicitor Wyatt asked.

"Yes, sir."

Having established the date, Luther Wyatt began calling witnesses to reconstruct, hour by hour, the events that had occurred on the day of Turner's murder. Mrs. Eula Baker, proprietor of the Greenville Cafe, located on the courthouse square, was the first witness.

In a sworn and signed statement, Mrs. Baker had said that at nine o'clock that morning she and her Negro cook, Willie Joe Copeland, had seen Henry Mobley arrive in town, followed a short time later by Herring Sivell. Henry Mobley parked on the courthouse square, Herring Sivell by the Standard Oil station, headed toward Newnan.

Their arrival in town on a Tuesday was unusual. Mrs. Baker and Willie Joe remarked on this. Later, when Henry Mobley came into the cafe for a Coke, Mrs. Baker had asked him why he was there.

"Just messing around," Mobley had replied. He had returned to his car, where he remained for the rest of the morning.

Sometime after twelve o'clock, Mrs. Baker had noticed that both Henry Mobley and Herring Sivell were gone. Busy with noonday customers, she had not noted the exact time.

These were the circumstances and events that Mrs. Baker had given to the investigating officer. On the witness stand, she denied everything. Handing her the sworn statement she had signed, Solicitor Wyatt asked her to read it to the court. She refused.

Declaring to Judge Boykin that he had been entrapped, Solicitor Wyatt then impeached his own witness. With the court's permission, he read Mrs. Baker's statement line by line, forcing her to answer.

In conclusion, Solicitor Wyatt said: "Mrs. Baker, did you or did you not make this statement to the investigating officer?"

Mrs. Baker, a grandmotherly woman with gray hair and rosy cheeks, peered from behind her steel-rimmed glasses, frightened and confused. "I don't think so."

"Is this your signature at the bottom of the page?"

Mrs. Baker took the paper that Solicitor Wyatt held out for her to see. "Yes."

"Do you know Cecil Perkerson?"

Mrs. Baker's breath caught in her throat. She covered her mouth with a trembling hand.

"Do you know Cecil Perkerson?" Solicitor Wyatt repeated.

"Yes."

"Did he speak to you concerning this statement?"

"No."

"Did he speak to your son, James, Junior, concerning this statement?"

"No."

Looking at Judge Boykin, Solicitor Wyatt said: "This witness is excused."

Mrs. Baker's son, James, Jr., then came to the stand, and in a strong, unwavering voice, described the events that his mother had denied. On the day that the investigating officer had taken their statements, he said, Cecil Perkerson had come to their cafe and called him outside.

"What did Cecil Perkerson say to you at this time?" Solicitor Wyatt asked.

"Is that material to this case?" Henson interrupted.

"It is indeed . . . to illustrate the relation of conspiracy."

Judge Boykin looked down at the solicitor. "The witness will answer the question."

"Mr. Baker, tell the court what Cecil Perkerson said to you on this date."

"He asked did I know that Herring Sivell was his brother-in-law."

The implication was clear. Solicitor Wyatt let a long silence fall

210

over the courtroom. The explanation for Mrs. Baker's strange behavior was in her son's reply.

Willie Joe Copeland, Mrs. Baker's cook, was called as the next witness. Her testimony supported that of Mrs. Baker's son. She told of seeing Henry Mobley and Herring Sivell waiting on the courthouse square that morning and the conversation she and Mrs. Baker had had concerning it.

C. E. Miller, an alert agent for the State Revenue Department, reported two unusual occurrences that had happened that day shortly before twelve o'clock. Going into Greenville's Production Credit Corporation, he had seen Herring Sivell conducting business with the woman behind the counter. A short time later, John Wallace walked in. Without speaking to Sivell, Wallace shook hands with Miller, exchanged a few pleasantries, and walked out again.

Wallace's not speaking to Sivell had struck Miller as strange. He had also found it unusual to see Sheriff Collier idling conspicuously on the courthouse square, talking with passersby.

Three other witnesses had seen John Wallace and Herring Sivell in town that day. Levy Garrett, chief of the Greenville police, had seen them waiting in a parked car that morning as he made his rounds. Hugh Martin, who ran the Standard Oil station, had seen them parked there, too. Also, a storekeeper named Frank Perkerson.

These three not only had seen John Wallace on the square that morning, they had seen him return alone at three o'clock in the afternoon.

"What did John Wallace do that afternoon?" Solicitor Wyatt asked Levy Garrett.

"He came up on the square, spoke to Sheriff Collier, and they left town in Collier's car, headed toward Carrollton."

This account dovetailed with Threadgill's earlier testimony that Wallace and Collier had come to his office in Carrollton on the afternoon of the murder.

Having established the time and movements on the courthouse square that morning, Solicitor Wyatt then turned the jury's attention to what was happening at the Meriwether County jail where Turner was being held prisoner.

Mrs. Vivian Matthews, the red-haired assistant jailer, told the court that she had not made an entry in the jail log when Turner was brought to jail, nor when he was released. This, often, was her way of doing things, she said—"to keep it in my mind until I have time to do it." Later, after Turner had left, she had logged the entries when she had gone into the office to do the dusting.

211

"Did you at any time see the warrant for Wilson Turner's arrest?" Solicitor Wyatt asked, referring to the warrant Wallace claimed Sheriff Collier had had with him when he transferred Turner from the Carrollton jail to the Meriwether County jail in the early-morning hours of Monday, April 19.

"Yes," Mrs. Matthews replied.

"Who signed the warrant?"

"Major Irvin, a Meriwether County justice of the peace."

Mrs. Matthews said she was not certain what time Turner had been brought to the jail on Monday because she did not own a clock and relied on the baby to waken her in the morning. Neither was she sure at what time he had been released on Tuesday because she had been busy with an upholstery job for her neighbor, Mrs. Jarrell, who lived in the house across the street from the jail.

Mrs. Jarrell had been drawn into the Turner affair because she had houseguests coming to visit. The dressing table in her guest room was beginning to look shabby, and at the last moment she decided to have it recovered. She asked Mrs. Matthews to do the job because she was close and convenient, and besides, she assured Mrs. Jarrell she could have the dressing table finished before her company arrived on Wednesday afternoon.

It was from Mrs. Jarrell's house that Mrs. Matthews had given the instructions for the noon release of Turner and his truck. Mrs. Jarrell testified that she remembered the circumstances quite well. Seeing that her upholstery job would not be finished by twelve o'clock, Mrs. Matthews had telephoned the jail from Mrs. Jarrell's house and delegated the job to the Negro trusty, Jake Howard.

On the witness stand, Jake Howard said he had followed the instructions given to him by Mrs. Matthews. He had backed Turner's pickup truck out of the yard and parked it in front of the jail. He released Turner, not at twelve o'clock sharp, as Mrs. Matthews had said, but shortly before twelve.

"Why was it," Solicitor Wyatt asked, "when you were told to let Turner out at exactly twelve o'clock, you released him a few minutes early?"

"Because," Jake Howard explained, a note of pride edging into his voice, "ever since I been made trusty, I goes to town and meets the noon mail train. That's my job."

"So that when the courthouse clock struck noon, both you and Turner were gone?"

"Yes, sir."

212

This, of course, was the error in time that had made it necessary for Wallace to chase Turner down.

Leon Flournoy, a State Highway Department employee, had spent the morning of Tuesday, April 20, helping repair the road near Luthersville, a small village on the highway between Greenville and Newnan. At twelve fifteen, he and his fellow workers had been eating their lunch under a shade tree.

"We could hear the tires squeaking and squealing as they come around the curve," Leon testified. "Then we seen a green-and-white pickup truck being chased by two cars. One car was green, one was black. We thought it was the revenooers after a truckload of liquor."

Forty minutes later, Leon Flournoy said, they saw the green car, driven by Sivell, return toward Greenville. They never saw the other car or the pickup truck again.

During the morning, a dozen witnesses were brought before the court, their testimony forming a composite picture of the circumstances and events preceding Turner's abduction and murder. Shortly before noon, Luther Wyatt called Steve Smith, the proprietor of Sunset Tourist Camp.

As he took the stand, there was increased tension in the courtroom. Reporters, seated across the courtroom from the jury, renewed their note taking, spectators edged forward, and the jury concentrated on the testimony.

At 12:25 P.M. on Tuesday, April 20, Steve Smith told them, he and his waitress, Geneva Yaeger, were serving lunch to four customers in the dining room at Sunset. A green-and-white pickup, followed by a green Ford sedan, raced into the driveway. The man in the truck jumped out and ran toward the cafe, yelling for help. The two men in the car, both with guns, ran after him and caught him just as he reached the cafe door. They began beating him and dragging him back toward their car.

"I walked outside and asked what the hell was going on," Steve Smith reported. "The men with guns told me they were officers . . . that this fellow was dangerous . . . wanted for murder. Then the fellow started yelling, 'Get some help quick. They're gonna kill me!'

"The two men began beating this fellow again. One, named Sivell, had a pearl-handled pistol, the bald-headed one, named Wallace, had a sawed-off shotgun. They dragged this fellow to their car door and tried to force him inside, but he braced himself against the door frame and they couldn't budge him. That's when Wallace took his sawed-off shotgun in both hands and brought it down against that fellow's head so hard that the gun went off. That fellow never hollered no more. He just fell limp inside the car."

"How big was the fellow that was hit?" Solicitor Wyatt asked.

"He was a weasly-looking thing . . . not more'n one hundred twenty-five pounds."

"And Mr. Wallace?"

"I'd say right at two hundred thirty or two hundred forty pounds."

Solicitor Wyatt allowed a thoughtful pause, then: "Did the fellow who was struck with the sawed-off shotgun ever make another sound?"

"No, sir. He looked like he was dead to me."

Henson was on his feet immediately, his face angry and red. "I object to that inflammatory statement and ask the judge to strike it from the record."

Judge Boykin sustained the objection, and Henson asked that the jury be sent out. "The evidence given is the opinion of a nonexpert witness not qualified in that particular field or science," he said. "A matter like this cannot be proved by a nonexpert witness."

Judge Boykin granted permission. "Let the jury retire."

"Why, Mr. Henson," Judge Boykin asked when the jury was gone, "would the witness not be justified in an opinion? He described the blow, the man who received it, his conduct before and after the blow."

"Because," Henson said, "a man receiving a blow like that could be utterly knocked out for a month instead. . . ."

"The burden to prove that he was only knocked out would be on *you*," Judge Boykin said emphatically. "I will let the evidence in. Let the jury return."

When the jury was reseated, Solicitor Wyatt repeated his question. "I will ask you, Mr. Smith, if the blow that struck Turner on the back of the head was or was not a mortal wound sufficient to cause death and did cause death?"

The answer to the question was important. It set the situs of the crime, establishing that William Turner was killed at that moment in Coweta County.

"Yes, sir," Steve Smith replied. "I would say the blow was hard enough to kill him."

"Please describe for the jury what happened after the man fell forward into the car."

Wallace, Steve Smith told them, grabbed the man's heels, stuffed them in the car, crawled in on top of him, and continued beating him. Sivell got behind the steering wheel and turned back toward Meriwether County.

"You said, Mr. Smith, that the defendant was still beating this fellow as they drove away?"

"Yes, sir. He had something in his hand, still beating this fellow. I don't know whether it was a piece of wood or a piece of iron. I just saw him beating him with something."

"Thank you, Mr. Smith. Your witness, Mr. Henson."

Henson's cross-examination began by challenging every statement that Steve Smith had made on the stand. For forty minutes, he taunted Steve Smith on every detail, but Steve Smith stood fast on his testimony. Finally, Henson turned his questioning to the instrument Wallace used to beat Turner as they drove away from Sunset.

"What did it look like?" Henson asked.

"I don't know."

"Was it a round object?"

"I couldn't tell whether it was round or square."

"Was it as big as a pencil or as big as a post?"

"Well, it wasn't as big as a post."

"Would you say it was five inches long or five feet long?"

"I told you. . . ." Steve Smith began.

"Don't tell me anything," Henson snapped. "Answer the question . . . five feet or five inches?"

"Well, it sure wasn't no five feet long."

"Was it black?"

"I don't know."

"Dark-looking?"

"I suppose maybe it was."

"Mr. Smith, please answer the question yes or no," Henson scolded, as though he were talking to an unresponsive child. "Yes or no?"

"Well, I guess, yes," Steve Smith said tentatively.

"But you're not sure?"

Steve Smith scratched his head.

"*Why* won't you tell the truth, Mr. Smith?"

Steve Smith clenched his big fists in his lap. "I *am* telling the truth!"

"Then *why*, Mr. Smith, did you sit there in the witness chair and tell Mr. Wyatt that you didn't know what it was that John Wallace used to beat Turner with, and then you sit there and tell me that he had a dark object five inches long? You did say that, didn't you?"

Henson's questions, hurled like a rain of bullets, began to confuse Steve Smith. He tried to remember and couldn't. "I don't know what I said."

215

Myer Goldberg, seated at the prosecution table beside Luther Wyatt, was outraged by Henson's tactics. "Your Honor, I protest this line of questioning. The defense is putting words in the witness's mouth . . . saying he has sworn things that he has *not* sworn to. I don't believe this is fair."

"The man is under cross-examination," Judge Boykin replied. "Objection overruled."

Henson allowed a satisfied smile to play on his lips as he watched Myer Goldberg sit down. As he turned back to Steve Smith, his voice was indulgent and deliberately patient. "Now, Mr. Smith, your last statement was that you don't know what you said. Let's go back over a few things. You don't know the real effect that blow had on that fellow's head, do you?"

"He looked to me like he was dead."

"How much education do you have, Mr. Smith?"

"Enough to get along in this world."

"Ever study medicine?"

"No, sir."

"Ever observe injured people in the hospital?"

"No, sir."

"All we have to go on is what you swore before this jury . . . and yet you admitted awhile ago that you didn't know what you had said."

Henson paused and let his gaze move around the room, waiting for his words to settle on the jury and the spectators who now sat tensely waiting for his next question.

Suddenly, Henson turned theatrically on his heels toward Steve Smith again, his face stern, his voice full of accusation: "*You* didn't know that this fellow who ran up to your door was running away from a cow-stealing warrant, did you?"

"No, sir."

"*You* didn't know that he had a false name, did you?"

"No, sir."

"*You* didn't know that he had a false draft card in his pocket that he had stolen from his brother, did you?"

"No, sir."

"Did you know that he and his brother looked alike?"

"No, sir."

"You didn't know that!" Henson exclaimed.

Steve Smith wore the bewildered expression of someone who has been caught in a lie he hasn't told. "No, sir."

Henson shook his head as though appalled by such ignorance. He picked up the photograph of William Turner, marked Exhibit No. 1, handed it to Steve Smith, and asked: "Can you swear before this jury whether this is a photograph of William H. Turner or Wilson Turner?"

"I would swear that is the fellow they got down at my place."

"Is this him or his brother?"

"*This* is the one they got," Steve Smith said, hitting the photograph with the back of his hand.

"You're sure?" Henson asked, letting amusement show in his eyes.

"I'm sure!"

"That's all, Mr. Witness. Step down."

Steve Smith heaved his big, boxer frame out of the witness chair. He was accustomed to physical confrontations that could be settled with his fists, and his shoulders sagged with fatigue from the ordeal of resisting verbal assaults. When he returned to the witness room across the hall from the courtroom, J. M. Phillips, the next witness, got up and went over to him. Alarmed by the change he saw in the man, Phillips put his hand on Steve's arm and asked: "What happened?"

Before Steve could reply, the bailiff was at the door. "You're next, Mr. Phillips." Phillips's Adam's apple bounced. Sucking in a deep breath of the hot, stale air, he followed the bailiff into the courtroom.

On the witness stand, he told the court that on twelve twenty-five on Tuesday, April 20, he was eating his dinner in the cafe at Sunset Tourist Camp when a pickup truck dashed into the drive and the driver raced to the door, hollering for help. From his booth by the window, he saw Wallace and Sivell overtake Turner, drag him to their car, beat him over the head, and push him inside. From where he was sitting, Phillips said, he got a good look at Wallace's face when he grabbed Turner at the cafe door, but did not see what happened after they got Turner in the car.

"What were you doing while this was happening, Mr. Phillips?" Solicitor Wyatt asked.

"I just kept on eating my dinner," Phillips confessed.

After hearing that Phillips had not seen the continued beating that Steve Smith described, Henson's cross-examination was brief. His questions to Phillips mostly concerned where Steve Smith was in the cafe and how it was possible for him to have seen all that was happening.

Henson's previous efforts had been to confuse, disqualify, or discredit the witnesses against Wallace. Now he was working for a plea of double jeopardy. Only three witnesses—Steve Smith, J. M. Phillips, and Mrs. Merle Hannah—had come forward to testify about the events at Sunset. If it could be proved that Turner had been killed in Meriwether—not Coweta County—John Wallace would walk away from his murder charge free and clear. Having been tried at first in Coweta for a crime committed in Meriwether, a plea of former jeopardy would guarantee his not being tried again.

To substantiate Steve Smith's testimony concerning the severity of the blow that Turner received when John Wallace hit him with the sawed-off shotgun, Luther Wyatt called as witnesses for the State three local doctors, each with more than thirty years' experience. Dr. C. C. Elliot had been a practicing physician for thirty-six years; Dr. J. D. Tribble, an army doctor for twenty-five of his thirty-four years of practice; Dr. George Kinnard, a surgeon, had served as chief of surgical services for the 110th Evacuation Hospital in Europe during World War II. All of them qualified as expert witnesses by virtue of their training and experience.

Called to the stand one at a time, and each having the circumstances described to him, all three physicians agreed that such a blow as received on the back of the head would, in most cases, cause death. Over Henson's strenuous objections, their opinion evidence was allowed under Section 38-1710 of the Code of Georgia of 1933, which states: "The opinion of experts, on any question of science, skill, trade, or like questions, shall always be admissible; and such opinions may be given on the facts proved by other witnesses."

With the opinion evidence entered as part of the record, Luther Wyatt returned to the timetable of Wallace's actions on the day of the murder. Mrs. Merle Hannah, the last of the three Sunset witnesses, was called to the stand.

Her hands nervous as usual, the anxiety in her eyes magnified by her glasses, Merle Hannah told the jury that at twelve twenty-five on that Tuesday she had been standing in her yard across the street from the Sunset Tourist Camp. She had seen Turner wheel his truck into Sunset with Wallace and Sivell in close pursuit. As Turner ran for the door, Wallace had raised his sawed-off shotgun and taken aim at him. She had cried out: "Don't shoot him!"

Wallace turned toward her, Mrs. Hannah reported, and motioned for her to hush, then ran to the cafe door and grabbed Turner. With Sivell helping him, Wallace beat and dragged Turner to Sivell's car. When Turner resisted, Wallace struck him full force on the back of the head with the shotgun.

"When Turner slumped over," Mrs. Hannah said, "they picked up his feet and shoved them inside the car. Wallace crawled in on top of him, still in the motion of beating him."

218

"Could you see what he had in his hand?" Solicitor Wyatt asked.

"No, I couldn't see what he had in his hand. He was in motion, as if he were beating him."

Henson stood up. "I move to exclude that last statement. She said he was in motion as if he were beating him . . . which would be her conclusion. She can state what she saw and leave it to the jury to form a conclusion."

"I don't see how else," Judge Boykin observed, "she can state in the motion of beating him."

"She can say in motion," Henson suggested.

Judge Boykin nodded permission to Mrs. Hannah. "State what he was doing."

Merle Hannah pursed her mouth into a wrinkled circle, annoyed at Henson's attempt to dilute her statement. "All right. He was *beating* him when he left."

This was precisely what Henson wanted. When his turn for cross-examination came, he derisively addressed Mrs. Hannah, an obviously middle-aged woman, as "young lady." Merle Hannah's plain face flinched when he said it: "Young lady, you said awhile ago that Wallace was motioning like he was beating Turner, and when I objected, you said he *was* beating him. How come you to change it?"

"Well, you didn't like what I said. . . ."

"I didn't ask you that. How come you to change it?"

"She was getting ready to answer that question." Judge Boykin scowled at Henson. "You stopped her. Don't do that anymore. Let her finish." To Mrs. Hannah he said: "Just answer the question he asked."

Merle Hannah, unsure of how to express what she had seen, began to twist the strap of her handbag. She bobbed her head in reply to Judge Boykin's instructions and turned back to Henson.

"*Now,* young lady," Henson said, exuding exasperation with every word, "you testified that Wallace was going through the motion like he was beating him, didn't you?"

"He *was* beating him."

"Would you mind answering the question!"

"Answer the question," Judge Boykin said patiently.

"With the permission of the Court, I will ask you again: *Why* did you change your testimony? First you said he was in the motion of beating him, then you said he was beating him."

"He *was* in the motion of beating him," Merle Hannah insisted, trying to make the words accommodate the truth.

Henson threw his hands in the air and walked away from the

witness stand. He stood, looking out the window, rubbing his chin, feigning perplexity. Slowly, he walked back to where Merle Hannah sat rigidly on the edge of the chair.

"Let me ask you the question again . . . you testified that he was going through the motion like he was beating him."

"I did say that," Merle Hannah answered, her eyes moist.

"Then a minute later you swore . . . changed it . . . and said he was beating him, didn't you?"

"I did say that."

"WHY DID YOU CHANGE IT?" Henson shouted.

"You wanted me to," Merle Hannah cried. "You can't beat anybody without being in a motion."

Turning to Judge Boykin, Henson demanded: "Will you ask her to answer the question?"

"I think her answer is all right," Judge Boykin replied. "Go ahead."

The predominantly male spectators had watched in dismay as Henson verbally bludgeoned Merle Hannah. Hearing Judge Boykin's reply, two of them joyfully clapped their hands.

Angered by the break in his court's decorum, Judge Boykin angrily smashed his gavel down. "Don't let that happen again," he warned, "or I'll clear this courtroom for the rest of the trial."

Gus Huddleston, sitting at the defense table between Wallace and Kiser Whatley, began hurriedly taking notes. When Merle Hannah's cross-examination was finished, he got up and asked that the jury be retired. After they had left the room, he announced: "If Your Honor please, at this time I would like to make a motion for a mistrial."

An audible gasp could be heard from the spectators. Luther Wyatt took off his glasses and stared in astonishment at Huddleston, now posturing before the courtroom.

"This is based on the ground," he said, "that when Your Honor remarked to counsel examining the witness that it seemed like a good answer, there was a burst of applause which clearly showed amusement of the crowd to the jury and demonstrated to them the feeling of this crowd."

A dead silence fell over the courtroom. The spectators, already warned and admonished by Judge Boykin, held their breath as Huddleston continued his astonishing request.

"I insist on this motion at this particular time. The crowd thinks that this was an expression of Your Honor's opinion in this matter. The jury might take it the same way, and I think it is irreparable and the mistrial should be granted."

Judge Boykin looked down at Huddleston. "Is that all?"

"That is all," Huddleston replied, satisfied with his surprise move. Judge Boykin laced his fingers and bent forward over his folded arms. "Now. The Court wishes to correct counsel as to there being an outburst of applause." Judge Boykin enunciated his words clearly and emphatically. "There were two persons applauding. They were reprimanded by the Court at the time, the Court stating that if it happened again, the courtroom would be cleared. *The motion is overruled.*"

Huddleston stood up, rising to his full height. He permitted himself a sardonic smile. "If Your Honor please, in order to preserve my rights, I would like most respectfully to renew my motion for a mistrial."

Judge Boykin returned his smile. "I most respectfully overrule it. Let the jury come back."

Huddleston's motion for a mistrial was headline news. Several reporters from afternoon newspapers quietly slipped out of the courtroom to ask their editors by telephone to hold the front page.

Four more witnesses were scheduled to testify. The first was Wilson Wood, the old Negro who had helped Wallace locate the lost well. He said Wallace had come to his house one morning in Mozart Strickland's pickup truck, asking for the location of the old wells in the woods. Wilson Wood gave him directions.

"Did you go with him to look?" Luther Wyatt asked.

"Naw, suh. He went off lookin' by hisself."

Mary Turner, Mozart Strickland's Negro cook, then told the court that on Wednesday evening, April 21, Wallace had come with Albert Brooks to Mr. Mozart's house to borrow Mr. Mozart's pickup truck. Wallace sent Albert Brooks and her husband, Ted Turner, down to the woodpile for a load of wood.

"Where is your husband now?" Solicitor Wyatt asked.

"I don't know," Mary Turner replied. "The next day he told me he was going to haul wheat at Mr. Tom Strickland's place. I ain't seen him since."

"He disappeared?"

"Yes, sir."

When Henson's turn came for cross-examination, he said: "No questions."

The clock in the courthouse dome was striking four when Robert Lee Gates was called to testify. The jury, hot and restless after listening to six and one-half hours of testimony, leaned forward with renewed interest as Robert Lee nervously took the stand as that day's twenty-first witness.

"Robert Lee," Solicitor Wyatt said, "tell us in your own words what happened on Tuesday, April twentieth."

Robert Lee began by telling of the arrival of Tom Strickland, Henry Mobley, and Herring Sivell at Wallace's farm that morning. Wallace had left in the car with Sivell, Tom Strickland in the car with Henry Mobley. At two o'clock that afternoon, Sivell had returned and given Albert Brooks a flat tire and two shotguns, directing him to repair the tire and set the guns in the dairy barn. Robert Lee did not see Wallace again until late the next day, Wednesday, April 21.

"Long 'bout quittin' time," Robert Lee said, "Mr. Wallace come down to the barn and tole me and Albert he had a job fur us to do that night. He tole me to go home for supper and he took Albert with him to get a load of cordwood down on Mr. Mozart's place. When they come back for me, they wuz in Mr. Mozart's pickup truck with the wood and two five-gallon milk cans full of gasoline. Mr. Wallace drove down to the swamp and we throwed off the cordwood and set the gas cans down at the edge of the woods."

Returning to the barn, Wallace got on his saddle horse, Robert Lee on Old Nell, and Albert, carrying ropes and well drags, walked ahead to open the pasture gate leading into the woods. There Wallace told them that they were to help find "a package" that he had lost. They searched until midnight in the brush and brambles before Wallace told them that "the package" was in a well. They continued looking until three o'clock in the morning.

"We wuz wore out then," Robert Lee said. So Wallace decided to return home and resume the search at daylight. Taking the horses, they left the ropes and well drags behind.

The next morning, Wallace stopped by to see Wilson Wood to ask him the location of the old wells in the woods. "Me and Albert wuz on the hill waitin' for him where us'd left the hosses the night before," Robert Lee continued. "When Mr. Wallace come up, he tole us he knowed where to look now. We followed him through the swamp till we come to this well. When I looked over in it, I seed there wuz a man inside."

Every eye in the courtroom was on Robert Lee's black, sweating face. The jury sat motionless, the spectators were intent.

"Who was that man in the well, Robert Lee?" Solicitor Wyatt asked.

Robert Lee's eyes widened with apprehension, and he searched out Sheriff Potts's face in the courtroom. Finding the reassurance he sought, Robert Lee turned back to Solicitor Wyatt and answered: "It was Mr. Wilson Turner down in that well."

222

There was a stir in the courtroom. Judge Boykin rapped his gavel: "Proceed."

Quickly, with the words tumbling over each other, Robert Lee told how he and Albert had gotten the well drags, hooked them in Turner's shoe, and with Wallace helping them, pulled Turner from the well with a rope. Obeying Wallace's instructions, they had wrapped the body in a burlap sheet, tied it to a pine pole, and carried it through the swamp to the hill they had started out from that morning. There, they had cut branches and concealed Turner's body.

While Wallace and Albert waited, Robert Lee, following Wallace's orders, had returned to the barn and brought the horses back again. After tying Turner's body on Old Nell's back, Wallace had led the way on his saddle horse through the woods, across the road, and into the swamp on the other side. There they had again concealed Turner's body with brush and left it in the swamp near a liquor-still pit. That evening, Wallace, driving Mozart Strickland's pickup truck, had taken Robert Lee and Albert back to the swamp again.

"That was Thursday evening, April twenty-second?" Solicitor Wyatt asked.

"Yassuh. Mr. Wallace drove us back to the woods where we had throwed off the cordwood the night befo'. He tole me and Albert to start totin' that wood down to the liquor-still pit where we had left Mr. Turner's body."

Robert Lee then described Wallace's racking of the wood, their putting the body on top, and Wallace's pouring on the ten gallons of gasoline.

"What happened then?"

Robert Lee, as well as his audience, was emotionally exhausted. Drawing in a deep breath and wiping his wet forehead on the back of his sleeve, he said: "Mr. Wallace throwed on a match and a big blaze blasted up."

After watching it burn for about thirty minutes, Robert Lee reported, Wallace had told them to go home and return again in the morning with shovels and burlap sacks. They were to clean out the pit, put the ashes in the sacks, and dump them in the nearby stream.

"Did you do that?"

"Yassuh. First thing Friday mawnin', me and Albert done just whut us wuz tole, and Mr. Wallace come down to see us'd done it."

"Robert Lee, weren't you afraid, handling a dead man like that? Why did you do it?"

"Yassuh, I was scart, but Mr. Wallace made us."

"What happened after you cleaned the ashes out of the pit and dumped them in the stream?"

"Mr. Wallace tole us to go back to the field and start plantin' cotton. He said he had some business in Newnan."

Solicitor Wyatt said nothing more. He turned toward the defense table and looked at John Wallace sitting expressionless between his attorneys. "Your witness, Mr. Henson."

Henson's face was stiff. He stood up and patted his buttoned jacket. "We have no questions."

Several reporters hurriedly left the room and dashed for the phones downstairs, not waiting to hear the day's last witness, John Wesley Ellison. One of Wallace's employees in the dairy barn, he told the jury that he had seen Wallace remove the sawed-off shotgun from the dairy barn on Friday, April 23, before he left for Newnan.

When the testimony was finished, Judge Boykin warned the jury that they were not to discuss what they had heard among themselves or with anyone else. Releasing them in the custody of the bailiffs, he adjourned court until nine thirty, Wednesday morning.

The spectators, held down tightly during the day by Judge Boykin, exploded with exclamations, talk, and conjecture. Dave Bowers, a young reporter from the *Columbus Inquirer* whose accurate accounts gave a verbatim report of the trial, made his way through the turmoil to the defense table where Henson was gathering his papers.

"What about Robert Lee Gates's testimony?" Bowers asked. "Any comment?"

"When you get a man on the stand who can do you no good," Henson replied stiffly, "the best thing is to let him alone. The less said about Gates's testimony, the better we like it."

The mood among Wallace's Meriwether friends was so ominous after Robert Lee's testimony that Sheriff Potts himself escorted Robert Lee and Albert back to the Coweta County jail, leaving Wallace in the custody of the other deputies. Sheriff Potts knew that Wallace's friends, for all their threats and bravado, were not fools. Their attacks were on the vulnerable; their prey, the unprotected. Their attempts were made only when the opportunity offered them a fair amount of success. He did not plan to afford them this opportunity.

When the jailer unlocked the cell door for Albert and Robert Lee, he told the sheriff: "A lady come by the jail this afternoon and brought a cake for Robert Lee and Albert. I left it over there on the table."

"Know who the lady was?"

"Yes, sir. It was Mr. Wallace's lady friend."

"Ummmmmm-ummmmmmm!" Robert Lee headed straight for the three-tier pink-frosted cake with coconut and maraschino cherries. "Ain't dat fine!" He ran his finger across the icing and almost had a scoop of it in his mouth when Albert slapped it off his hand onto the floor. Snatching the cake away, Albert began tearing it into chunks and throwing it down the toilet.

"Albert, whut fo' you doin' dat?" Robert Lee asked plaintively.

"You done forgot whut I tole you last night?" Albert demanded. Robert Lee looked stunned.

"You want to wake up tomorrow sayin', 'Good mawnin', Jesus'?" Robert Lee shook his head.

"Me, neither. I aims to say *my* piece at that cotehouse tomorrow."

"You don't have to worry about that, Albert," Sheriff Potts told him. "We'll see to it that you get to say your piece."

To the jailer he said: "Put a guard on this door. See to it that no one goes in or out."

"Think they'll try something, Sheriff?" the jailer asked.

"Can't tell. If they do, we'll be ready."

Chapter Twenty-one

Overnight the mood had changed. The spectators, back on Wednesday, crowded the courthouse square, waiting for the trial to begin. They spoke in solemn, subdued tones of what they had already seen and heard. The curiosity that had brought them to the opening of the trial on Monday, had given way on Tuesday to spellbound horror as they listened to the twenty-two witnesses.

Their stunned reaction to Robert Lee Gates's chilling account of burning the body had, during the night, changed from shock to awe to abhorrence. Not one among them could recall a crime where the body of the victim had been so deliberately desecrated.

When Sheriff Potts arrived on the square with John Wallace, the crowd parted to let Wallace pass. This was not the homage they might have offered him on Monday, nor the deference they might have shown him on Tuesday. Wednesday's opened path was a sign of withdrawal . . . a standing back from something incomprehensible and evil.

Wallace took no notice of the spectators' reaction. He walked briskly through them, swinging his arms energetically, his white Stetson snapped down over his eyes. He no longer wore Monday's festive mood. This had disappeared with his expectation of having the charges against him dropped through his legal counsel's clever manipulation. His face now was stony, void of all emotion.

With his Meriwether friends it was different. The carnival crowd that had come on Monday to see him make short work of the Coweta sheriff was now hostile, and ready to fight at the slightest provocation.

Aware of the changing mood, Sheriff Potts instructed J.H. that everyone admitted to the courtroom must not only check their firearms but submit to search if it seemed necessary. This, Sheriff

Potts said, was to be done for *anyone* who seemed suspect, not just from Meriwether County, but from Coweta as well.

Upstairs in the courtroom, the forty-three pieces of physical evidence to be introduced by the State during the day's testimony had been arranged in front of the judge's bench. This included the door panels and floor mats from Herring Sivell's and Henry Mobley's car, the milk cans used to carry the gasoline, the pine pole and branches used to transport and conceal Turner's body, the stumps from which they were cut, the ax, the knife, the well drags, all the paraphernalia used by Wallace to destroy William Turner's body and the cartridge box that held Turner's remains . . . white chips smaller than a dime.

John Turner, father of the murdered William and the idiot Wilson, stood trembling before the collection of bloodstained evidence that crowded part of the courtroom floor. Scheduled to testify that morning, Mr. Turner was wearing his white Sunday shirt, his only tie, and a secondhand suit, bought so long ago that it no longer fitted his shrunken body. He was old and ailing, stooped from years of backbreaking work, and his mouth hung open now as though he had received a staggering physical blow.

"Wilson," he said unsteadily to the son who stood beside him, "that there is all that's left of yore brother." His eyes brimmed over with tears as he pointed out the small box.

Wilson, in his late twenties, had a child's gentle face. He stood awkwardly in his stiff new overalls, both hands tucked inside the bib. He could not in any way understand the things he saw before him. He only knew that his father suffered and somehow he wanted to help relieve the pain. Not knowing how, he took his father's arm and supported his stumbling steps.

"There, there, boy," Mr. Turner gave Wilson's hand an appreciative pat. "I'll be all right."

No matter what the government said about Wilson's being mentally deficient and giving him 4-F status, Wilson was the one Mr. Turner depended on. Wilson was the one who helped with the hard, unrelenting work on the farm, and it was Wilson who tried to ease his burden even when he did not understand the nature of the burden. What difference did it make that Wilson couldn't never learn how to read and couldn't never do no figurin'? Maybe to the army, but not to Mr. Turner. William was smart, but . . . a sob shook Mr. Turner's frail shoulders.

Seeing the old man's grief, Sheriff Potts went to him. "Mr. Turner, could I help you to your seat?"

"I'm much obliged to you, Sheriff, but I got Wilson here to help me."

Recognizing the pride in this reply, the sheriff held out his hand. "How are you, Wilson?"

Wilson, unaccustomed to formality, took Sheriff Potts's hand uncertainly and give it a timid shake.

"Sheriff, I want to shake yore hand, too," Mr. Turner said. "Bad as it is to see what's left of my boy spread out like this, it's powerful good to know that what happened to him didn't go unnoticed."

"I'm sorry it happened, and sorry you have to see this, Mr. Turner."

"It's a sorrowful sight. Somethin' his ma wouldn't no way be able to stand. But she'd sho' be proud to see all these lawyers an' legal folks turned out to see that justice gets done. Why, it's just like William was really somebody!"

Sheriff Potts laid his hand on the old man's shoulder. "William *was* somebody, Mr. Turner, and he'll get justice the same as anyone else."

Mr. Turner nodded thoughtfully, then glanced in Wallace's direction. "But with the likes of him, it ain't often folks like us gets it."

"You will in this court," Sheriff Potts assured him. "*Everybody* is entitled to full justice under the law, and neither money, power, nor influence should dilute that right."

Mr. Turner smiled. "Them's powerful words, Sheriff, and I know his ma would be proud to hear them, but it ain't likely. . . ."

"Wait and see," Sheriff Potts said. "Now, let me show you to your place in the witness room."

"Wilson, too?"

Sheriff Potts nodded. "Wilson, too."

By nine fifteen that morning, so many spectators had crowded into the courtroom that every available seat, downstairs and in the balcony, had been taken. Metal folding chairs from McKoon's funeral home were brought in and set under the windows along the sides of the courtroom. Those who could find no seats stood along the walls. Spectators who had heard Robert Lee Gates's awesome account of the cremation on the day before, waited now to hear Albert Brooks tell it again.

When court began, Albert took the oath and sat down in the witness chair. He and Robert Lee were as unlike in their reaction to stress as they were in appearance. Thin, black Robert Lee had been a mass of jangled nerves on the stand, rolling his eyes, rubbing his legs, twisting, turning, and twitching. Albert, big and broad-shouldered, resorted to frozen immobility. His yellow-skinned face was set and expressionless. He kept his pale-green eyes lowered, concentrating on a shaft of sunlight that spilled a pool of gold on the courtroom floor. When spoken to, he raised his eyes quickly, and quickly returned them to the sunlit floor.

In a voice full of apprehension, Albert told the jury of the unsuccessful search for Turner on Wednesday night, of finding him on Thursday morning, taking him from the well, carrying him on the cut pole to the hilltop overlooking the road, and later loading him on horseback for the trip to the liquor-still pit.

As Albert described what had happened, Solicitor Wyatt had him identify each item they had used to accomplish the task. Asked could he be sure these were the items used, Albert replied, "Yassuh. That prong on them well drags there got bent when Robert Lee hooked 'em in Mr. Turner's shoe and we pulled him out of the well. That crooked-handled ax b'longs to Mr. Wallace, and that knife is mine. I'd know it anywheres."

"When you pulled the man from the well, Albert, did you know who he was?"

"Yassuh, I knowed who he was. Mr. Wallace tole me and Robert Lee to hurry and wrap him up like we wuzn't s'pose to see, but I knowed all the time it was Mr. Wilson Turner."

"You could recognize him?"

"Yassuh, I could see his face good, but the back of his head was knocked off."

The twelve jurymen watched grimly and intently as Solicitor Wyatt continued: "Tell the jury what happened after the body was taken to the pit."

Albert explained how they had unloaded the body at the pit, left it until evening, and returned at night to build a pyre and burn it up; how the next day, following Wallace's instructions, they had scraped the pit clean, put the ashes in three burlap sacks, and dumped the contents in a nearby stream.

"Are these the ones you used?" Wyatt asked, showing him the three feed sacks.

"Yassuh."

"Albert, tell the court what happened when the defendant set the match to the gasoline that he had poured over the body."

"A big blaze went up . . . down the ditch and clear to the tops of them trees. Me and Robert Lee run for cover."

"What did Mr. Wallace do?"

"He just stood there aside a tree and watched it burn."

229

Albert's words stunned the courtroom. Robert Lee's description of the cremation had, on first hearing, seemed almost unbelievable. Confirmation of the grotesque act came with Albert's quiet words, and a perceptible shudder ran through the crowded courtroom.

The silence and the shudder did not disturb John Wallace. Bent over the defense table, he did not look up but continued writing on the yellow legal sheets that had claimed his attention since the trial began.

The next witness was Major Irvin, the aged Meriwether County justice of the peace, who Mrs. Matthews claimed had signed the warrant authorizing the transfer of Turner from the Carrollton jail to the Meriwether County jail during the early-morning hours of April 19.

Questioned by Solicitor Wyatt about his visual disability, Major Irvin said: "Yes, sir. I do have a disability. My eyes are atrophied." In explaining this, he said he was unable to read and had to depend upon someone else to tell him what he was signing.

"You have no way of knowing what you are signing unless you are told?"

"That's true," the old man admitted.

Solicitor Wyatt dismissed the witness and called Charles Hixon, an attendant at a service station in Greenville. On Friday, April 23, the day of Wallace's and Sivell's arrest, Herring Sivell had brought his green 1947 Ford to the service station to be cleaned. The floor mat, door panels, and rear seat cover were heavily stained with blood.

"What instructions were you given?" Solicitor Wyatt asked Hixon.

"Mr. Sivell said he wanted his car cleaned out good, 'cause he had to go to Newnan that morning."

"So he brought it to a *public* service station to have it done?" The solicitor's tone was an indictment of Sivell's arrogance.

"Yes, sir."

The last witness before the law enforcement officers would begin to testify was old Mr. Turner. Weak and still trembling, he took the oath and identified the photograph shown him as that of his son William.

"Did you know, Mr. Turner, that William was using his brother's name?"

"No, sir, I didn't."

"Did you know he had stolen his brother's Four-F card?"

Mr. Turner, an anguished father who knew that his boy had gone bad, defended him as best he could. "No, sir, I didn't rightly know he took it. William trained good in the army. They even give him a medal for expert marksman."

230

"Why did he take his brother's Four-F draft card?"

"I don't know," Mr. Turner said, shaking his head. "William come home from the army one day and left the next. After that, Wilson . . . that's my son whose mind ain't good . . . couldn't find his Four-F card no more. We couldn't figure what went with it, but we never no time figured William took it."

"This caused a name mix-up," Solicitor Wyatt said, "and it was reported that Wilson Turner had been killed."

"Yes, sir, but that wasn't right. William is the one what's dead. Wilson's here with me, standing right yonder." Mr. Turner pointed a gnarled old finger toward the witness-room door where Wilson stood listening.

When the attention of the courtroom was directed toward him, Wilson self-consciously dropped his eyes and blushed, understanding only that he had been singled out.

"That will be all for this witness," Solicitor Wyatt told Judge Boykin.

Seeing his father's feeble efforts to get down from the witness chair, Wilson came over, put his arm around his father's shoulders, and led the rickety old man away.

The last of the disclosures by the State's witnesses had been made. The prosecution was now ready to verify their testimony with material evidence collected by the law enforcement officers for State exhibits.

"The State calls Sheriff A. Lamar Potts to the stand," Solicitor Wyatt said.

Responding to questions in a calm, even voice, Sheriff Potts described the pit where the burning had taken place. Henson objected to everything, including designating it as "the pit" instead of "a pit."

When Luther Wyatt handed Sheriff Potts the box of bone chips and asked about the contents, the spectators strained forward to see. "This box," Sheriff Potts said, "contains bone chips that we found at the pit."

A muted murmur rose from the courtroom and died with Judge Boykin's threatening look.

Item by item, Solicitor Wyatt went down the list of things used to conceal and destroy Turner's body. Each time he said: "I hand you this . . ." Sheriff Potts identified the item and told where it was found.

"Who directed you to the pit, Sheriff Potts?"

"Robert Lee Gates and Albert Brooks led us down there."

Pete Bedenbaugh, confidently swinging his long arms, next took the stand and identified the bloodstained pole that had been used to transport Turner's body from the well.

"Who directed you to the well?" Solicitor Wyatt asked.

"We followed directions given us by Robert Lee Gates."

"What did you do with the items that were found there?"

"Turned them over to Sheriff Potts."

At eleven forty-five, Judge Boykin recessed court for lunch. Pierre Howard, attorney for Herring Sivell and Henry Mobley, had spent the last three days in the courtroom, observing the conduct of the trial. Deeply concerned by the direction it had taken, he went during the noon recess to see his clients in the Coweta County jail.

"Henry, I want you and Herring to give serious thought to entering a consent plea of guilty," he told them.

"I ain't done nuthin' but drive a car," Henry Mobley said, "and I ain't goin' to prison for that!"

"Me, either," Sivell said.

"That jury up there at the courthouse is in no mood for lies or fancy footwork," Howard warned. "They aim to see that justice is done. You can feel it in the air. The jury you get won't be any different."

"Nuthin' doin'," Mobley said. "I'm goin' to trial and come clean."

"Not a chance," Howard replied. "I've never seen a better-prepared case. The chain of evidence is solid and overwhelming. The best I can do is save your lives with a consent plea of guilty."

Mobley rubbed the cuff of hair on the back of his almost bald head. "No, sir! Not me."

"Me, either," Sivell added.

Pierre Howard shrugged his shoulders and got up to leave. "Think it over."

When court reconvened, J.H. described the discovery of the well and its contents. Hanging his battered straw hat on the arm of the witness chair and leaning forward with his elbows on his knees, in an attitude as informal as during an office conversation, J.H. told the silent courtroom:

"In a pine thicket, twenty or thirty yards from the well where the body had been concealed, we found the stump and treetop from which the pine pole was cut. Inside the well we found a fifty-pound, bloodstained rock. Beneath it, erupted brains and a mass of coagulated blood."

"Mr. Potts," Solicitor Wyatt asked, "did you personally go down in the well and retrieve these items?"

J.H. smiled self-consciously. Without explaining that he was too fat

232

to fit in the well, he replied: "No, sir, I took custody of them when they were brought out."

"Who went down in the well to get them?"

"Sergeant J. C. Otwell, Georgia State Patrol."

Called to the stand, Otwell explained how he had been let down in the well on a rope held by J.H. and Pete Bedenbaugh. After identifying the rocks, brains, and blood, he added: "I also found a letter written on three cigarette papers."

"Whose name was signed to the letter?"

"Wilson Turner."

In a courtroom of spectators already appalled by three days of astonishing testimony and evidence, the letter came as a stunning surprise, ending the testimony of the investigating officers.

It now remained for Dr. Herman Jones to confirm his findings on the items tested in the Crime Lab. Qualifying on the stand as an expert in chemistry and biochemistry with twenty-four years' experience, Dr. Jones, speaking in a calm, clinical voice, began with Wallace's bloodstained shirt and pants.

Henson objected. "It has not been established that these garments belong to Mr. Wallace."

Interrupting his direct examination, Solicitor Wyatt asked Dr. Jones to step aside. "I recall Sheriff Lamar Potts to the stand."

Asked to identify the shirt and pants, Sheriff Potts explained that they had been found in the laundry hamper in Wallace's house on the day of his arrest. Confronted with the two bloodstained items, Wallace had admitted that the clothing was his. The bloodstains, Wallace said, had come from scratches on his hand received while riding his horse in the pasture.

"To establish the extent of his wounds at that time," Sheriff Potts reported, "a photograph was taken."

Picking up the picture that showed the three slight briar scratches across Wallace's hand, Solicitor Wyatt said: "I submit this photograph, marked State Exhibit Number Twenty-five, in evidence."

When Dr. Jones returned to the stand, he identified the items offered in evidence, explaining his laboratory conclusions. The door panels and floor mats from Herring Sivell's and Henry Mobley's cars, he said, "had apparently been washed or cleaned because the blood was diffused, not visible to the naked eye, and showed up only with the aid of fluorescent light."

In verifying the identity of the ax used to cut the pine pole on which Turner's body was carried, Dr. Jones explained: "The cutting edge of each ax has distinctive gaps and grooves that leave marks as easily distinguished under the comparative microscope as bullets fired from a specific gun."

Test samples from the treetop and tree stump brought to him by Sheriff Potts had been cut with the ax. Under the comparative microscope, the grooves made by the ax in cutting the pole matched the grooves made by cutting the test samples. The same was true of the knife used to cut the branches that covered the body.

As he continued his testimony on the mound of evidence piled in front of him, Dr. Jones pointed out the fifty-pound rock found by Otwell at the bottom of the well. "Microscopic examination of this rock showed one side to be imbedded with brain tissue and blood. Intermingled with the brain tissue and blood was a black hair."

The jury stirred restlessly at this statement, remembering that the photograph used at the beginning of the trial to identify William Turner showed that the young man had black hair.

Handing Dr. Jones the bucket containing the coagulated blood, Solicitor Wyatt asked him for an explanation of his findings.

"Analysis showed only that this was blood. We could not determine if it was human blood because it had become putrefied, decomposed, and had lost its normal protein nature."

"Was this also true of the brains found in the well?"

"Yes, the same was true of the brains."

"Could you tell whether or not they were human brains?"

"Chemically, no. Judging by the size and quantity of the brains, we know it's too much of a fragment to have been the brain of an animal. Our conclusion, therefore, is that the large amount of brains brought from the well was the brains of a human being."

Picking up the small box of bone fragments, Solicitor Wyatt said: "Dr. Jones, I now hand you Exhibit Number Three and ask you to tell the Court what it is and what your findings were."

Dr. Jones took the exhibit and placed it in the palm of his hand. "This box contains bone fragments mixed with charcoal. In the laboratory, chemical analysis showed that the chips in this box have the qualitative amount of calcium, phosphorus, and magnesium in the same ratio as that found in human bones. Our conclusion, therefore, is that these are human bones."

A spectator in the balcony, leaning over the rail to get a better look, lost his footing and accidentally dropped the Coke bottle he was holding, barely missing an elderly woman seated in the courtroom below. Judge Boykin immediately stopped the testimony and instructed the bailiffs to see that no more bottles were brought into the courtroom.

Returning again to the testimony, Luther Wyatt said: "This concludes our examination of this witness."

Judge Boykin nodded and turned to Al Henson. "Any questions from the defense?"

Fred New, a hollow-eyed attorney from Hamilton, Georgia, was introduced by Henson as added counsel to cross-examine Dr. Jones. "Mr. New is a technical expert along the same line as Dr. Jones," he explained.

Fred New sought to establish his expertise in much the same manner as Henson, but he had not Henson's energy. Large and lethargic, with multiple bags under empty eyes, he had a jaded, dissipated look. His verbal thrusts, intended to have a cutting edge, were inept and impotent.

"Dr. Jones, you say you received your medical degree from Vanderbilt University. Did you have occasion to study the circulation of blood in the human body?"

"From beginning to end," Dr. Jones replied coldly.

"How much blood is there in an average human body?"

"Five quarts."

"Ten pints," Fred New corrected, implying the answer was wrong.

The spectators exchanged glances and shifted in their seats as Fred New continued his elementary examination for more than half an hour. Finally, he asked: "When does the circulation of the blood cease?"

"The moment the heart stops beating," Dr. Jones replied.

"How long after death does the normal corpse stop bleeding?"

"So variable, it would be hazardous to say."

Fred New then proposed that had William Turner received a fatal blow at Sunset Tourist Camp, the automobile floor mats would have been soaked with blood.

"I pointed out earlier," Dr. Jones reminded him, "that the mats had been washed. There is no way to determine the amount of blood that might have been there originally."

Fred New continued to haggle until finally, wearied by his own words and unable to extract the answers he wanted, he dismissed Dr. Jones.

George Cornett, assistant to Dr. Jones, concluded the testimony for the State by explaining the positive and negative casts he made of the tire tracks found at the edge of the woods near the pit and of the matching tracks made from Mozart Strickland's pickup truck.

Solicitor Wyatt introduced the last of the State's evidence by recalling Sheriff Potts to the stand to identify the pearl-handled pistol taken from the glove compartment of Herring Sivell's car on the day of his arrest, and a blackjack found in Henry Mobley's car.

"Is there anything further for the State?" Judge Boykin asked.

"We wish to tender in evidence State Exhibits One through Forty-three," Luther Wyatt replied.

"Any objections?"

Henson rose from his seat at the defense table, his face showing disdain. "There are forty-three sets of objections, and I want to urge them all."

"You have your chance right now," Judge Boykin told him.

The tedious task began. Luther Wyatt tendering the evidence, Henson objecting to each item as: "Immaterial, irrelevant, harmful, and prejudicial." When the process was done, Judge Boykin sustained Henson's objections only to the stump of the pine tree, the two milk cans, and the casts made by George Cornett.

"I don't think there is enough identification to be certain about these items," he said.

Henson argued that the note found by Otwell at the bottom of the well could not be certified as having been written by Turner. Although it bore Turner's signature, only a handwriting expert could certify that Turner himself had actually written it.

"What say you, Mr. Solicitor?" Judge Boykin asked.

"Give us a minute," Luther Wyatt said, going to the prosecution table to talk with Myer Goldberg. After a brief consultation, it was decided that with the preponderance of evidence tendered by the State, it was more important to maintain the momentum of the presentation than to ask for a handwriting expert, which would mean delay.

"Your Honor," Luther Wyatt said, "we don't insist on it."

"The note is withdrawn. Is that correct?"

"That is correct."

"What else now for the State?"

The long ordeal of witnesses, testimony, and presentation of evidence was over. In a solemn voice, Luther Wyatt announced: "The State rests."

"What says the defendant?" Judge Boykin asked.

Huddleston, who had been chosen to conduct the defense presentation, stood up and placed his glasses ceremoniously on the end of his nose. "We would like to recess, Your Honor. We have a large number of witnesses, and it is necessary at this time to confer with them."

Judge Boykin nodded his approval. "Court is adjourned until nine o'clock tomorrow morning."

236

Members of the press, seated in chairs across the room from the jury box, had chafed with impatience for the proceedings to be done. Judge Boykin had barely left the courtroom before they were swarming around the defense table, firing questions at Henson and Huddleston.

"What response will you have to the thirty-eight witnesses who testified against Mr. Wallace?" Celestine Sibley asked.

Henson smiled smugly. "We have forty witnesses."

"Will Mr. Wallace be one of them?" Hugh Park wanted to know.

Henson's eyes twinkled behind his glasses. "He will take the stand in his own defense."

"Will he tell what happened in Coweta?" Dave Bowers asked.

"No more questions, boys, no more questions," Henson said good-naturedly, waving them away. "Come back tomorrow and you'll hear the *truth* about what happened to William Turner."

Some of the spectators had crowded around the reporters and craned their necks to see what was going on. Overhearing Henson's words, they rushed down the steps and into the crowd on the courthouse lawn.

"Did you hear that! Did you hear that!" they cried. "*Tomorrow,* John Wallace is going to tell what *really* happened."

Chapter Twenty-two

John Wallace arrived at the courthouse Thursday morning, radiating self-assurance. With his white Stetson hat set at a rakish angle and a thick roll of yellow legal sheets in his back pocket, he waved and called to friends in the crowd, exhibiting the same confidence he had shown the morning the trial began.

Anyone with access to any conveyance at all—car, truck, horse, or mule-drawn wagon—was in town that morning to hear Wallace's explanation of what "really" happened to Turner. Enterprising schoolboys had come at dawn, filled all available places, and before court began, auctioned them off to the highest bidder. The better seats downstairs sold for five dollars each, those in the balcony, for two.

Learning of this, Judge Boykin was filled with judicial rage. His first order of business was to instruct the bailiffs that if they came upon any further evidence of such transactions, they were to take custody of both the seller and the purchaser and hold them until court adjourned: "I will take care of them then."

The trial began with Wallace's fourth defense counsel, Fred New, calling Henry Mobley to the stand. Herring Sivell, he said, would follow.

Pierre Howard, attorney for both Mobley and Sivell, stood up. "Mr. Mobley and Mr. Sivell decline to testify in this case, since any evidence they give might tend to incriminate them."

The announcement hit the courtroom like an exploding shell. Wallace, seated at the defense table, was visibly stunned. Leaning forward, he hurriedly conferred with his three attorneys. Fred New bent over and listened intently, then told the judge, "We wish to ask the witness himself."

238

"Mr. Mobley and Mr. Sivell have employed me to advise them, and they will follow my advice," Pierre Howard said.

"We won't know that until we ask the witness himself," New insisted.

The bailiff brought Henry Mobley to the stand, and Judge Boykin advised him of his rights under the Fifth Amendment. "Now, Mr. Mobley, what do you wish to do in this case?"

Henry Mobley, pale and subdued, did not even glance in John Wallace's direction. "I refuse to testify."

When Mobley was led away, Judge Boykin asked: "Do you want to call Mr. Sivell?"

This time, Huddleston got up and answered: "If the same applies to Mr. Sivell, it might be just as well to let Mr. Howard so state in his place."

"Mr. Sivell takes the same attitude in this matter and does not wish to testify," Pierre Howard said.

Huddleston asked for and received a short recess. While Wallace's defense counsel conferred furiously, the courtroom buzzed over this latest development. If Wallace's two best friends refused to testify, what about the rest of the forty witnesses that Henson said yesterday were ready to come forward in Wallace's behalf?

Before the speculation could go any further, court resumed and Wallace himself took the stand for an unsworn statement with Huddleston advising him: "Mr. Wallace, you are not under oath. You are permitted to make any statement to the jury in your behalf that you wish to make. I will not ask you any questions, nor will the solicitor here ask you any questions. Take your time and make whatever statement you wish."

Spectators who had been sitting back as they listened to the proceedings were now on the edge of their seats. Members of the press, their pencils poised, were ready to take down Wallace's every word.

Relaxed and confident again, Wallace sat back in the witness chair and looked benignly over the courtroom until he saw Mayhayley Lancaster and her heavily veiled sister sitting in the balcony. Turning a grave face toward Judge Boykin, he began: "Thank you, Mr. Court and gentlemen of the jury. I am fully aware of the serious charge against me. I think in all fairness to myself that I should make some statement about the early part of my life."

From his back pocket, Wallace pulled out the thick roll of yellow legal sheets that he had worked on throughout the trial. He began by

239

telling the jury where he was born, where he went to school, when he served in the army, and how he became involved in the liquor traffic. He explained the circumstances of his two convictions, and the sentences he served in the Atlanta Penitentiary.

"I have in my possession a complete and unconditional pardon signed by the President of the United States," he said proudly. "That was twelve years ago. I have tried to make a good citizen. I have worked hard for what I have."

Following this, he outlined in exhausting detail how he had gone into the dairy business, where he had bought his cows, and how much he had paid for them. Members of the press were now jotting down only occasional notes. Finally, after more than an hour, he began telling of his first meeting with Turner in November 1945 when Turner came asking him for a job.

"I told Turner I didn't want to mix white people with my colored help on the farm. My experience had shown me that this promoted social equality and caused serious problems. Over my better judgment, I let him begin work because I was interested in helping any young man who wanted to get a start."

Turner proved to be a very efficient worker. By the fall of 1946, he had earned twelve hundred dollars as his share of the crops. Wallace advised him to save his money. Instead, Turner bought a car.

Remembering this, Wallace's eyes flashed angrily. "This automobile was really his undoing. The average salaried man or farm laborer who has to work for a living is not financially able to operate a car. It takes him away from his work."

Since Turner was a good worker, Wallace said, he allowed him to continue, and increased the acreage he sharecropped from the original fifteen acres of cotton and fifteen acres of corn to fifty acres of each. Then in March 1947, Wallace learned from Broughton Myhand's wife, whose uncle, Rob Carter, was a Troup County policeman, that Turner was under surveillance for making illegal liquor. Several days later, while out riding his horse in the pasture, Wallace said he came upon Agent C. E. Miller, who said he was looking for Turner.

"I was thoroughly distressed with Turner's behavior. I wanted him to leave before he created the opinion that *I* was involved in the liquor business. I asked my sheriff, Mr. Collier, wasn't there some way to make this man leave the county. Mr. Collier said he didn't know how it could be done."

Warming to the subject of Turner and his liquor making, Wallace's face reddened and he punctuated his statement with angry gestures as he told how Turner involved his Negro tenants. Returning from a trip

240

to Mexico in September 1946, Wallace learned that Turner had used his influence on Robert Lee Gates.

"He had taken this Negro's cow, his hogs, and fifty dollars which he had given him for making liquor, and bought this Negro a pickup truck which he had no need for. All the means in the world this Negro had for milk, butter, and meat was gone. The burden was on me to feed him. Besides, it gave the Negro a way to get away from his work. Also, to load up others and take them away from their work, too."

Wallace paused and asked for a glass of water. He had been talking now for nearly three hours and sweat was pouring off his bald head and hairless face.

"I told Turner: Go home and gather your crops. Stay away from my Negro tenants and cut out this liquor traffic. You're going to get ever' Negro I've got in the chain gang and me along with them!"

This, Wallace reported, made Turner very angry and he began hearing reports from all over the county that Turner was out gunning for him with a .45 pistol that he was carrying in the side pocket of his car.

The next day, on a train trip back from Atlanta, Wallace was taken off before he reached his station by Cecil Perkerson, a Meriwether County deputy, who escorted him to Sheriff Collier's waiting car. They had heard that Turner was going to shoot Wallace when he got off the train in Greenville.

Wallace's earlier attitude of arrogance and anger had now changed to perplexity and an appeal for understanding.

"I asked Mr. Collier, 'What am I to do?' Mr. Collier replied: 'Use whatever means necessary for your own protection.'"

The next day, when Wallace drove out to get the Sunday paper, he found Turner parked on the roadbed across the dam of his lake. Pulling alongside, Wallace saw that his uncle Mozart Strickland was there talking to Turner.

"I passed on," Wallace said, describing the scene to the jury, "but I admit to you gentlemen that I was afraid at that moment for my life. I didn't know but what Turner might shoot me in the back."

The jury's reaction was not responsive to Wallace's fearful claims. The jurors had a decidedly sour and skeptical look, for it was both incredible and insulting to be asked to believe that this powerful man had been in mortal fear of his frail tenant who at that moment had been talking to his uncle.

Sensing a loss of rapport, Wallace returned to his more productive tirade about his labor troubles, seeking to identify with the farmers on the jury. In October, during a noon rain, he said he had set out to look for Albert Brooks and Robert Lee Gates to do some inside work in the barn. "You gentlemen who are farmers know how disruptive a rain can be. You have your labor scattered all around the farm and you have to call them in to do a rainy day job."

The two Negroes could not be found. Robert Lee's wife said he had left in the truck—the one Turner had helped him buy.

"I was tired of this truck-riding up and down the road when they ought to be home working!" Wallace said, emphasizing his anger by smashing his fist down on the arm of the witness chair.

Determined to find his Negroes and put them back at their duties, Wallace followed the truck's tire tracks down to the woods and into the swamp. There he found Albert, Robert Lee, Tommy Windham, who was Turner's brother-in-law, and another Negro named Rube McGruder, operating two small stills and one very large one.

"I'm going to tell you gentlemen," Wallace said in a confidential tone, "that this still was as big as any I have ever seen . . . and I've seen some big ones. It was eight feet tall, eight feet wide, and had a fermenting capacity to produce two thousand gallons of liquor." Wallace sat back and took another sip from his glass of water. Letting the jury digest these facts, then feigning bewilderment, he continued, "I hardly knew what to do. What would happen if I were caught at a still in operation?

"I have lived in my county for thirty-five years, and I have never been hailed into county court on any charge. I am proud of that. I have never been sued or prosecuted on any charge in my county. The only time I have ever been in county court was to help someone else," Wallace said, assuming the role of a good citizen. He paused. He was a powerful and persuasive man, satisfied and certain that he could manipulate the jury's judgment by utilizing a wide range of emotions . . . anger, fear, pride, and repentance. . . .

Like a remorseful sinner, he averted his hooded eyes and told the jury: "I'm ashamed of the conduct that sent me to the penitentiary. I wish I had never seen a drop of liquor. It was the beginning and the end of the saddest part of my life. I have tried hard to live down that mistake.

"I tried to steer Wilson Turner on the straight and narrow so that he would not experience these same mistakes. He ignored what I said and continued to endanger me with his liquor making. I could not understand why the Federal officers did not stop him. I hardly knew how to proceed."

That afternoon, Wallace said, he went to Chipley to see Roy Askew, the man who had been his guardian during the probationary period of his two liquor sentences and the cashier of his bank. "My freedom is at stake," Wallace told him.

"Notify the proper authorities at once," Roy Askew advised.

Leaving Askew's office, Wallace drove to Greenville to his attorney, Gus Huddleston, and requested that he call the Alcohol Tax Unit in Atlanta. That night, Federal Agent Earl Lucas and State Agent Pete Bedenbaugh arrived. Nothing was done.

Recalling this, Wallace's eyes flamed with anger. He abandoned his calculated account and began to bog down in accusations against the Federal officers. Gus Huddleston rose to interrupt his tirade. "If Your Honor please, the defendant is tired. If we could take the noon recess at this time, we will allow him to resume the stand after lunch without any further interruptions."

Judge Boykin agreed and the recess was called. Not one spectator got up to leave for fear of losing his place. John Wallace had talked all morning long. He had outlined in interminable detail everything that had preceded Turner's death, but he still had not told what had happened, and those with seats aimed to stay there until he did.

At the defense table, Huddleston and Henson hung over Wallace and conferred with an intensity that could be seen but not heard. The only audible words concerned Wallace's complaint about Mayhayley Lancaster and her black-garbed sister.

"Gus, I want you to get that goddamn witch and her spook sister out of here."

"John, you know we can't do that," Huddleston said patiently.

"I tell you I want her *out!*" Wallace said, slamming his fist on the table between them. "Every time I look up, I see Mayhayley's glass eye glaring at me . . . she's trying to cast a spell."

"For God's sake!" Henson snapped indignantly. "Stop talking superstition and let's get to the issue at hand."

"This *is* the issue at hand."

"The issue at hand," Henson reminded him coldly, "is if you don't get off that witness stand, you're going to hang yourself with your own words."

When court reconvened after lunch, Wallace chose to ignore Henson's warning. To Huddleston's dismay, he resumed his attack on the officers who had refused to remove Turner from his midst, who had ignored his information, and had not captured Turner or destroyed the still.

"Utterly hopeless," is how Wallace described his situation. He himself was not legally authorized to do anything about it and Sheriff Collier was too ill to take the necessary action. In the meantime,

Turner just drove up and down the road. He refused to harvest his corn crop and let it lie rotting in the field. Wallace took his own labor over to do the harvest. When he offered to buy Turner's share, Turner refused. Arranging to furnish the money, Wallace had Broughton Myhand buy Turner's corn crop, thereby salvaging the senseless waste.

In November 1947, Turner moved away. Wallace said he could not figure out why . . . Turner just took his family and left. He heard no more about Turner until March 1948, when the spring chores began on his two-thousand-acre farm. He and his hired hands rounded up the seventy-five head of cattle that had been turned out for winter grazing on honeysuckle vines and found he was twenty head short.

In April, he discovered that one of his purebred Guernseys was missing. Four days later, his dairyman reported that two more purebreds had been taken from the lot. This amounted to a total of three thousand dollars in all . . . a rate that would soon bankrupt him.

As he and his hired hands searched the woods and pastures for the missing cows, they discovered a man's footprint along the fence . . . a small footprint. Turner, of course, was a small man. People suggested that Turner had taken the cows.

On Monday, April 12, when the cows had not been found, Wallace called Sheriff Collier and asked that all law enforcement agencies be notified. Sivell, Mobley, Myhand, Tom Strickland, and Sheriff Collier all went in different directions to cover cattle sales barns all over the state.

In long and tedious detail, Wallace described Threadgill's finding the cow in Carrollton on Wednesday, April 14, Turner's arrest and transfer to the Meriwether County jail . . . "with the full authority of the law."

On Monday, April 19, he went on, Sheriff Collier called Solicitor Wyatt and explained Turner's case. Forming his opinion from Collier's description, Wyatt said the case was weak. Collier told Wallace that there was nothing to do but turn Turner loose. "I told Mr. Collier," Wallace said imperiously, "I would be up there at the jail the next morning to decide what to do about Turner."

As he finally approached the day of the murder, the spectators, bored by hours of unnecessary detail, roused themselves and began to listen.

"I gathered some friends who were interested in helping me locate the rest of my cows: my cousin and kinsman Tom Strickland, my

244

friend Henry Mobley, and Herring Sivell, who was under some obligation to me. Broughton Myhand was supposed to go, too, but failed to show up. We four men drove two cars to Greenville on Tuesday morning."

Wallace stopped, then turned an earnest face to the jury. "I am not going to mislead you. I had a shotgun in that car. I didn't take that gun along to kill anybody with. I didn't leave home with murder in my heart. I am an average churchgoing man. I go to Sunday school and church. I love my God just like you love your God. I am no cold-blooded headhunter. I have never wanted to harm any man."

He looked at the twelve jurymen, trying to assess the effect he was having on them, unaware that his effort was coming across as theatrics. Recognizing the fact that he had spent a long time on the stand, he said: "I have gone into quite a few details. They might not seem so essential to someone else, but they are essential to me. It is my statement and it is the truth."

Returning to his narrative, he said: "When we four men got to Greenville, I was not excited. I was not out manhunting. I meant to talk to Turner, but I didn't mean to talk to him in jail. I meant to talk to him somewhere else.

"It is not the first time that a man was ever taken out of jail and talked to. Sheriff Potts told me out of his own mouth that he took Herring Sivell out of jail and back down to his home in Chipley for the purpose of obtaining a written confession in connection with this crime he has been charged with.

"Although I am not an officer of the law," he asserted, assured and arrogant now, "I have got the right of an officer of the law with a man guilty of a felony up until the time this man can be delivered to the proper authorities.

"When we reached Greenville, I told Mr. Sivell to park his car just above the Standard Oil filling station where the road turns off to the Meriwether County jail. Mr. Mobley, with Mr. Strickland, parked alongside the courthouse. Mr. Mobley commanded all the avenues of travel in Greenville."

Confirming earlier testimony, Wallace said: "Mr. Sivell and I had some business at the Production Credit Association. I saw Mr. Miller of the Alcohol Tax Unit there. I greeted him. When our business was finished, I went down to the jail. Sheriff Collier was having his noon meal. When I asked, 'What's become of Turner?' Sheriff Collier said: 'I turned him out this morning.' 'Where did he go?' 'I gave him a dollar for gas to put in his truck. He said he was going to LaGrange.'"

Wallace stopped. His face was red and sweating, showing the strain of the daylong testimony. "If you don't mind," he said hoarsely to Judge Boykin, "can we have a little recess?"

Judge Boykin agreed to ten minutes and asked the jury to leave the room.

It was four thirty in the afternoon, the time that court normally adjourned for the day. The spectators were exhausted, the jury was weary, the whole courtroom was blanketed by the heat. The testimony had lasted for six and one-half interminable hours, and Wallace had not yet explained how Turner had died.

Judge Boykin called Henson and Huddleston before the bench for consultation. "We can't do a thing with him," Henson admitted, "he just keeps on talking."

During a brief break at two thirty, they had begged Wallace to cease his marathon disclosures. "These endless details are damaging your case," Henson had told him. "You're telling them things that would better be left unsaid."

"What are you talking about?" Wallace scoffed. "Fred New and I have been working on this speech all week."

Fred New laced his hands together and looked down at the floor.

When the testimony resumed, the courtroom was dismayed to hear Wallace still telling of his conversation with Collier.

"Sheriff Collier was having his dinner when I went in, and he asked me to have a bite to eat with him. I will tell you in detail, if I may. The reason I remember so well is because they had string beans on the table. I don't like string beans. I had some mashed potatoes, some iced tea, some sliced peaches, and a small piece of cake.

"I did not mention to the sheriff that I had come there to talk to Turner, I just asked him where he was. I left the jail, walking back to where Mr. Sivell had parked his car. I glanced down the street past the service station and saw Turner in his truck headed toward Newnan. I got in Sivell's car and we left in pursuit. My reason for that was that I wanted to talk to Turner about this cattle-theft business. I meant to put him back in jail. I had never consented for Sheriff Collier to turn him out.

"Turner was driving as fast as his truck could run. We did not overtake him until we reached this Sunset Tourist Camp. The testimony that has been given by the witnesses here about entering Sunset . . . I admit that much of it is true. I got out in pursuit of Turner with a shotgun in one hand and my other hand empty. I caught hold of him as he reached the cafe door."

246

Wallace stopped. A deathly quiet settled over the courtroom. He leaned forward in his chair, his eyes on the jury. "Now, gentlemen, I ask you in all earnestness to follow me from this minute on, especially."

As Wallace spoke these words, the clock in the courthouse dome began to strike five. Wallace waited for the tolling to end. The vibration from the sound, directly overhead, rumbled through the courtroom, heightening the suspense of the spectators and reminding the members of the press to resume their note taking.

"I never willfully struck Turner with that gun at that time. I never struck him with anything. I shoved him toward the car. When I reached the car, I attempted to push him in. He caught hold of the car with both hands, and with his foot on the fender, he pushed back. In the shoving, the shotgun struck his ear and broke the skin. That place did bleed, but not profusely.

"When I pushed Turner in the car, the barrel of the gun struck the top of the car and fired. Now, you heard in this courtroom that I took that gun in both hands and struck him with my full force. That testimony against me won't bear out. If I had turned loose my hold on Turner, he would have been free. He would have escaped.

"You have heard the testimony of this lady who witnessed what was happening. I have the greatest respect for any lady, and I don't want to give the lie to what she said, but I do say she is mistaken. She didn't see what she told you she saw, because it did not happen.

"Mr. Smith swore against me, too. He said I struck Turner with all my might. Well, now," Wallace threw up his hands. "I don't say the man lied. I'm not going to get up here and use a lot of vicious language in my defense. I'm not mad with anybody. I was only trying to apprehend the man who had stolen my cattle and have him brought before the proper authorities and dealt with as a man guilty of the crime he had committed. Now, gentlemen, *I* am stating the facts . . . not half of them, but *all* of them.

"We got Turner in the car. I got in the car with him. I never struck him a blow with any instrument in that car as Mr. Smith swore to you I did. I held my hand over his mouth to stop his hollering. I didn't do it with any effort to injure the man. I placed my hand over his mouth to stop the alarm that he was making. There is nothing unnatural about that. I did the natural thing that any man would have done. I was holding him down in this car with my left hand, and I held my right hand over his mouth."

At the defense table, Wallace's attorneys wore expressions of

247

sustained pain. Kept silent by the rule of law that prevents stopping or advising a defendant making an unsworn statement, they could only endure the disastrous testimony.

"When we drove away from Sunset Tourist Camp," Wallace continued, "Turner was as much alive as you and I are at this minute. He had no deadly injury. *That is a fact!* Just as much as anything else I have told you in this statement is a fact. I have not tried to cover up anything. I am going to tell you gentlemen the *truth* about how the man lost his life.

"Turner never tried to holler anymore after we drove off. I just held him in the foot of the car. About a mile from Sunset, we met Mr. Mobley and Mr. Strickland headed toward Newnan. They had followed us from Greenville as I had instructed them to do. Mr. Sivell pulled his car off onto a sideroad, and Mr. Mobley turned in, too. Here, we discovered Mr. Sivell had a flat tire.

"Of course, at that minute I was excited," Wallace admitted, his words coming faster and his hands beginning to tremble slightly. "I am not an iron man. I had been under a terrible strain for many days and nights out in the Carrollton pasture, watching my cows. I had had no sleep. Naturally, I knew that there was going to be some investigation of this incident that had happened up there at Sunset Tourist Camp.

"Turner and I got in the car with Mr. Mobley and Mr. Strickland, leaving Sivell there to fix his flat tire. We turned off the paved highway. I was sitting in the back seat of Mobley's car. Turner was offering no resistance. He was sitting, at my direction, in the foot of the car . . . just as any man would sit in the foot of any automobile. He didn't complain about his ear. He was talking. He remarked about the poor fitting of the doors in the new automobiles . . . how the dust came in. He had no tobacco and asked me for a cigarette. I gave it to him and he lighted it under his own power."

Wallace edged forward in his seat, satisfied with his delivery and the courtroom's rapt attention. He adhered to the thesis that, given enough details, anything could be made to sound reasonable and true.

"I took Turner back to the scene where I had first lost the cows in my herd . . . the same as Sheriff Potts took his man Sivell back to the location where Tom Strickland, indicted along with me on this charge, had told him this happened. Sheriff Potts had a prisoner and he wanted a confession from him. My reason for taking Turner down there was the same . . . to try to gain a confession from him, to make him tell me where my cattle were. I had not planned at that time to harm this man. I had no premeditated determination to take this

248

man's life." As proof, he added: "I have never even killed a quail in my life. I am not what you call a hunter.

"Now, gentlemen, I have got a very helpless feeling." Wallace paused to appeal for understanding. "I need some backing up on this statement I am making to you. My only hope in the world is resting on whether or not you believe this statement I am making without oath. The testimony I so badly need in my defense has been denied me. I don't know why those boys, indicted along with me in this case, are not here to testify. They promised me they would come here and tell the truth. Now I have got to do it alone, with nobody to help me. I don't see why the law is not fixed where a man can be made to tell what he knows."

Wallace shook his head, saddened by such a melancholy state of affairs. "I have got nobody to call in here to substantiate these statements I have made to you. Before any one of you gentlemen were qualified for this jury," he reminded them, "*I* passed on you . . . *every one of you* . . . out of my own heart, trusting that you were good men, law-abiding men, fair men, who could give me a fair trial up here.

"I know this is a hard case. I am charged with the worst crime a man can be charged with, but what I am telling you is the truth . . . the whole truth. If this is not the truth, then nothing I have told you is the truth."

Wallace looked once more at each juryman in turn. Then, reassured by the words he had spoken, he returned to his narrative.

"Mobley drove to a certain location in the woods, where Strickland, Turner, and I got out. I told Mobley to go on home. As I got out of his car, I took a shotgun. I don't know whose shotgun it was. It was not the same shotgun that I had at the tourist camp. We walked along the pasture where I had had my cows during the winter. We came upon an old well. Strickland, Turner, and I stopped there. Turner looked down in the well. I did *not* say: 'I am going to throw you in the well.' I didn't tell Turner anything.

"For some reason"—Wallace shrugged, unable to pinpoint a cause—"Turner said to me, 'Mr. John, put me in that well and let me stay two or three hours, then I will move back down here and help you find your cows.'

"That was this man Turner's statements and request to me. I don't know why he made that request, but that is what he said. Strickland was standing by the well, facing Turner. I walked within about five feet of Turner . . . for what reason, I don't know. Just as I reached this point, I heard somebody to my right holler.

"I turned my head in the direction of the noise. As I did so, I transferred this shotgun that I was holding in my right hand to the bend of my left arm. I don't know why I did this, I just did. As I turned toward the noise, the gun fired. When I looked back, Turner was lying full-length on the ground with the top of his scalp torn off."

The jury was tight-lipped and taut. Judge Boykin bent forward. The spectators sat motionless, transfixed by this dark side of the human soul.

"It was horrible," Wallace said, managing to look appropriately shocked and bewildered. "Tom Strickland was looking at Turner when this accident happened. He is just as innocent of this crime as I am. He could have come up here and made this statement. I needed this man's testimony. I need it now. I needed all these boys' testimony.

"This man Sivell had no more to do with Turner's death than any of you. Mr. Mobley is just as innocent as any of you. I am just as innocent as any of you. I did not willfully take this man's life. I had no control of that gun."

Dismissing all the incongruities, Wallace said: "Now, gentlemen, I have told you all I know about this case. This is the end of it, so far as I know. When I looked at this man on the ground . . . the horrible sight of him with his scalp blown off . . . I had lost so much sleep during the time leading up to this that I don't remember anything of what happened for several days after that. I don't remember his being put in the well, I don't remember what happened to the gun. I don't remember what became of his body . . . I just don't remember."

Wallace's incredible conclusion hung like motionless smoke over the courtroom. Of all the explanations he could have given, the least expected was sudden loss of memory, for until now, his recall had been total.

Judge Boykin straightened up, the jury stirred restlessly, and the spectators sat back in their seats. Wallace, expecting acceptance because he said it was so, continued on his unalterable course.

"I have prayed with my God over this thing," he said, affecting humility. "I have done no crime. The most terrible accident has happened. I am sorry about it. I am fifty-two years old. At best, I won't live so many more years." His eyes grew sad as he looked over the courtroom. "I have got nobody down there with my family, or with my business set up the way it is. Everything I have will be lost. I have no way for my wife to be supported, and at this particular time, she is in poor health."

In a final appeal to the jury, he said: "Let me go back to my family and my home. I asked God to guide me through the presentation of this statement in telling you the truth. Go in there and commune with my God and find out the truth of this thing." As though his request had already been granted, he nodded an acknowledgment to the jury. "I thank you."

He started to leave the witness stand, but Huddleston sprang forward to stop him. Wallace had spoken to the jury for seven and one-half hours. The statement was the longest ever on record in the Coweta Circuit, and yet he had failed to tell the jury the most important part . . . where the accident had happened.

Huddleston's voice held restrained desperation. "May I state what county?"

Judge Boykin scowled down at Huddleston. "You *know* you can't tell him. You *know* the rule on unsworn statements. You don't tell him anything."

Henson had now joined Huddleston before the bench. "We want to direct the statement and ask if he wants to make that statement."

"No," Judge Boykin replied firmly.

Realizing that in his effort to overwhelm the jury he had omitted the pivotal point of the trial, Wallace quickly seized the opportunity. "May I continue?" he asked Judge Boykin.

"If you have any further statement, you may make that, but there will be no suggestion from counsel."

Wallace drew in a deep breath, filling his bearlike chest, his face radiating triumph. "The pasture and well where this accident happened are in Meriwether County."

It was now ten minutes before six o'clock in the evening. Judge Boykin struck his gavel and announced: "Court is adjourned until tomorrow morning at nine o'clock."

Wallace had narrowly averted a disastrous omission. As he stepped down from the witness chair, he strode victoriously back to the defense table. Flushed with success and rubbing his hands together, he waited . . . ready to receive the accolades he felt he deserved for his daylong statement on the stand. From the four attorneys seated at the table there was not a glance, not a word.

"*Well* . . ." Wallace demanded. "What do you think . . . about the whole thing?"

Henson's small, tight mouth was drawn. Huddleston forlornly passed his hand over his creased forehead. Fred New sat in slack-jawed apathy. Only Wallace's young cousin, Kiser Whatley, spoke up.

"John, you just played hell."

The Verdict

Chapter Twenty-three

Not one witness testified in John Wallace's behalf. When trial resumed Friday morning, Judge Boykin asked if there was anything further for the defense. Wearily, Huddleston rose. "We rest, Your Honor."

Solicitor Wyatt recalled six witnesses to rebut Wallace's seven-and-one-half-hour statement: Dr. Herman Jones, Albert Brooks, Robert Lee Gates, Sheriff Potts, J.H., and Earl Lucas.

After a noon recess, closing arguments began, with both Huddleston and Henson stating flatly that John Wallace had spoken the truth. In conclusion, Huddleston said: "The jury should find it was accidental death because that was what it was."

Henson, rising to more impassioned heights, made what he called a "mother-home-and-heaven" speech, ending it by saying: "If John Wallace is made to pay the death penalty, it would be like the crucifixion of Christ!"

The jury stirred indignantly. Even making allowances for courtroom eloquence, this was blasphemy.

Myer Goldberg, the first to speak in the State's closing arguments, rose in righteous indignation.

"John Wallace's statement on what occurred is the most incredible I have ever heard," he told the jury. "He is a persuasive, brilliant man with a two-sided personality . . . capable of warmhearted charity and cold-blooded killing. When he is aroused, his brilliance obviously deserts him, for on April the twentieth, 1948, he *willfully, feloniously, and with malice aforethought* did kill and murder William Turner."

Goldberg leaned with one hand on the jury rail. "He would have us believe," he said, "that nothing these thirty-eight witnesses have said is so. Nor should we believe the forty-three pieces of corroborating

255

evidence. *Instead*"—his flashing eyes encompassed the jurors—"*instead,* he asks us to believe the incredible story of shooting Turner accidentally near a well in Meriwether County.

"*Meriwether County!*" He let the words hang in the air. "You know, of course, why he insists that death came in Meriwether County. If he could persuade you to believe Meriwether County, he could walk away from this murder charge free and clear. But John Wallace did *not* kill Turner in Meriwether County. He ran Turner down and killed him in *Coweta County,* violating the laws of this state and the good order and peace of this county."

Swinging around, Myer Goldberg walked across the courtroom to face Wallace, sitting with his attorneys. "Let me say to you, Mr. Wallace," he admonished, shaking his finger in Wallace's face, "and to every other defendant in this case . . . and to every criminal in the nation . . . keep your murder and devilment out of Coweta County!"

Wallace gave him a cold stare, unwrapped a stick of chewing gum, and snapped it into his mouth. With a sweep of his hand, Myer Goldberg presented Wallace's insolent reaction to the courtroom.

"In the name of justice," Goldberg said, raising his clenched fist, "I ask you, gentlemen of the jury, to convict this man for the unspeakable crime he has committed. *And,* in the public interest, do *not* recommend mercy!"

Compared to Goldberg's fiery delivery, Solicitor Wyatt's was grave and solemn. In conclusion, he said: "Gentlemen of the jury, you have seen and heard the evidence presented in this case. The State asks that you reach a verdict of truth."

When the closing arguments were finished, Judge Boykin charged the jury for twenty-five minutes. "Before you consider the guilt or innocence of the defendant," he told them, "you should first determine venue. All criminal cases must be tried in the county in which they are committed. If you are not convinced, beyond a reasonable doubt, that the mortal blow was struck in Coweta County, as alleged in the indictment, *go no further.* Acquit the defendant on trial.

"If you find, from the evidence, that William, alias Wilson, Turner suffered a mortal blow in Coweta at the hands of the defendant, John Wallace, that ultimately resulted in death, it would not be material whether he *died* in Coweta or elsewhere. Venue is established where the mortal blow is struck.

"John Wallace enters upon trial with the legal presumption of innocence in his favor," he reminded the jury. "That presumption goes with him throughout the trial until the State has proved him guilty beyond a reasonable doubt. *The burden is upon the State to prove each and every material allegation:* that John Wallace is guilty of the offense of murder on the twentieth day of April 1948, in Coweta County, that he then and there unlawfully, willfully, feloniously, and with malice aforethought did kill and murder William, alias Wilson, Turner with a pump shotgun.

"There can be no murder without malice, either expressed or implied. Express malice is the deliberate intention unlawfully to take away the life of a fellow creature, manifested by circumstances capable of proof. Malice shall be implied where no considerable provocation appears and where all of the circumstances of the killing shall show an abandoned and malignant heart.

"When homicide is shown to have been committed with a deadly weapon, the law presumes it to be malice until the contrary appears from circumstances of alleviation, justification, or excuse. Malice may be rebutted by the defendant, and the *burden is upon the defendant, John Wallace, to make out such circumstances to the reasonable satisfaction of the jury.*"

Judge Boykin then told the jury that one of three possible verdicts could be rendered. Guilty of murder, which carried the penalty of electrocution, guilty with a recommendation for mercy, which would mean life imprisonment, or not guilty, in which case the defendant would be acquitted.

In weighing the evidence, he said, they could believe the sworn testimony of the witnesses or the unsworn statement by the defendant, giving it such weight as they saw fit.

"If you find that William, alias Wilson, Turner, came to his death from any cause other than that stated in the indictment, you should acquit the defendant, John Wallace."

In conclusion, Judge Boykin warned the jury not to take into consideration any newspaper accounts they might have read prior to the trial, nor any expression by the trial judge that might imply opinion. The latter was a reference to the remark he had made during Merle Hannah's testimony that Huddleston had charged showed judicial prejudice and constituted grounds for mistrial.

"I charge you now, gentlemen of the jury, to determine what is the truth in this matter, and let your verdict speak the truth."

The courthouse clock was striking four as the jury retired to the mahogany horseshoe table in the jury room. The foreman, G. Y. Chestnut, an elderly farmer who lived near Sunset Tourist Camp, reminded the jurymen of the gravity of the decision that it was their duty to make. Before starting deliberations he prayed, asking for

257

God's guidance in reaching a decision, then requested that each member of the jury take time for a silent prayer to ask individually for guidance.

The spectators remained in the courtroom, standing in front of their seats, waiting for the verdict. Seventy minutes later, the bailiff took a message to Judge Boykin, informing him that the jury had reached a decision.

The jury returned and the foreman handed the verdict to the assistant prosecutor, Myer Goldberg. John Wallace and his attorneys rose, but before the verdict could be read Judge Boykin warned the courtroom against any expression . . . favor or disfavor. Then he asked: "How does the jury find the defendant?"

A hushed courtroom heard Myer Goldberg read: "We, the jury, find the defendant, John Wallace, guilty as charged."

Without a word or an expression, John Wallace, aloof and unshaken, sat down in his chair. Then Judge Boykin called him before the bench for sentencing.

Looking down at Wallace standing between Henson and Huddleston, Judge Boykin said: "John Wallace, you have been duly tried according to the laws of this state and found guilty of the charge of murder as alleged in the indictment. The penalty for murder in this state is death by electrocution."

He paused. "On the thirtieth day of July, between the hours of ten A.M. and two P.M., you will be put to death in the electric chair."

John Wallace in no way believed this solemn pronouncement. Returning to his seat, he tilted his chair back and coolly chewed his gum. Huddleston sank down beside him, his shoulders drooping with despair. Henson, angry and disappointed, spoke to no one.

The spectators had been profoundly impressed by Judge Boykin's solemn words. Even after court was adjourned and the judge had retired to chambers, they made no audible comment about the verdict. They had come to the courthouse hoping to see justice done, but expecting that Wallace's circumstances would somehow mitigate the letter of the law.

Instead, they had witnessed an historic happening. Never in the history of Georgia had a man of Wallace's prominence and wealth been convicted of so serious a crime, and never had a man of such power been sentenced to the electric chair.

There was a new awareness of justice and protection under the law and an assurance that the violation of human rights would not go unnoticed. In this case, ordinary men had accomplished an extraordinary thing. Beginning with the sheriff, each man had brought his best

258

effort to the challenge. Courage had fed upon courage, and the witnesses, judge, and jury had discharged with integrity the duty that had to be done.

Henson, unable to conceal his anger and disappointment with the verdict, began snatching up papers and stuffing them in his briefcase. Approached in the courtroom by members of the press who had covered the trial from the beginning, he told Celestine Sibley of the *Atlanta Constitution*, Hugh Park of the *Atlanta Journal*, and Dave Bowers of the *Columbus Inquirer* that not since the 1916 trial of Leo Frank had a legal battle created such furor. He was implying an analogy with the case of Leo Frank, a Jew, who was convicted on circumstantial evidence for the rape-death of fourteen-year-old Mary Phagan. Awaiting execution, Frank was taken from jail by a prejudiced mob and publicly hanged near Mary Phagan's grave.

"The prosecution," Henson complained, "resorted to everything from sorcery to science, and the jury had prejudice popping out of them like fleas on a dog. We'll be in court Monday morning and immediately appeal for a new trial."

Meanwhile, Pierre Howard, attorney for Herring Sivell and Henry Mobley, had gone to the Coweta jail to urge his clients to plead guilty at their trial on the coming Monday. John Wallace's case, he told them, had been judged strictly on the evidence offered. There had been no consideration of clemency because of *who* Wallace was. "My recommendation to the two of you is to make a consent plea of guilty and throw yourselves on the mercy of the court. It's the only chance you've got."

Herring Sivell shook his head. "I ain't got no stomach for pleading guilty. I ain't had nothin' to do with all that killin' and burnin', and all I got to do is tell them dumb bastards up at the courthouse what happened."

Pierre Howard leaned back in his chair. "Wallace said the same thing. This afternoon he was convicted and the judge sentenced him to the electric chair. Execution is set for six weeks from now."

Henry Mobley stepped forward, his dark eyes squirrel-bright. "Well, I can tell you this much . . . *I* ain't making no consent plea. It wasn't none of my idea to kill Turner. Killing Turner was *John's* idea, and I ain't about to go to no chair for somethin' I didn't do."

"Well, *I* can tell you this much," Pierre Howard snapped back, "the climate in that courthouse is for upholding the law. You use the same brand of asinine arrogance that John Wallace used, and you'll get what he got."

Mobley and Sivell were adamant. They refused even to consider a

259

consent plea of guilty until the next morning when Pierre's father, head of the law firm, came down to talk with them.

"Considering the circumstances, the best we can do," he told them, "is try to save your lives with a life sentence. With good behavior, you could come up for parole in seven years. That's a damn sight better than what you're likely to get if you go in that courtroom with the kind of denial *you* propose."

Grudgingly, they agreed, as did Tom Strickland, who was also to stand trial on Monday and whose Greenville attorney, Jack Allen, recommended that he, too, offer a consent plea of guilty.

On Monday morning, June 21, Al Henson filed an appeal for a new trial for John Wallace. Sivell, Mobley, and Tom Strickland, after making a consent plea of guilty, were sentenced to life imprisonment by Judge Boykin.

Old Mozart Strickland was scheduled for trial on Tuesday, June 22. This, however, had to be postponed until the September session of Superior Court because of the disappearance of a witness, the cook's husband, Ted Turner, who had helped Albert Brooks gather the cordwood used to burn William Turner. Ted Turner had gone to the wheat field one morning to work and was never seen again.

When September came, the case against Mozart Strickland was nolle prossed for want of sufficient evidence. The following day, the grand jury, hearing the case of Albert Brooks and Robert Lee Gates, originally charged with accessory to murder, returned a verdict of not guilty.

Sheriff Hardy Collier was also scheduled to come to trial during the September session of Superior Court, but he was never tried. On July 13, 1948, scarcely a month after John Wallace's trial, Sheriff Collier dropped dead of a heart attack while making an arrest.

Al Henson and Gus Huddleston, meanwhile, had been busy preparing John Wallace's appeal for a new trial that was to be considered by Judge Boykin on August 14. The amended motion for a new trial claimed eleven grounds of error: the admission by the trial judge of testimony by the three physicians who qualified as expert witnesses, the admission of testimony by nonexpert witnesses Steve Smith and Merle Hannah, the remark of the trial judge constituting judicial prejudice.

Grounds nine and ten complained of the admission of certain photographs (the picture of William Turner, admitted for identification, and photographs of the well where Turner was thrown and the pit where he was burned). "These photographs," the charge read, "were not shown to have been made by persons competent and skilled in the operation of a camera in such a manner as to bring about a correct result."

Ground eleven claimed that ashes that Sheriff Potts gathered at the creek, admitted as Exhibit No. 4 and turned over to Dr. Jones for chemical analysis, were not properly identified, nor was the chain of custody established.

John Wallace remained in the Coweta County jail while he awaited a decision on his appeal for a new trial. On July 16, three days after the death of Sheriff Collier, he arranged with Gus Huddleston to hold an auction at his farm to sell off all his holdings in livestock and machinery.

Despite the withering heat of the July day, seven thousand buyers in five thousand vehicles drove to Wallace's farm to attend the auction, creating a massive traffic jam with cars parked for two miles down both sides of the highway. Throngs of people, curious to see the spot where the burning had taken place, walked over Wallace's two thousand acres of farmland, climbing barbed-wire fences, wading creeks, and looking at land that had always been barred from public view.

The dam for Wallace's forty-acre lake had given way at an earlier date, and the area reeked with the odor of rotting fish.

At noon, the auction began. Tractors, trucks, tools, cows, and calves went on the auction block. By five thirty that afternoon, everything had been sold but a stud horse and a jackass.

"The only reason we didn't sell those," Huddleston reported to Wallace, "was because we couldn't catch them. The sale was complete, right down to the striped cat."

"In other words," Wallace said, "I don't own a foot of land or a piece of property."

"That's right," Gus replied.

"Good."

Having divested himself of all landholdings when he transferred the property deeds to his friend Pope Davis, Wallace now legally owned nothing. The seventeen thousand dollars realized from the auction, Huddleston announced, when asked by newspaper reporters, would be used to satisfy some outstanding debts. When the bill for court costs for Wallace's five-day trial in June was submitted to his attorneys, they filed a pauper's plea, and Wallace Gray, clerk of the Superior Court for Coweta County, had to pay the additional five-hundred-dollar expense for added clerical help out of his own pocket.

"John Wallace," his lawyers claimed, "is a pauper."

To improve Wallace's chances for further appeals, he and his friends decided that Gus Huddleston should run for solicitor general in the September election. Luther Wyatt had decided not to stand for reelection because the demanding duties of a solicitor had necessitated his neglecting his own law firm in LaGrange, Georgia.

Although Gus Huddleston's election as solicitor general would have been a distinct advantage to John Wallace, the role of a politician seeking solicitorship of five counties—Coweta, Meriwether, Carroll, Heard, and Troup—suited him badly. He had always been comfortable as a county lawyer. The aggressive rough-and-tumble of a political campaign was just not his style, but because Wallace asked him, he tried. Despite the support of Wallace's wealthy and influential friends, when September came, Huddleston was soundly beaten by an energetic young Coweta County lawyer named Wright Lipford.

Huddleston's defeat was a disappointment to Wallace. A far greater disappointment was Judge Boykin's denial of his motion for a new trial. Henson continued the effort by appealing Wallace's case on October 2 to the Georgia Supreme Court. One of the justices sitting on the case was Lee B. Wyatt, who had, in 1947, presided over a three-judge tribunal trying Nazi war criminals in Nuremberg, Germany.

The presiding judge of the Georgia Supreme Court at this time was William Y. Atkinson, Jr., son of the former governor whose 1894 portrait hangs in the Coweta County courtroom, commemorating his contribution to law and justice.

While Wallace's fortunes floundered, those of the mystic Mayhayley Lancaster flourished. People from as far away as California, who had read the newspaper accounts of Mayhayley's foretelling the future, called, wrote, and came to see her for consultations. On weekends, the country dirt road leading to her cabin in sparsely populated Heard County was lined with the cars of people waiting their turn to have their fortunes told with tea leaves, cards, or dice.

Business was so brisk that Mayhayley increased her price for readings from one dollar and a dime to two dollars and a dime, storing the money in her mattress, since she had no faith in banks. Miss Sally, her seventy-year-old sister, added to the family fortune by selling sardines and corn muffins as refreshments to the visitors who waited to see Mayhayley on the falling-down porch and under the shade trees in the bare, grassless yard.

When word got out that her earning power had so dramatically increased, Mayhayley found herself the victim of a number of robberies. Uncannily correct so many times about the fortunes of others, she was strangely unable to predict her own.

When she was interviewed by Celestine Sibley, of the *Atlanta Constitution*, Miss Mayhayley said: "The law won't even let me and my sister sleep here anymore for fear of our lives. We been robbed of three thousand dollars, and nary a trace of it has been found." She told Celestine Sibley that every night they had to lock the chickens up in the kitchen and go up the road to a cousin's house with their pack of thirty-three dogs.

With John Wallace's case pending a decision from the Georgia Supreme Court, Miss Mayhayley refused to make a prediction on the outcome. "I don't want to influence the judges' minds by telling what's gonna happen," she said modestly.

On the first day of January 1949, Wright Lipford took office as solicitor general, replacing Luther Wyatt. On January 11, the Georgia Supreme Court denied John Wallace's appeal for a new trial.

The conclusion of the justices was: (1) that the trial judge was not in error to admit expert and nonexpert testimony; (2) that the remark of the trial judge, *reasonably* construed, did not amount to judicial prejudice; (3) that no injury was shown to the defendant by the admission of the photographs; (4) that the complaint of the admission of the ashes was without merit; and (5) that the evidence amply supported the verdict.

All the justices concurred, and on January 28, Judge Boykin resentenced John Wallace to the electric chair. The execution date: February 11, 1949.

Chapter Twenty-four

With the electrocution date less than two weeks away, Henson and Huddleston moved quickly to appeal for a hearing before the Pardon and Parole Board. Since there was not sufficient time for the board to consider the case, Georgia's Governor Herman Talmadge was asked for a stay of execution. This he granted at the request of the board.

Hurriedly, hundreds of petitions were circulated in Meriwether, Troup, and Harris counties, asking that John Wallace's death sentence be commuted to life imprisonment. Every friend and every person for whom John Wallace had ever done a favor was approached and urged to sign the petition.

Whole families of ten or more had their names on the petition; even the names of babies in high chairs were signed. When the Pardon and Parole Board met on February 24, cardboard boxes filled with signed petitions were ready to be presented.

So that the board would be overwhelmed by the public sentiment supporting John Wallace's cause, seventy-five of his neighbors attended the hearing in Atlanta. Since the hearing room normally used by the board could not accommodate so large a crowd, the meeting was transferred to the Georgia Senate Chambers. There, the Reverend W. G. Harvey, minister of the Presbyterian churches in Greenville and Manchester, Georgia, whose services had occasionally been attended by the late President Franklin D. Roosevelt, spoke eloquently for an hour. He traced Wallace's life from the time he was a child, brought up and influenced by his iron-willed uncle, John Strickland, who taught him to make illegal liquor.

The minister pointed out that despite this disadvantaged beginning, and his own two convictions for making illegal liquor, Wallace had in 1933 renounced it all and had become a valuable citizen, concerned

264

with his church and community, renowned for his Christian charities.

"A man of such value should not be forever taken from our midst," the Reverend Harvey said. He appealed to the Pardon and Parole Board for compassion, asking it to commute Wallace's death sentence to life imprisonment.

In order to contrast effectively the worth of John Wallace's life with that of William Turner's, Henson presented an affidavit to the board signed by Crawford County Sheriff L. R. O'Neal, of Roberta, Georgia, which stated that he "had never known anything good about William Turner. Turner had been in trouble all his life, even with his own family." Henson explained to the board that O'Neal was the sheriff of the county in which Turner had grown up.

Myer Goldberg, representing the Turner family at the hearing, was incensed by the remarks of the preacher and the shocking statement offered by the sheriff.

"There is no accurate measure to determine how much more valuable one man's life is than another's," Myer Goldberg told the board. "To these people"—he swept his hand across the crowded Senate Chamber—"John Wallace's life is worth more than that of William Turner, but *not*"—and he smashed down his fist on the table in front of him—"to this wife and child!" Here he pointed to Julia Turner, sitting beside him, holding her child on her lap.

"John Wallace willfully, feloniously, and maliciously murdered William Turner. He was tried by due process of law, found guilty, and convicted. Turner had no trial . . . no judge . . . no jury. *John Wallace was Turner's judge and jury!* On his own judgment, Wallace killed him . . . murdered him . . . burned his body . . . and threw his ashes away!"

Myer Goldberg's impassioned words filled the Senate Chamber. "Murder in this state is punishable by electrocution. I say to you, members of the board, that capital punishment should not be reserved for the poor whites and Negroes. John Wallace's sentence should be upheld as theirs would be!" Gesturing once more across the Senate Chamber, he concluded: "John Wallace's friends and money should not make *his* case any different."

Henson hastened to tell the board that Wallace was innocent of the murder charge, that he had shot Turner accidentally and was convicted of a crime he did not commit because the trial had been held in a hostile atmosphere.

Although John Wallace was not present for his hearing before the Pardon and Parole Board, he was confident of its outcome. The board had promised an early decision, possibly within two months, and

265

Wallace felt certain that at that time he would receive a commutation. After all, he had said from the witness chair during the trial that Turner's death was an accident, a statement that should have been sufficient. Unquestionably, the board would find him an innocent man.

On March 28, while awaiting the decision, Julia Turner, represented by Myer Goldberg, filed a $74,280 damage suit against John Wallace, Herring Sivell, Henry Mobley, and Tom Strickland. All four were charged with conspiracy to deprive her of her survival rights by transferring property after her husband was slain. The amount of damages was computed on her husband's life expectancy of 37.14 years and his annual earning power of $2,000 per year.

Three weeks later, on April 18, 1949, the Pardon and Parole Board denied John Wallace's appeal to commute his sentence to life, and on April 22, Judge Boykin sentenced John Wallace for the *third* time to the electric chair. The date of execution, May 6, 1949, was only two weeks away.

Henson was very upset by the decision. He told Wallace's friends in Meriwether County that he had defended a total of 106 capital felony cases, and not a single one had ever been executed. Meanwhile, Wallace, his most prominent client, told him: "*Do* something before you fool around and let me get electrocuted."

On April 30, 1949, Henson filed an extraordinary motion for a new trial based on three grounds: first, that a juror named Homer Lasseter, who had served at Wallace's trial, had publicly declared before the trial "that regardless of the evidence, he would give John Wallace the electric chair." This statement was supported by a joint affidavit signed by Frank Odom and Mr. and Mrs. E. L. Gross, of Senoia, a small mill village in Coweta County.

More startling were the second and third grounds based on affidavits signed by Herring Sivell and Henry Mobley, indicating their willingness to *now* testify that William Turner was alive when he left Coweta County.

To reinforce the strict state requirement that an extraordinary motion for a new trial be based on newly available evidence, John Wallace did a curious thing. He sent for Howard Norris, a former member of the Manchester police force, who, after the death of Sheriff Collier, had been transferred to Meriwether County to assist the new Sheriff Gill. Wallace instructed Norris to go to the abandoned well on his farm where Turner's body had been thrown and to look under a large rock nearby. There, Wallace told Norris, he would find the brains of William Turner.

When he accidentally shot Turner, Wallace said, his brains had fallen out, and he had put Turner's body in the well and his brains under this rock. Even though a year had passed since Turner's death, Wallace wanted Norris to take the brains to Dr. Herman Jones at the Fulton County Crime Lab in Atlanta for chemical analysis. They were to be presented as new evidence at his trial.

For additional evidence, Wallace told Norris to go to his cow pasture where his little calves had been kept, draw the water off the well, and there he would find Turner's hat, shirt, and a towel. These items, too, Wallace wanted presented at the new trial.

Taking GBI Agent Reuben Smith with him to verify his findings, Norris went to the well and found some decayed material under a rock, which he put in a cigar box to take to Dr. Jones. But when they went to the cow pasture to retrieve the other items Wallace had described, Josephine Wallace, dismayed with her husband's manufactured explanations, refused to allow them to drain off the well. "Everything has been done for John that can possibly be done," she explained. "There's no use in doing this."

After analyzing the material found under the rock, Dr. Jones reported that it contained no brain tissue nor any other matter pertaining to a human being.

The State, represented by Solicitor Wright Lipford, countered the charges brought by Wallace in his extraordinary motion for a new trial. A positive affidavit, signed by the accused juror, Homer Lasseter, stated that he had entered without bias upon trial. Supporting affidavits as to his good character were signed by six prominent Coweta County businessmen, including one banker and one county commissioner. These affidavits stated: "Homer Lasseter is a man of good moral character, worthy of belief."

In response to the second and third grounds (that Sivell and Mobley, who had invoked the Fifth Amendment and refused to testify at Wallace's trial, were now willing to testify), Wright Lipford introduced an affidavit signed by Sheriff Potts, stating that the joint defendant, Tom Strickland, had been in his custody throughout the trial and available to testify had he been called upon. Lipford also pointed out that the defendant, John Wallace, had chosen to rely upon his own unsworn statement.

On May 7, 1949, Judge Boykin denied John Wallace's extraordinary motion for a new trial, and the same day, Henson appealed this decision to the Georgia Supreme Court.

Wallace considered the consistent denials a personal affront and felt that those who judged had judged erroneously. He could not

267

understand what he termed "this persistent prejudice against him," and he spoke about it to Sheriff Potts.

During the year he had spent in the Coweta County jail, they had come to know each other well, the sheriff stopping by to see him whenever he made his rounds at the jail. Their relationship was courteous and cordial, with their conversations ranging over crops, cattle, baseball, hunting dogs, and horses, but never about the trial or its ultimate outcome—not until the day Judge Boykin denied his extraordinary motion for a new trial.

"I simply can't understand it," Wallace told Sheriff Potts. "I am *not* a violent man. I'm fifty-three years old, and I've killed only four men. . . ."

"Man, what do you mean *only* four?"

"Hell! Every one of them was an accident. Take for instance that time I was helping Sheriff Collier. He had a nigger in jail he had arrested for stealing. No matter how hard he tried, he couldn't get that nigger to tell him what he had done with what he had stole. The nigger kept claiming he was innocent."

"What happened?"

"Well, suh," Wallace continued, "Sheriff Collier asked me could I help him out, and I told him to bring the nigger on out to my creek that afternoon and I'd see what I could do. I asked that nigger where them things were, and he started carrying on with me that he didn't know, so I hit him and held him under the water by his overall straps. When I pulled him up, he said the same thing again. The third time, I reckon I held him under a little too long, 'cause he was dead when I pulled him up."

"Did it ever occur to you that the Negro might be innocent?"

Wallace was indignant. "When has a nigger ever told the truth?"

Sheriff Potts shook his head. Wallace was incorrigible. "Didn't your action ever strike you as wrong?"

"Wrong?" Wallace looked mildly surprised. "What's wrong about it?"

"Killing a man like that."

"If you mean Bible-wrong, and you mean my conscience," Wallace smiled, "that's something for women and children. My ma always told me: 'Do what you gotta do and don't let your conscience get in your way.'"

"What about the law?"

"Hell, that nigger gave me cause."

"How's that?"

"Stealing and lying about it."

268

"The same way Turner gave you cause?"

Wallace nodded. "He stole my cow."

Sheriff Potts studied Wallace's implacable face. The appalling fact was that Wallace *believed* what he said. Over the years, the undeterred progression and escalation of evil deeds and illegal acts had stripped him of all humanity. In his mind, the law, as applied to ordinary men, did not apply to him. Always allowed his own discretion, it had become his *right* to execute whatever judgment he made.

"What was done about the Negro?" Sheriff Potts asked.

"Hell, I don't know. Collier threw him in the back of his car and carried him off. That's the last I heard of it."

John Wallace spent the summer of 1949 in the Coweta County jail, awaiting his appeal to the Georgia Supreme Court. On September 14, the court handed down its decision. The justices unanimously held that the lower court was not in error and that "a party is bound at his peril to submit on trial all competent evidence in his favor. A new trial will not be granted where the defendant makes no explanations of his failure to use the evidence at hand."

Judge Boykin sentenced Wallace for the *fourth* time to the electric chair. This time, the date was set for October 14, 1949.

As Henson's effectiveness dwindled in the eyes of John Wallace's friends, they held an emergency meeting to see what could be done to salvage the situation. They had seen Henson's every legal effort fail. Their conclusion was summed up by their leader: "Henson ain't done a damn thing but brag about his prestigious connections. That conceited sonofabitch is gonna keep mouthin' around till they get John down at Reidsville and electrocute him. We gotta *do* something!"

Their only recourse, they decided, was to break John out of jail, like in the old days, in the twenties and thirties. They began making their plans. When word of this got back to Sheriff Potts through his information sources, he recommended to Solicitor Wright Lipford that Wallace be transferred to the Fulton Towers jail in Atlanta for safekeeping. Lipford agreed, and the transfer was made before Wallace's friends had time to make their move.

Immediately, Henson swore out a writ of habeas corpus against Fulton County Sheriff A. B. Foster. Filed on September 16, 1949, the petition alleged that Wallace's conviction had resulted from the perjured testimony of the two Negroes, Albert Brooks and Robert Lee Gates; that their place of imprisonment prior to the trial was unknown, therefore the defense attorneys had been limited in

269

preparing their defense; that the Negroes had been induced to give perjured testimony by the threat of physical violence, the promise of immunity if they did, conviction and electrocution if they did not.

The allegation further stated that Sheriff Potts had induced Wallace's codefendants to claim constitutional immunity by promising them less than the maximum sentence, and that by suppressing the favorable testimony of the codefendants, John Wallace's constitutional rights, guaranteed under the Fourteenth Amendment, had been violated.

Sheriff Potts, the charge continued, had assumed the role of prosecutor when he offered a five-hundred-dollar reward from his personal funds for evidence against the defendant, and in this role as prosecutor, had been allowed to summon the jurors.

The coverage by the press was also singled out for condemnation in the writ of habeas corpus: "Their articles went far beyond objective reporting, parading the defendant before the people as arrogant and mean, steeped in the crime of being 'wealthy,' and concealing the fact that Turner was a cow thief and an army deserter."

The petition went on to charge that Wallace had been robbed of an impartial consideration before the Pardon and Parole Board by the publication of "letters from the people" objecting to the dilution of Wallace's sentence, inflammatory material that "violated his rights as a citizen under the Sixth Amendment."

The writ of habeas corpus was brought before Judge Virlyn Moore in Fulton County Superior Court and denied by him on October 4, 1949. Henson wanted the decision appealed to the higher court, and on October 15, Judge Moore signed a *supersedeas* allowing the petition to go before the Georgia Supreme Court.

Five months later, on March 15, 1950, the rehearing was denied. The judgment of the Georgia Supreme Court was that "a writ of habeas corpus could not be substituted for appeal or review of alleged assignment of error in the trial court, that a defendant could not assert his defense by piecemeal nor substitute the writ of habeas corpus when his motion for a new trial is denied. Habeas corpus is appropriate only where the court exceeded its jurisdiction or was without jurisdiction."

Henson resorted to the last chance he had left to save John Wallace from the electric chair: He appealed to the United States Supreme Court on the grounds that the trial had been held in a hostile atmosphere. Having patterned his appeal after the 1916 Leo Frank case, and even though the Supreme Court had upheld the judgment in that case, Henson hoped that the dissenting opinions then by Justices

Oliver Wendell Holmes and Charles Evans Hughes would now work in Wallace's favor.

Henson's failure so far to bring about a reversal in the Wallace case was, for him, a crushing defeat, and although he was in despair, Wallace was not. During the two years he had spent in jail, his confidence had never wavered. He was certain he would be absolved.

"I'm not going to die for a murder I didn't commit," Wallace resolutely told Celestine Sibley when she came to Fulton Towers for an interview. "Don't you think a man would know inside if he was facing death? I honestly do not believe I'll go that way.

"Besides," he went on, "I've been studying the Bible a good deal since I've been in here. I got religion now." Wallace paused to see the effect of his statement, then blinked his hooded eyes and leaned forward confidentially. "You know, religion is a good thing to have in these parts. People really set store by it.

"There's a verse I rediscovered," he said, reaching for the Bible that he kept in his cell. "It's Verse Twenty-two in the Twenty-first Chapter of St. Matthew: *And all things, whatsoever ye shall ask in prayer, believing, ye shall receive.*"

He had appropriated, from Holy Writ, the text that supported what he wanted to believe, and was convinced that God would not let him die for something he had decided he did not do. While he serenely awaited divine intervention, he contented himself with prison food, which he thought wholesome, the guards, whom he considered kindly, and the other prisoners, whom he thought an interesting lot.

Josephine, Wallace told Celestine Sibley, was penniless and was allowed to live in their house only through the kindness of the people who had bought the farm. "We haven't a dime left in the world or a foot of land. Josephine will have to get a job."

Meanwhile, he looked forward to the time when he would get out of prison. "It's good planting weather . . . makes it hard to sit here when the land is waiting."

The waiting for the Supreme Court decision on Henson's appeal continued through the summer of 1950. In August, Julia Turner was awarded $7,500 in her $74,280 damage suit against John Wallace and the three others now serving life imprisonment. She returned to her relatives in Griffin, Georgia, and went back to work at the cotton mill.

Finally, on October 9, the United States Supreme Court handed down its decision: *Denied.* On October 18, Judge Boykin sentenced John Wallace to the electric chair for the fifth time. The electrocution was set for November 3, 1950.

In a final effort, Henson appealed to the Pardon and Parole Board once again to commute the sentence to life. A rehearing was scheduled for October 23. Meanwhile, Solicitor Wright Lipford received a call from a man of prominence, offering a "substantial amount" if he would just not oppose Wallace's appeal for commutation when it came up before the board. The "substantial amount" was rumored to be twenty-five thousand dollars—five times the annual salary for the office of solicitor general. Wright Lipford declined the offer.

The day after the rehearing was held, the board refused to commute the death sentence. "Every resort has been taken by John Wallace's counsel. There was no error in procedure, no lack of sufficient evidence revealed in the judgment of the courts of review."

Governor Herman Talmadge, when questioned by newspaper reporters, said he had received no formal request for a pardon from Wallace's attorneys but that he would not go over the denial of the Pardon and Parole Board.

From Meriwether County, the rumor was that Wallace's friends would band together and overtake Sheriff Potts and his deputies when Wallace was transferred on November 1 from Fulton Towers in Atlanta to the State Prison at Reidsville where his sentence would be carried out.

On the morning of the transfer, Sheriff Potts, having taken the necessary precautions, arrived at Fulton Towers with his deputies: J.H., Sergeant Otwell, State Agent Pete Bedenbaugh, and GBI Agent Jim Hillin.

"Well, John," Sheriff Potts said, "it's time to go."

Wallace smiled. "I hate to put you to any unnecessary trouble, Sheriff."

"I'm just doing my duty," Sheriff Potts said.

Wallace grinned, putting on his broad-brimmed white Stetson hat. "You know you'll just be going to Reidsville for nothing. They ain't going to electrocute *me*."

272

Chapter Twenty-five

John Wallace went to Reidsville with the complete conviction that before the final moment arrived, he would be pardoned by the governor, saved by God, or rescued by his friends. Robust and confident, he sat in the back seat of the sheriff's car beside Pete Bedenbaugh, his hands manacled, waiting for deliverance.

To avoid any confrontation or shootout with Wallace's friends, Sheriff Potts had carefully planned the two-hundred-mile route from Fulton Towers in the northwest section of the state to Tatnall Prison in the southeast. Avoiding the congested cities, he chose the less-traveled state roads through small towns with checkpoints all along the way with the Georgia State Patrol. As one patrol point was passed, the lookout began at the next. Radio contact was constant.

They traveled in a heavily armed three-car convoy. Sergeant Otwell and three other patrolmen led the way, followed by Sheriff Potts and J.H. in the sheriff's car with John Wallace and Pete Bedenbaugh in the back seat. GBI Agent Jim Hillin, in a second State Patrol car with three more patrolmen, drove close behind. In the beginning the pace was fast and the atmosphere tense, but as the distance from Meriwether County increased, the probability of a takeover dwindled.

"I figure they aren't going to try anything too far from home," J.H. said.

"Not likely. They'd have too far to run for cover."

From the back seat Pete Bedenbaugh said, "Hell, I heard they planned to take him clear to Mexico."

Sheriff Potts smiled. "It's been my experience that mostly what they do is talk."

Wallace, sitting in the corner of the car, said nothing—his poker face inscrutable, his eyes constantly on the road ahead. Since the start

273

of his trouble with Turner, his friends had wanted to take action to free him, but they had not yet been able to muster the strength—or courage—to outmaneuver Sheriff Potts. As the miles passed, Wallace waited. The trip to Reidsville would be their last opportunity.

One hundred miles out of Atlanta, he leaned forward and spoke for the first time. "Sheriff Potts, I'd like to ask a favor."

"What's that, John?"

"In this next small town coming up, I have a cousin whom I haven't seen since we were boys. I'd like to stop and tell him good-bye."

Under the circumstances, it was an incredible request. Sheriff Potts looked in the rearview mirror at Wallace to gauge his intentions. Taking a prisoner to Reidsville was, for the sheriff, an unpleasant duty, and refusing a last request went against his nature.

Pete Bedenbaugh, always cautious, spoke up immediately. "Sheriff, if it was up to me, I wouldn't do it. Most likely it's a trap."

Wallace gave Pete a cold, hard look. To Sheriff Potts he said: "I assure you it's not."

J.H. shook his head. "We got him halfway to Reidsville, I can't see taking any risks now."

"Me, neither," Pete said.

Wallace gave Pete another withering look. "Sheriff, if you were on your way to the electric chair, wouldn't you want to tell your kinsman good-bye?"

"What's your cousin's name and where does he work?" Sheriff Potts asked.

When Wallace told him, Sheriff Potts radioed ahead. "Locate this man and give me a report." Satisfied that the cousin constituted no part of a conspiracy, Sheriff Potts stopped the convoy when they reached the town and sent Otwell to get him.

The cousin, a local dentist, wearing a white starched jacket and an annoyed expression, outdistanced Otwell as he crossed the street to the convoy. Getting out of the car, Sheriff Potts introduced himself and they shook hands. The dentist slipped into the sheriff's empty seat, turning to face Wallace in the back.

"John, what in the hell are you doing here?"

Surprised by his cousin's tone, Wallace said solemnly: "You may have heard. I'm on my way to the electric chair. I stopped to say good-bye."

The cousin's face was flushed with angry accusation. "You didn't get one thing more than you deserved."

274

"I'm innocent, I tell you. I didn't do a damn thing that anyone else wouldn't have done!"

Wallace's cousin gave a furtive look at the curious passersby who craned to see the occupants of the three strange police cars. "Have you any idea, John, how many lives you've destroyed with your unbridled acts? Have you ever once stopped to take count?"

Wallace, expecting solace and family support, was stunned by his cousin's condemnation. This, from a kinsman, was more than he could take. The great stone facade that he had maintained from the beginning began to crack. Tears no one had ever expected to see filled his eyes.

An elderly lady walking past called out: "Good morning, Doctor."

The cousin paused, smiled stiffly, and replied: "Good morning, Mrs. Davis."

Turning back to Wallace, trembling with outrage, he snapped, "Can you imagine what it's like for those of us who try to live decent, useful lives . . . to be forever in the shadow of your disgrace?"

Wallace covered his face with his manacled hands and wept. The cousin got out of the car and addressed himself to Sheriff Potts. "You see, Sheriff, we've always known it would come to something like this. It was bound to." He stopped and took a deep breath, his anger subsiding. "I'm sorry if this appears callous, I don't mean it to be, but there are other branches of the family who have achieved worth and respect in their communities. All of us . . . thank God . . . are not like that same roughshod strain who ruled that half-moon corner of Meriwether County."

He gave a brief nod. "If you'll excuse me, I must return to work. I have patients waiting." Without another word, he walked briskly across the street to his office.

Completely disoriented by Wallace's sudden and surprising breakdown, J.H. stirred uncomfortably and stared out the car window. Pete Bedenbaugh looked down and studied his fingernails. It was an awkward and embarrassing moment. Getting into the car, Sheriff Potts took his handkerchief from his back pocket and handed it to Wallace, whose handcuffed hands prevented his getting his own.

Over the car radio, the sheriff said: "Okay, Otwell, let's get back on the road."

Wallace wiped his face and returned the handkerchief. "It's a killing thing to see a family dynasty die," he said. "There was a time when the whole clan stood shoulder to shoulder . . . proud and powerful. Now, except for Uncle Mozart, all the *real* Stricklands are

275

gone. There's nothing left but little watered-down warts like *that*. No honor, no pride, no sense of family loyalty."

As they drove out of town, Wallace settled back in his corner and never looked back. By the time they reached the State Prison at Reidsville, he had completely recovered from his single, momentary lapse into emotion.

Confident and cocky, he got out of the car. Although his friends had failed him, there were still God and the governor. Looking around at the State Prison, where the execution would take place, Wallace grinned. "Yes, sir, we've come a long way for nothing."

While Sheriff Potts went to find Warden Balkcom, J.H. and Pete took Wallace to the clerk's office to turn in his personal belongings.

"You're gonna kill a poor, innocent man," Wallace told the astonished clerk. "I ain't got a thing in this world but my wallet and my watch. My wallet's empty, and my watch don't work."

As he took off his broad-brimmed Stetson to turn it in, Pete Bedenbaugh spoke up. "How 'bout giving me that hat?"

Wallace turned an angry, acid look on Pete. *"Why?"*

Taken aback by Wallace's sudden change from teasing taunts to genuine anger, Pete blurted out: "Because I ain't never seen a case like this before, and I want something to remember it by."

"By God, you oughta remember it! You convicted an innocent man, rigged the trial, and railroaded it through the courts. If you and Earl Lucas had told the truth on the stand about William Turner . . ."

"All Turner ever did," Pete interrupted, "was steal a few cows and make a little liquor."

"And try to kill me."

"Turner was the scaredest man I've ever known. Anytime he'd see *anybody* coming, he'd take off running."

Hearing the angry voices as he returned with the warden, Sheriff Potts asked, "What's the trouble?"

Wallace's smile was cold. "Pete here wants my hat."

Angered by this impropriety from one of his officers, Sheriff Potts demanded: "What in the hell for?"

Before Pete could answer, Wallace held up his hand. "I'll be glad to oblige. I want Pete to pass this on to his grandchildren."

Taking his fountain pen, he wrote across the white hatband: "From John Wallace, a man not guilty of the crime charged."

Later, after Wallace had been led away by the prison guard, Sheriff Potts turned to Pete. "If you're going to be a law officer, Pete, you're going to have to learn about people's feelings."

276

Pete looked down at Wallace's hat. "Hell, I didn't think he'd mind."

Sheriff Potts's reproving look put a stop to any further comment. "Get Otwell and the others," he said to J.H., "and let's go back to Newnan."

On the steps outside, Warden Balkcom asked: "Will you be back for the execution, Sheriff?"

Sheriff Potts shook his head. "No. Our job is done. I would like to know when the sentence is carried out."

"Mr. Wallace seems rather certain that it won't be."

"I know. He still feels that he has been misjudged. Killing Turner was, to him, no crime." The sheriff was leaving now. "Notify me when it's over," he said.

Throughout the night, Wallace conducted himself in so confident a manner that it was unnerving for those around him to watch. The following morning, the day before execution, he summoned his banker from Chipley. "I'm doing this solely as a matter of administrative routine. I don't believe for a moment that they're gonna pull that switch on me tomorrow," Wallace told him. "But just to go along with a superstition, I'll have my affairs in order." He stopped and grinned. "You know that old saying about it never happens to those who are ready."

Handing his banker a sheaf of papers, he said: "Pope Davis has all my holdings. I have written out a will, and here is how my property is to be distributed."

The banker looked through the listings and said: "I see two hundred acres of land listed here to be given to Mrs. Henry Mobley and four hundred acres to your young friend, but nothing for Josephine. She's penniless, you know."

Wallace shrugged indifferently. "She can find a job."

Concern crossed the banker's face. "John, Josephine is outside. She wants to see you."

Wallace did not reply.

"John, this whole thing has had a devastating effect on her. You really should see her."

"All right," Wallace agreed, "but only for a moment."

Afterward, when Josephine returned in tears from Wallace's cell, she went to the telegraph office and made one last desperate attempt. At twelve forty-one, on November 2, 1950, she sent a wire to the Pardon and Parole Board: "Please reconsider or extend the time of John Wallace. I know he is innocent."

For reasons known only to herself, she signed the telegram: "Smilingly, Josephine Leath Wallace (Worldye)." The parenthetic addition was the pen name she used in writing her songs and fantasies about children.

Other friends from Meriwether County were waiting to see Wallace. Grief-stricken, they had come to comfort him in his remaining hours. Wallace swept away their melancholy with joking, laughing, swapping stories.

"Hell, there ain't gonna be no electrocution tomorrow," he assured them, slapping one after another on the back. "They're talking about JOHN WALLACE!" His face was fierce and proud. "And there ain't never been a hole so deep that I couldn't find *my* way out!"

His friends cheered his words, but the sadness never left their eyes. When the prison chaplain came to pray, Wallace urged them all to stay. For hours they prayed and sang hymns with Wallace joining in. The guards who kept watch outside his cell marveled at his high, good spirits, his absolute disregard for the coming day. One guard reported to the warden: "It's just like a prayer meetin' in that cell."

"More like a camp meetin', I'd say," the other guard observed.

It was the chaplain's fervent hope that at the last, John Wallace would repent his sins and save his soul, but Wallace's only regret was for having to wait so long for the pardon he knew would come.

Toward the end of the day, the warden, as was his duty, went to Wallace and asked if he had any last requests. Wallace threw back his head and laughed. "Yes, sir," he replied. "I want my own personal embalmer and I want to be buried in blue silk pajamas."

Distressed by the frivolity, the warden, nevertheless, treated it as a genuine request. "For your last meal tonight, you may ask for whatever you choose."

Wallace's face was serious for a moment as though he were really considering. "Warden, I'd feel like a fool getting you to go to all the trouble of frying chicken and making strawberry shortcake and then show up for supper tomorrow night." He slapped his knee and grinned, his decision made. "No, sir. I'll have the regular prison fare."

When his tray was brought to him, he ate the chili, creamed potatoes, corn bread, and egg custard, thoroughly cleaned his plate, and thanked the guard for bringing it to him. Afterward, he lay down on his bunk and went to sleep.

The guards outside his cell were astounded by the soundness of his sleep. "I ain't never in all my years working on Death Row seen a fellow facing death in the morning sleep so peaceful the night before," one remarked to the other.

278

Almost persuaded by Wallace's absolute confidence, the other replied: "Maybe he ain't gonna die. He says he ain't."

"No way. That fellow's gonna walk that last mile in the morning. Do you *remember* what he's in for?"

"Killed his tenant, didn't he?"

"*Publicly* killed him in front of eight eyewitnesses, threw his body in a well, later dragged him back out, burnt him up, and threw his ashes away."

"Whewwwwww . . . he really meant to get that fellow, didn't he?"

"That's just it . . . he really *meant* to get him."

When morning came, Wallace calmly ate the regular prison breakfast. Two hours before the scheduled electrocution, he decided to call a press conference. The reporters, many of whom had covered the trial and the appeals, crowded into the room where Wallace calmly waited to receive them. Having expected a last-minute change in his undaunted attitude, they were dismayed when Wallace began by saying: "I am innocent of William Turner's murder. It was an accident. I never laid my hands on him to kill him. My gun went off."

When asked about the burning of Turner's body, Wallace replied coolly between puffs on his cigarette: "I had nothing to do with that. After the accident, I had intended to have his body sent to his folks, but they put me in jail before I could attend to it."

The *Atlanta Journal*'s Hugh Park, whom Wallace had come to know well during the years of trial and appeals, asked: "Mr. Wallace, in case no reprieve comes, are you frightened?"

Wallace tilted his chair back nonchalantly and smiled confidently. "I've never been afraid of anything in all my life. I fear no man. I fear no evil." Concluding his news conference, he said: "I hold no malice toward anybody."

Shortly before ten o'clock, the warden went to Wallace's cell to tell him there was no indication of a reprieve. Wallace received the news without a sigh. His friends had failed to rescue him and the governor had not granted the reprieve, but Wallace was undismayed. He thumped the Bible he held in his hand and said, "The good Lord will take care of me."

At 10:30 A.M., the three rows of seats in front of the electric chair were filled with witnesses: newsmen, prison officials, a few of Wallace's friends, and Pete Bedenbaugh. Before bringing Wallace down, Warden Balkcom arrived to make certain that all was in order for the execution.

At ten thirty-five, the prison chaplain began reading the Twenty-third Psalm as he led Wallace to the death chamber: "The Lord is my shepherd, I shall not want. . . ." When he finished, he said: "John, this is your very last opportunity." His voice trembled with hope. "Is there *anything* you want to say?"

Wallace, standing straight, his voice calm, replied: "No." As he approached the chair, he seemed to reconsider. Turning to the warden, he asked: "May I pray?"

The warden nodded his consent. Silence sealed the room. The chaplain's face shone with the expectation of repentance and redemption.

Wallace knelt down before the electric chair, leaning his folded hands on the seat as though it were an altar. His voice was strong and without a tremor:

"Almighty God, I want to say before you, I am not guilty of this crime for which I am about to pay the penalty. I pray for the officers responsible. Forgive them, for they know not what they do. I pray for the governor and the Pardon and Parole Board, who did not know the facts. Stand ready, Lord, to receive me in Your house."

The prison chaplain, who had hoped so much and prayed so hard, turned his back and wept.

Wallace remained kneeling, waiting for the Lord to respond. But there was only silence. Mildly astonished, he got up and looked around expectantly. The silence continued. Still confident that, at the last, something would happen, he sat down in the electric chair. The electrodes were attached. The warden gave the signal.

The moment had come. Realizing that God had failed him, too, Wallace's last words were: "Good-bye, men. I love everybody."

The switches were pulled, and one minute later, John Wallace was dead.

At the courthouse in Newnan, Sheriff Potts read the account in the *Atlanta Journal.* Written by Hugh Park, and on the street an hour after the execution, the story covered the murder, trial, conviction, and conclusion. As the sheriff finished it and laid the paper aside, there was a knock at the door.

Willie, once the run-around-boy at the jail, stood in the doorway, beside him, a young woman holding a baby. Older now by two and a half years, Willie grinned and said: "Sheriff, I got a boy of my own now. This is my wife Pearline."

Sheriff Potts acknowledged the introduction and shook hands with Willie. "Good to see you."

"And this is my son, Roosevelt Potts. Me and Pearline decided

280

with a name like that, he was bound to grow up strong and stay out of trouble."

"He looks like a fine boy."

"Yes, sir," Willie said, gathering his family up to leave. "We just wanted you to know."

The telephone rang. Sheriff Potts picked up the receiver. "Sheriff's office . . . yeah, Joe . . . when did this happen?" He took his notebook from his pocket and jotted down the information. "Okay, I'll be right out."

And so it went for more than a quarter of a century. Lamar Potts became a legend in his own time and a strength to his people. He was sheriff of Coweta County for thirty-two years.

Index

283

286